Global Corporate Citizenship

Global Corporate Citizenship

EDITED BY

Anuradha Dayal-Gulati and Mark W. Finn

Introduction by Daniel Diermeier

Northwestern
University Press
Evanston, Illinois

School of Management
Evanston, Illinois

Copyright © 2007 by Global Initiatives in Management, Kellogg School of Management. Published 2007 by Northwestern University Press. All rights reserved.

Printed in The United States of America

10 9 8 7 6 5 4 3 2 1

ISBN-13: 978-0-8101-2383-0

Library of Congress Cataloging-in-Publication Data

Global corporate citizenship : edited by Anuradha Dayal-Gulati and Mark W. Finn.
    p. cm.
Includes bibliographical references and index.
ISBN-13: 978-0-8101-2383-0 (pbk : alk. paper)
ISBN-10: 0-8101-2383-5 (pbk : alk. paper)
1. Social responsibility of business. 2. Social responsibility of business—Developing countries. 3. Business enterprises—Developing countries. 4. International business enterprises—Moral and ethical aspects. I. Dayal-Gulati, Anuradha. II. Finn, Mark W.
HD60.G557 2007
    658.408—dc22
                                    2007019572

The paper used in this publication meets the minimum requirements of the American National Standard for Information Sciences—Permanence of Paper for Printed Library Materials, ANSI Z39.48-1992.

CONTENTS

Foreword, ix
Preface, xi

1 Introduction: From Corporate Social Responsibility to
  Values-Based Management   1
  Daniel Diermeier

PART 1
ACCOUNTING, TRANSPARENCY, AND MONITORING   25
2 Labor Standards in Thailand: The Players and Their
  Impacts   27
  *Julie Boris, Kaya Davis, Michael Gross, Jessica
  Keintz, and Jami Totten*
3 The Impact of Labor Audits in Vietnam   41
  *Janice Farrel, Gregory Merchant, Andrew Sofield,
  and Mareike Willimsky*
4 Preventing Labor-Standards "Explosions" in
  Thailand and Vietnam   57
  *Jared Cluff, Andrew Knuckle, Carlo Libaridian,
  R. David Smith, and Wonita Williams*

PART 2
ECONOMIC EMPOWERMENT AND GLOBAL CITIZENSHIP   75
5 The Impact of Foreign Direct Investment on
  Chinese Women   77
  *Alison Curd, Amelia Julian, Adam Sabow, and
  Leigh Seligman*

6 Avon in Brazil: Direct Selling and Economic
Empowerment   89
   Helen Cha, Polly Cline, Lilly Liu, Carrie Meek,
   and Michelle Villagomez
7 Corporate Social Responsibility: A Case Study of
Multinational Corporations Investing in India   97
   Scott Benigni, Brandon Davito, Adam Kaufman,
   Andy Noble, and Risa Sparks

PART 3
Partnering for Change in South Africa   119
8 Education for Change in South Africa's Auto
Industry   121
   Kannan Arumugam, Akeshia Craven, and
   Jackie Statum
9 Black Economic Empowerment in the South
African Wine Industry   133
   Liliahn Johnson, Laura Koepke, and Amie Wang
10 Venture Capital and Black Economic
Empowerment in South Africa   151
   Stephanie Davis, Marene Jennings, Srikanth Reddy,
   Yuji Sadaoka, and Guhan Selvaretnam
11 Closing the Skills Gap in Post-Apartheid South
Africa   165
   Piotr Pikul, Kathy Wang, and Craig Wynn

PART 4
Meeting the AIDS Challenge   175
12 Sustainable Foundations for HIV/AIDS Care:
Treatment and Delivery in South Africa   177
   Stephanie Chan, Deepa Gupta, Kara
   Palamountain, and Aparna Saha
13 Meeting the HIV/AIDS Challenge in Brazil   189
   Joshua Bennett, Nageswara Pobbathi,
   Andy Zhilei Qiu, and Ryan Takeuchi

PART 5
CORPORATIONS AND THE ENVIRONMENT   **203**

14   Green Management in the European Union   205
*Lamtiurida Hutabarat, Marc Major,
and Doug Stein*

15   Ecoefficiency in Chile and Peru   217
*Stacy Gibbons, Maren Lau, Stacy McAuliffe,
and Jessica Watson*

16   Flex-Fuel Technology in Brazil   233
*Henry Lai, Matt Lippert, Guilherme Silva,
Avi Steinberg, Pratish Sthankiya, and
Justin Twitchell*

17   Environmentally Friendly Technologies in
China's Auto Industry   251
*John Eisel, Jonathan Glick, Adrienne Kardosh,
Coleman Long, David Mayer, and Doug Roth*

Acronyms, 263
Index, 267

FOREWORD

In 2003, the Ford Motor Company Center for Global Citizenship of the Kellogg School of Management announced two $1,500 Best Paper Awards for graduate student papers from the Global Initiatives in Management (GIM) classes of 2003. One of the awards was for papers on social corporate engagement, the second for those concerned with environmental sustainability. "The Impact of Labor Audits in Vietnam," included as a chapter in this book, was the paper awarded the first of these prizes. The paper on which the chapter "Green Management in the European Union" is based won the other award. The other papers in this volume were among the nearly two dozen submitted to this competition. They ably document the range and diversity of management challenges associated with the increasing globalization of business.

The Ford Center, like the Kellogg School of which it is a part, is committed to the idea that in a global context, basic management skills such as accounting, finance, strategy, and marketing are necessary but not sufficient conditions for business success. Global leaders of the current century must also recognize that businesses thrive where people and societies thrive. Thus, an essential part of building successful businesses is enabling successful societies—societies that are educated, healthy, and rich in opportunities for all citizens. Societies that allocate education only to elites fail the first test; societies that pollute or destroy their natural resources fail the second; and societies burdened by corruption or regimentation fail the third.

The chapters included in this volume deal with specific issues within the broad domain of corporate social responsibility. How does foreign direct investment influence economic and social opportunities for women in China? In Vietnam, do labor audits to verify the safety and healthfulness of workplaces actually have an adverse impact on the availability of jobs or the incomes of employees? What are the hurdles for providing opportunities through microfinance in Brazil? Can Avon develop strategies to sell its products to wealthier Brazilian consumers with the same success it has had with less affluent ones, for many of whom the company also provided employment? How can South African firms compensate for a century of racial and gender discrimination to create an economy and broader society in which all citizens may participate freely? Education and capital are crucial, as many of these chapters point out, but providing them is complex. In several chapters, the authors discuss the need for partnerships between corporations and nongovernmental agencies. Two arenas for such partnerships are disease education/management and environmental initiatives. Healthy employees are essential for healthy enterprises, but health can be threatened by global disasters such as HIV/AIDS or pollution. Only the most shortsighted firms would fail to see the value in eliminating such epidemics or sources of environmental damage.

These chapters represent efforts to grapple with the problems that arise from the inevitable interaction of business and its physical and social environment, an interaction that we expect to evolve into an even more varied source of challenges and opportunities in the decades ahead. We are proud to share these works with the reader.

David M. Messick
Morris and Alice Kaplan Professor of Ethics and
Decision in Management
Codirector, Ford Motor Company
Center for Global Citizenship

PREFACE

The movement toward global outsourcing and manufacturing and the expansion of overseas marketing, distribution, and sales operations have had far-reaching implications for businesses and the countries in which they invest. Although multinational corporations (MNCs) are motivated by the prospects of lower costs or acquiring local customers more easily by increasing their presence overseas, there are spillover benefits to the local economy, usually in terms of higher wages and overall standards of living. However, these shifts have not been without controversy. For instance, MNCs have been accused of having a negative impact on the environment, working conditions, and culture of the countries they occupy. These accusations are predicated in part on the growing belief that businesses have obligations to society—both to their home countries and to the local economies they affect—that go beyond making money. Since 1990, in fact, more than 100,000 new citizens' advocacy groups have emerged around the globe. In response to these pressures, there has been a rising trend toward corporate social responsibility (CSR), driven by both investors and consumer interest and reflected in the CSR initiatives featured prominently on the Web sites of most of the companies in the Fortune 500.

Corporate social responsibility has been broadly defined as the ways in which a company's activities affect its stakeholders and fulfill its perceived obligations to society, including the environment. Some businesses are on the cutting edge of the movement to make corporations more socially responsible. Others are driven to join it by unfortunate disclosures or the consequences of missteps in regard to social responsibility. Nevertheless, most large companies grapple with a broad range of CSR issues ranging from global poverty to renewable energy.

This volume is a product of the class Global Initiatives in Management (GIM), a course offered by the Kellogg School of Management for the past decade. The GIM program and Kellogg's Ford Center for Global Citizenship compiled this book based on student research related to global CSR, in part to address the increased attention to this area. Each year the GIM program offers classes that span the globe. Recent courses have focused on China, Japan, India, South Africa, Chile, Peru, Brazil, Southeast Asia, and the European Union. Kellogg students in GIM capped their classroom experiences with visits to the countries of focus over spring break. In addition to the lectures and country visits, the students undertook in-depth research on the issues included in this book. Many of the results and findings presented here are based on first-hand, in-country interviews.

Corporate social responsibility is clearly a broad topic with many facets. The chapters in this book illuminate how companies may move toward CSR, along with the form it may take in different countries, encompassing issues ranging from education and health to environmental responsibility. Similarly, the impetus for CSR may vary across companies and countries. Despite these differences, this book's findings suggest that companies with effective CSR policies typically share one or more of the following features:

- Their CSR programs are closely linked to their business interests in the local market. Thus, as companies play a leadership role in addressing social problems such as education or AIDS, they seek to reconcile profit realization with the welfare of local communities. In emerging markets such as those included here, small CSR programs can have a large impact because of the lack of locally based social initiatives.
- Their CSR programs are aligned with their business competencies. This ensures effective leverage of company expertise for the CSR program and that the program in turn offers tangible benefits to the business.

- They have staff dedicated to implementing and monitoring CSR programs.
- They have built-in annual reviews and planning processes for their programs to ensure that the programs will be sustainable, effective, and responsive to changing needs. Monitoring achievements over time may facilitate the CSR programs' development into long-term commitments that add much greater cumulative value.
- They have senior level buy-in regarding the vision underlying CSR. This helps to make the importance of such efforts clear to all employees and institutionalizes philanthropy.
- To implement their CSR programs, they partner with the government, nongovernmental organizations (NGOs), and other local companies. These partnerships leverage local expertise and networks to provide significant benefits to both the company and the targets of their CSR efforts. Some analysts argue that such partnerships can prevent public controversies that may damage a firm's global reputation and business.

There is growing evidence of the positive effects of CSR on bottom lines through increased consumer and brand loyalty, reduced risk, and the creation of goodwill among consumers and investors. Companies can no longer afford to ignore CSR's potential benefits—or the costs of neglecting efforts in this domain. These chapters provide some insight into the costs and benefits of CSR in a global context.

The book is organized as follows. First we present an overview of conceptual issues in corporate global citizenship. The author of chapter 1 is Daniel Diermeier, IBM distinguished professor of regulation and competitive practice at the Kellogg School of Management. The remainder of the book is made up of five parts.

Part 1, Accounting, Transparency, and Monitoring, examines the interplay among social accounting, labor standards, and the methods used to uphold them, and it reviews the returns gained— at both corporate and societal levels—in Asia. These chapters suggest that shareholder value and social responsibility are not incompatible. However, compliance with worker safety and welfare regulations in overseas markets, where the civil foundations of society may differ from those of the home country, pose unique challenges. Nonetheless, addressing these issues can protect the company's reputation and returns. Chapter 2, "Labor Standards in Thailand," examines the key players responsible for developing and maintaining labor-related policies and practices in that country: the Thai government, international and local NGOs, MNCs operating in Thailand, and local companies. Despite the proliferation of agencies concerned with labor standards in Thailand, a general lack of resources and the population's ambivalence toward the enforcement of labor standards pose significant challenges to progress. Chapter 3, "The Impact of Labor Audits in Vietnam," discusses the effects of labor audits on wages, working conditions, and employment opportunities in Vietnam. Many companies, particularly in the apparel and footwear industries, participate in these audits, which are performed by independent parties. As the chapter reveals, the audits have had direct and indirect effects on the Vietnamese economy and society, and these effects have been positive (for example, increased wages) and negative (for example, movement away from nonfarm household enterprises). In Chapter 4, "Preventing Labor-Standards 'Explosions' in Thailand and Vietnam," the section's final chapter, the authors assert that the benefits of measures taken by MNCs to avoid public relations crises usually outweigh their costs. Among these benefits are increased credibility among U.S. stakeholders—including customers—and better service of the needs of local employees.

Part 2, Economic Empowerment and Global Citizenship, concerns the effects of MNCs' policies and operations on local citizens, with a focus on disenfranchised groups such as low-income women. Chapter 5, "The Impact of Foreign Direct Investment on Chinese Women," reveals how overseas investment, despite media attention to the poor conditions of many factories (for example, news segments on sweatshops), has improved the status of women in China on multiple measures. For example, the authors estimate that foreign investment contributed to 35 percent of the growth in female labor participation in the country from 1980 to 2000. Still, ample opportunities for improvement exist, and the policies of several socially minded MNCs in China are paving the way for progress toward these. "Avon in Brazil: Direct Selling and Economic Empowerment," chapter 6, examines how the cosmetic giant's sales model has had a significant economic impact on the women of Brazil's poorest segments. Complementarities between Latin American culture and Avon's direct selling method allowed the company to leverage low-income women as both direct-sales agents and customers, to great mutual benefit. However, as the company strives to capture greater cosmetics wallet share from elite customers, this sole distribution channel may become a liability. The authors examine how Avon can successfully target upscale consumers without losing its existing base of customers and saleswomen. Chapter 7, "Corporate Social Responsibility . . . in India," presents brief case studies of the CSR efforts of Ford and General Electric in India. Based on forward-thinking philosophies and monitored rigorously, these companies' CSR practices embody several of the success factors outlined earlier, including alignment of CSR programs with business interests and collaboration with local organizations, including NGOs.

Part 3, Partnering for Change in South Africa, shifts the focus to one of geography: Each chapter covers a different facet of MNCs' and other organizations' contributions toward black economic empowerment (BEE). BEE is defined officially as a strategy for "redressing the imbalances of the past by seeking to substantially and equitably transfer ownership, management and proportionate control of South Africa's financial and economic resources to the majority of its citizens" through measures such as job creation, rural development, education, and access to business financing. As this section indicates, the legacy of apartheid cannot be the purview of solely the public or private sector. Rather, partnerships between the government and private enterprises may lead to the most profitable and sustainable changes in South Africa. Chapter 8, "Education for Change in South Africa's Auto Industry," considers how BMW, Nissan, and Ford, in partnership with local interest groups, are working to improve the educational levels of unskilled autoworkers.

The authors discuss the implications of each company's strategy—
they are distinct on several dimensions—and provide recommendations for effective changes. Next, chapter 9, "Black Economic
Empowerment in the South African Wine Industry," reveals how
South African government and winemaker initiatives, including
equity and education, have resulted in several successful black-
owned vintners including New Beginnings Winery and Fair Valley.
Despite this progress, several obstacles to future success remain,
including insufficient funding and administrative shortcomings. In
chapter 10, "Venture Capital and Black Economic Empowerment
in South Africa," the authors examine collaborative efforts between
the South African government and venture capital firms to fund
small and medium enterprises (SMEs). A promising example of this
type of public/private partnership is the Progress Fund, which faces
the ongoing challenges of balancing public good with profitable
returns and attracting and retaining qualified black investment professionals. Finally, chapter 11, "Closing the Skills Gap in Post-
Apartheid South Africa" details how BEE initiatives have moved
beyond granting more blacks ownership and control of corporations to focusing on improvements in procurement, distribution,
and social investment.

Meeting the AIDS Challenge, Part 4, concerns corporate
attempts, as influenced by governmental and nongovernmental
organizations, to address the HIV/AIDS crises in South Africa and
Brazil. Drug access for HIV/AIDS treatment has become a major
CSR issue, in response to which firms have implemented multiple
solutions: drug donations; licensing drug manufacturing to a firm
in a developing country to decrease costs and, subsequently, local
retail prices; differential pricing for home and select foreign markets. Chapter 12, "Sustainable Foundations for HIV/AIDS Care:
Treatment and Delivery in South Africa," focuses on Abbott
Laboratory's partnership in that country with Axios International
and International Healthcare Distributors in AIDS treatment and
drug distribution. Such partnerships are extremely valuable, especially in the face of a government far from proactive in addressing
HIV/AIDS. Fortunately, some governments are much more willing
to combat the disease, as revealed in chapter 13, "Meeting the

HIV/AIDS Challenge in Brazil." The authors discuss Brazil's AIDS treatment model, which includes the successful application of pricing pressure on pharmaceutical manufacturers, leading to customized prices. With such success, however, have emerged several risks, including those of reimportation of AIDS drugs to the United States and potential reductions in AIDS-related research and development investments. This chapter also proposes ways in which pharmaceutical companies may address these risks.

Part 5, Corporations and the Environment, presents several chapters on corporate, governmental, and NGO efforts to reduce threats to the environment and promote greener technologies. The chapters examine the factors driving increased environmental awareness, the measures resulting from this emerging perspective, and their impacts on multiple dimensions of developing countries. Chapter 14, "Green Management in the European Union," examines the factors that make some companies more environmentally friendly than others. The authors profile Unilever, Otto Versand, and BP Amoco to demonstrate that while regulatory requirements may be a factor prompting corporate environmental initiatives, such movements must be internally driven and reflect top management's attitudes to be more successful. Chapter 15, "Ecoefficiency in Chile and Peru," profiles management philosophies and practices that create value by reducing companies' harmful environmental impacts. Specifically, the authors discuss the efforts of TetraPak's Chile and Peru organizations toward increasing consumer recycling and corporate environmental responsibility. Chapter 16, "Flex-Fuel Technology in Brazil," analyzes factors related to the success of flex-fuel vehicles in that country. First introduced in 2003, flex-fuel automobiles run on a combination of gasoline and ethanol. The convergence of consumer demand, technology availability, and Brazil's strong ethanol infrastructure has led to these cars' success. Chapter 17, "Environmentally Friendly Technologies in China's Auto Industry," the section's final chapter, details the explosive growth of automobile use in China, along with the implications of this trend for auto manufacturers, consumers, the Chinese government, and the environment. The authors suggest that China, aided by the government's central planning processes, may overcome the environmental hazards posed by the surge in automobile use, but that it will take a thoughtful and dedicated approach on the part of all stakeholders.

We would like to thank the people and organizations who have been instrumental in making this book a reality. The Ford Center for Global Citizenship and, in particular, Dave Messick, the codirector of the center, have supported the GIM program over the years and provided the impetus for this book. We are deeply grateful to Dave for his invaluable assistance. We would also like to thank the authors for their time and effort in crafting the chapters, making revisions, and meeting deadlines. The faculty advisers for the GIM classes—Fran Brasfield, Dave Gent, Raj Gupta, Dean Emeritus Don Jacobs, Patricia Ledesma, Dave Messick, Judy Messick, Johannes Moenius, William Ocasio, and Ed Wilson—have provided significant input on these projects over time. We gratefully acknowledge Donna Shear, director of Northwestern University Press, who persisted with us in bringing this volume to print, and Rich Honack, assistant dean and chief marketing officer, Kellogg School of Management, for his enthusiastic commitment and backing. Many others have played a part in bringing this book to fruition. We would like to thank Laura Bunch, Alisha Fund, and Regina McKie, who have provided endless administrative support, as well as Tom Truesdell, Elizabeth Ungar, and Sachin Waikar, who have assisted in carefully editing and preparing these chapters for publication. Last but not by any means least, we would like to thank Dean Dipak Jain for his vision and encouragement for this series.

Anuradha Dayal-Gulati
Mark Finn
Kellogg School of Management
Evanston, Illinois

Chapter 1

INTRODUCTION: FROM CORPORATE SOCIAL RESPONSIBILITY TO VALUES-BASED MANAGEMENT

Daniel Diermeier

CORPORATE SOCIAL RESPONSIBILITY AND MANAGEMENT PRACTICE

There is little doubt that we have witnessed a surging interest in corporate social responsibility (CSR) over the past decade. The number of annual sustainability and corporate citizenship reports has skyrocketed, and chief executive officers (CEOs) increasingly rank CSR as a "central" or "important" concern for senior managers (Simms, 2002; Friedman, 2003). Yet the increasing interest in corporate social responsibility is not just limited to talk. Companies are also making significant changes in their business practices. Examples range from global labor standards (Nike, Adidas, Ikea), sustainable supply chains (the decision by Home Depot and Lowe's not to sell wood from old-growth forest), and animal welfare (McDonald's and Yum Brands poultry policies) to general public-policy issues such as global warming and human rights (British Petroleum [BP], Shell). Even Wal-Mart, the current bête noire of political activists, is now aggressively moving in this direction. It has began to work with nongovernmental organizations (NGOs) such

1

as Conservation International and the Natural Resources Defense Council on various sustainability initiatives ranging from sourcing from sustainable fisheries to attempts to reduce waste production and energy use (Baron, 2006b). Particularly striking are the recent attempts of major global corporations to rebrand themselves as ecologically responsible companies. Examples include BP's Beyond Petroleum initiative and its carbon footprint campaign as well as General Electric's Ecoimagination initiative.

Of course, corporate social responsibility is not a new phenomenon. Procter and Gamble pioneered disability and retirement benefits (1915) and an eight-hour workday (1918) long before such policies were required by law. Henry Ford paid his workers twice the market rate, and companies such as Heinz, IBM, and Hershey's subsidized education and other community benefits (Crook, 2005). More generally, corporate philanthropy has a long tradition, especially in U.S. corporate history, from the nineteenth-century robber barons to the "5 Percent Club" in the 1960s and 1970s, so named because its members (for example, Levi Strauss, Cummins Engines, and Control Data) donated at least 5 percent of their earnings (Vogel, 2005) to charitable causes.

What is new is an emerging consensus that corporate social responsibility is no longer a luxury for a few prosperous companies but a necessary component of sound business practice. Companies are increasingly held accountable by standards other than maximization of shareholder value, and they need to develop strategies and policies to address these challenges. In a recent article in the *McKinsey Quarterly* followed by an op-ed piece in the *Financial Times,* Ian Davis, worldwide managing director of McKinsey & Co. (Bonini, Mendonca, and Oppenheim, 2006) lists the need for companies to gain sustained social acceptance as one of the five key global, emerging trends:

> The role and behavior of big business will come under increasingly sharp scrutiny. As businesses expand their global reach, and as the economic demands on the environment intensify, the level of societal suspicion about big business is likely to increase. The tenets of current global business ideology—for example, shareholder value, free trade, intellectual-property rights, and profit

repatriation—are not understood, let alone accepted, in many parts of the world. . . . Business, particularly big business, will never be loved. It can, however, be more appreciated. Business leaders need to argue and demonstrate more forcefully the intellectual, social, and economic case for business in society and the massive contributions business makes to social welfare.

It is important to understand that this claim is not about a question of morality. The issue is not what companies *should* do ("What is the social responsibility of business?") but what they *need* to do to be successful in today's economy, whether their goals are purely motivated by profits or they also include references to ethical motives not captured by shareholder value. In other words, the debate is less about business ethics and more about management practice.

It is conceptually useful to first consider these issues from the point of view of a firm whose sole goal is to maximize profits because it helps to clarify whether and to what extent CSR is indeed a successful strategy (for example, Vogel, 2005). (We will discuss the case of morally motivated managers and owners later in this chapter.) The issues are whether and when CSR improves performance of a business unit, which companies should adopt it, and how CSR strategies should be implemented. From this perspective, the issue of whether a company should engage in CSR activities is not fundamentally different from whether it should pursue a high-quality or a low-cost strategy. It also suggests that we should expect significant variation in the patterns of CSR activities and when CSR activities lead to better business performance.

CSR AS A STRATEGY

Perhaps the most basic question about CSR as a strategy is whether the strategy works. In the management literature, this question has been expressed as whether it "pays to be green" or whether companies are "doing well by doing good" (for example, Dowell, Hart, and Yeung, 2000; Fisman, Heal, and Nair, 2006; Heal, 2005; Porter and van der Linde, 1995). The existing literature on this topic is empirically motivated. It tries to establish whether firms that engage in CSR activities exhibit better financial performance than companies that do not. There is much debate among management scholars about this issue, but the evidence for a positive association between CSR and financial performance is at best mixed. Some studies find a small positive effect, others find no effect, and yet others find a negative effect (for example, Dowell, Hart, and Yeung, 2000; Margolis and Walsh, 2003; Vogel, 2005). In addition, there are serious problems measuring CSR (what exactly counts as CSR activities?) and questions about the direction of causation (are firms more profitable because they engage in CSR, or can they afford to engage in CSR because they are more profitable?).

Irrespective of the validity of the existing findings, from a strategy perspective this line of research is not very fruitful, since (as would be the case with any other business strategy) we would expect the effect of CSR activities to heavily depend on the market or the product. Recall that the existing literature has tried to establish whether *on average* socially responsible companies do better. But markets are frequently characterized by product differentiation. Some firms in an industry may rely on a high-quality/high-price strategy, others on a low-quality/low-price strategy. In many markets, ranging from consumer goods to financial services or retail, such differentiated markets are highly stable. However, were we to ask whether *on average* high quality pays off, we may find no relationship whatsoever. Both Tiffany and Wal-Mart may be highly profitable in their respective retailing segment, one adopting a high-quality/high-cost strategy, the other a low-quality/low-cost strategy. Similarly, in a market that is differentiated by CSR activities, it is entirely possible that both the socially responsible *and* the "regular" firms can be profitable. In other words, there may an "ecological niche" for socially responsible firms and another one for companies that do not care at all for CSR (Vogel, 2005). Empirical studies that correlate social and financial performance are only useful if they can address the question of why and under what circumstances firms can benefit from adopting socially responsible business practices.

Proponents of the business case for CSR have pointed to various benefits of CSR activities, of which the following is a partial list (see, for example, Heal, 2005):

1. Reducing costs and waste
2. Accelerating product innovation
3. Creating and improving brand equity
4. Lowering the cost of capital
5. Improving employee productivity and attracting or retaining talented employees
6. Reducing various forms of risk (legal, regulatory, political, reputational)
7. Improving relationships with political and regulatory entities

It is important to understand that the listed motivations operating suggest conceptually different justifications for CSR. The proposed rationales 1 and 2, for example, are purely operational, not strategic. They use CSR (especially environmental CSR) as a heuristic to improve process performance. A well-known example is BP's adoption of a firmwide cap on greenhouse emissions combined with corporate emissions trading system (Reinhardt, 2000). That decision led to great success. Not only were emissions reduced significantly, but, according to BP, the trading system increased net income by more than US$600 million. A similar example is Dow Chemical's decision to adopt aggressive pollution controls, which led to the capture of tens of millions of dollars' worth of valuable solvents (Heal 2000, 2005). Both cases are straightforward examples of increased operational efficiency. Both Dow and BP had hidden sources of cost efficiencies, unbeknownst to management. For example, BP was flaring natural gas from some of its wells. But these costs were difficult to identify. They did not show up as cash costs on a balance sheet but constituted hidden opportunity costs. Simply polluting the environment, somewhat surprisingly, turned out not to be the least expensive way for the companies to dispose of their waste. CSR played the role of a heuristic that made it more likely for management to identify such cost savings.

The same argument (or its mirror image) holds in the context of innovation, item 2 in the previous list. Here the argument is that a focus on sustainability and environmental responsibility will lead to faster rates of innovation in high-impact technologies. GE's Ecoimagination initiative is one of the better-known examples of this approach. CSR again serves as a heuristic, now with a focus on the innovation process.

Both rationales should be utterly uncontroversial. They should be adopted by any company interested in improving its operations. To put it differently, even if ExxonMobil fundamentally disagrees with BP about the fact or the causes of climate change, imitating BP's trading scheme would be advisable, provided the system indeed leads to the stated cost savings. What may vary across companies are the extent to which such heuristics are fruitful and which CSR domain will be most important. For example, a focus on environmental CSR may be a very useful heuristic in the energy sector or the chemical industry but much less important for software companies. On the other hand, a focus on improving access to health care may spur innovation in the medical-device industry but may be of no importance to the financial service sector. The bottom line is that whether and to what extent CSR can serve as an operational heuristic is largely an empirical question and will vary widely from market to market and firm to firm. Unfortunately, we lack empirical studies that would allow us to assess or measure the operational impact of CSR for a large set of companies.

The remaining five proposed benefits (items 3 through 7) have an entirely different rationale. They are based on the belief that adopting CSR will improve a company's competitive advantage in the marketplace. While the focus of competition may vary—the competition may be over customers, talent, or capital—these five benefits all suggest that companies are well advised to consider CSR as a significant component of their business strategy. In contrast to the operational benefits discussed above, this strategic approach is based on the fundamental premise that some significant segment of the actors in the company's business environment care about values other than their own monetary gain. In other words, CSR strategies presuppose the existence of moral agents whose concerns are not addressed by shareholder value maximization and who are willing and able to act on these motivations. These agents may be part of the value chain (customers, employees, investors) or external stakeholders (NGOs, journalists, politicians, and so on). In the first case, CSR is intended to satisfy a (latent?) "demand for virtue" (Vogel, 2005). It provides value to the "moral self" of customers, employees, and investors and therefore would make a company more competitive in the market for customers, talent, and capital. CSR therefore is frequently thought of as a benefit-focused, competitive strategy. That is, it provides a company with a competitive advantage that is based on providing higher value to customers, in contrast to providing lower costs to the company or lower prices to customers. Note that this approach is conceptually distinct from the operational rationale discussed previously. The demand-for-virtue rationale only works if there are agents who care about something other than personal income or profit, whereas the operational rationale does not depend on such a premise. It works even if the world were solely populated by actors straight out of an economics textbook.

Viewed from this perspective, CSR works in the same way as a strategy that focuses on providing customers with high quality. This strategy makes sense if there is a customer segment willing to pay sufficiently more for a high-quality product to more than compensate the company for the higher cost of providing it. There are many successful examples for such strategies, frequently in small companies created by visionary entrepreneurs. Well-known examples are Ben & Jerry's, Patagonia, Seventh Generation, the Body Shop, Whole Foods, and the British retailer Green & Black's. What is striking about this list of companies is that such firms largely provide high-end products to niche markets of well-to-do customers (Vogel, 2005). It is much less clear whether these strategies can be extended to large multinational companies, especially if these companies offer a wide range of products. This is one reason why experiments such as BP's Beyond Petroleum campaign or Toyota's success with the Prius are particularly interesting. To assess the prospects for such strategies, in general we need to understand their logic in more detail.

SATISFYING THE DEMAND FOR VIRTUE

Let us first consider competition for customers. This is best considered in the context of socially responsible brands. Socially responsible brands are based on the idea that customers prefer to buy their products from companies that abide by certain moral rules or principles. This may result in a higher willingness to pay or in a larger market share. In other words, socially responsible brands allow customers to express a demand for virtue. The existence of such a demand, however, is not enough for a sustainable business model. Companies must also be able to capture this value by building sustainable competitive advantages.

From a strategic management perspective, socially responsible brands are examples of product differentiation on nonprice attributes (here virtue), similar to differentiation on quality (Lexus versus Kia) or location (local drugstore with higher prices versus remote discounter). That is, the company tries to attain a competitive advantage over other firms in the industry that cannot easily be imitated. This can in principle be done through a benefit position (that is, creating higher value for customers) or through a cost position (that is, producing at lower cost than competitors). Socially responsible brands, because they try to satisfy customers' demand for virtue, fall in the category of benefit position. They are intended to create and capture value for customers concerned about the social and environmental aspects of producing, marketing, and consuming goods and services.

To attain a competitive advantage through a product-differentiation strategy, various conditions need to hold. First, there must be a segment of customers willing to pay sufficiently more for the socially responsible product to cover the additional costs of providing it. In other words, if the variable costs of providing a socially responsible brand are higher than the costs for providing a customary brand, the additional willingness of consumers to pay extra must be sufficiently high and the customer segment must be sufficiently big to cover fixed costs. Note that this argument implies that (contrary to widespread belief) the ability to charge higher prices is not necessary for CSR strategies to work. It may be sufficient that customers prefer to buy from a socially responsible provider at the same price to experience the warm glow of having done the right thing. Such behavior would lead to an increase in volume or market share, which would lower the impact of fixed costs and improve profitability.

Second, to qualify as having a competitive advantage, socially responsible brands cannot be easily imitated. This suggests that in markets where there is room for socially responsible brands, we will find product differentiation. This is indeed the case in all the examples listed previously. For example, Ben & Jerry's is differentiated from Häagen-Dazs on the social-responsibility dimension, while both are differentiated from, for example, Dreyer on the quality dimension. Modern competitive strategy (for example, Tirole, 2002) suggests that such differentiated outcomes may constitute stable outcomes in markets with various customer segments. That is, no competitor has an incentive to imitate the other, and both can be profitable.

It is important to note that in contrast to other nonprice attributes such as quality, convenience, or location, consumers cannot directly verify whether a company or product makes good on its promise of social responsibility. In the language of strategic management, they constitute "credence goods" (Feddersen and Gilligan, 2001). That is, the goods possess attributes that are important to the consumer but that the consumer cannot directly experience in the act of consumption. Rather, the consumer must *believe* the credence-good quality. This suggests that companies that try to differentiate themselves along a social-responsibility dimension need to invest in building a reputation. This in turn may make it difficult for other firms to quickly imitate such a positioning strategy.

Although the rationale for a brand-focused CSR strategy is clear, we know very little of whether and how such strategies work. In a recent empirical study, Fisman et al. (2006) investigated the effects of brand-based CSR strategies. The authors focus on a measure of "visible CSR" based on ratings collected by Kinder Lyderberg Domini (KLD) Research & Analytics on community-related activities such as generous giving programs, innovative support for local charities, and so on. As a measure of the importance of branding, they use advertising-to-sales ratios, based on the assumption that brand-conscious firms will be more likely to advertise widely. Fisman et al. first show that heavy advertisers are indeed more likely to also invest in visible CSR activities. This is consistent with viewing CSR as a competitive strategy. Fisman et al. also investigate whether the strategy works. Specifically, they investigate the effect of visible CSR on a company's financial performance. Interestingly, they find that although the overall relationship is slightly negative, for heavy advertisers the negative effect is mitigated. However, only for the very top segment of advertisers (above the ninetieth percentile) can a positive effect of CSR strategies be documented.

The study by Fisman et al. is an important first step in understanding whether customer-based strategies work, but it has important limitations. Their study focused on large public companies. Yet it is small companies, many privately held, that have pioneered the use of socially responsible brands. Unfortunately, there are no quantitative studies of this market segment to assess the validity of CSR as a competitive strategy.

In summary, for benefits-based CSR strategies to work, they must play by the rules of competitive strategy. They must be able to establish a sustainable competitive advantage and a market segment that is willing to pay for the extra value offered. At this point in time, the most successful examples of such strategies are boutique businesses serving a high-end market. To date, little evidence exists whether this strategy is applicable to other industry segments.

A similar line of reasoning can be applied to competition for talent and capital. The rationale is similar to that for the case of socially responsible brands. Like consumers, employees may also be motivated by moral concerns. Therefore, a socially responsible firm may be able to attract and retain more talented and productive employees. The underlying assumption is that employees value working for a company that has an ethical reputation. This may mean that workers are willing to accept a lower monetary compensation package or that a given compensation package will attract more productive employees. In addition to helping to attract more productive employees, CSR may help to retain them and improve morale, which may improve overall productivity.

A well-known example of the success of this strategy is Merck. After Merck decided to develop and then donate a drug to cure river blindness, the company found it much easier to attract scientists to its staff. Merck recruiters mentioned the river blindness episode in job interviews, and a statue of a boy leading a blind man was displayed in the entrance area of the company's headquarters. Other companies that have used this strategy include Starbucks (in addition to its commitment to sustainable sourcing and introduction of fair trade coffee, it provides health-care benefits for all of its employees at a cost that is higher than the cost for coffee) and Timberland (in addition to its other support of charities, according to Vogel, 2005, it allows its employees to dedicate one week a year to work for a charity at full pay).

Despite these success stories, caveats remain. For example, no quantitative evidence establishes a link between CSR policies and successful hiring, retention, or productivity of an employee. To put it differently, many factors influence people's decisions to take a job at a company and their productivity on the job, including the CSR activities of an employer. What needs to be established is whether, holding these other factors constant, companies recover the additional costs of engaging in CSR activities by achieving better success in the market for talent. At this point, only anecdotal evidence suggests that this is, indeed, the case.

Similar caveats apply to competition for capital. It is important to distinguish two distinct rationales for why CSR lowers the cost of capital. The first rationale is analogous to the morally concerned customer discussed previously, presupposing the existence of "virtuous investors"—that is, investors that evaluate the returns on their investment not only by the financial performance of a portfolio company but also by its impact on society. We will use the term "socially responsible investing" (SRI) in this case. The market share of socially responsible investment has rapidly grown over the past decade and currently accounts for about 12 percent of all U.S. assets under professional management in 2001 (Geczy, Stambaugh, and Levin, 2003). The second rationale is based on risk assessment strategy and does not depend on the existence of socially responsible investors. It will be discussed in the next section.

Socially responsible investors have not only financial but also social, moral, and political goals. Therefore, only a company that satisfies certain CSR criteria will have access to the capital of SRI funds, value-motivated individuals, or institutional investors that have a social or political agenda (for example, labor or faith-based pension funds). Socially responsible investors use various approaches to influence business practices (for recent overviews, see Heal, 2005, or Vogel, 2005). Many investment funds (for example, the FTSE4Good fund) and institutional investors such as the California Public Retirement System (Calpers) commonly use "screens" listing criteria that eliminate company segments from consideration—for example, any interest in the tobacco, alcohol, gambling, or weapons industries. Others use ratings such as the Domini 400 Social Index, which is based on the ratings provided by KLD Research & Analytics. Finally, morally or politically motivated investors have increasingly used shareholder resolutions to change corporate practice. Even though legally such resolutions are rarely binding, proxy resolutions have led to demonstrable change in many instances on issues ranging from same-sex benefits and working conditions to greenhouse emissions and recycling. Companies that have adopted changes in response to shareholder pressure include Wal-Mart, Home Depot, Unocal, Baxter International, and many others.

There are two potential effects of socially responsible investing. The first effect concerns the investor side. As in the case of socially responsible brands, most research has focused on the question of whether SRI funds outperform typical portfolios, and as in the case of socially responsible brands, we find little empirical evidence for this claim (see Heal, 2005, or Vogel, 2005, for overviews). As posed, however, this question is conceptually flawed. Consider an investor who has both financial goals and social goals. Suppose there is no conflict between financial and social goals—that is, the socially responsible portfolio also maximizes financial returns. Then we should expect no difference between well-run standard portfolios and SRI portfolios. In this case, an SRI approach is equivalent to a good investment heuristic in the same way that sustainable management may be a good operational heuristic to minimize costs (see previous discussion about operational rationales for CSR business practices). Suppose now there is a conflict; then, a socially responsible investor, by definition, would be willing to give up some return to accomplish his or her social or political goals. Therefore, we should expect a somewhat lower financial return, depending on the conflict between the two goals. What we should not observe is a higher average return for SRI portfolios.

To see this, consider the following example. Suppose tobacco stocks underperform other stocks. In that case, neither a return-maximizing investor nor an SRI fund would hold tobacco stocks. Of course, the rationales are different. A standard investor would avoid tobacco stocks because such an investment strategy would lead to lower returns; an SRI fund would avoid them because holding tobacco stocks (presumably) would violate the ethical values of the fund. Suppose now that tobacco stocks perform better than other stocks. Then, a standard investor would add them to his or her portfolio and thereby increase returns; a socially responsible investor would not do so, which would result in a lower relative return.

Hong and Kacperczyk (2006) have provided some compelling evidence for this claim. They investigate the financial performance of "sin stocks"— publicly traded companies with involvement in the alcohol, tobacco, or gambling industries. They first show that sin stocks are held in smaller proportion by institutional investors expected to be more constrained by moral concerns, either because their investors care directly or because they are subject to more pressure from shareholders. Examples are universities, pension funds, religious organizations, banks, and insurance companies. In contrast, other classes of investors, such as hedge funds, do not hold sin stocks in smaller proportion. The difference is substantial; sin stocks have about a 13 percent lower institutional ownership ratio than other companies. Following an argument by Merton (1987), the neglect of sin stocks by a substantial segment of investors will depress the price of those stocks relative to their fundamental value due to limited risk sharing. In other words, sin stocks should be underpriced compared with other firms in the market, which in turn means that they would tend to outperform the market. Hong and Kacperczyk (2006) provide substantial evidence that this is indeed the case. Interestingly, this effect should emerge when about 20 percent of investors shun a certain stock for moral reasons, which is very close to the estimated share of current investors that are subject to moral constraints.[1]

Of course, to the extent that individual investors in SRI funds are willing to make such trade-offs between financial and social goals, this finding is not all problematic. (The same argument applies to social entrepreneurs. We will revisit this topic later in this chapter.) SRI funds and their investors need to satisfy potentially conflicting goals. To put it differently, since socially responsible investors value financial *and* social goals, it is a mistake to only measure financial performance. This means that we also should consider to what extent socially responsible investing affects *social* outcomes. We will return to this issue.

The second effect of socially responsible investing focuses on companies competing for capital. The idea is that if a significant amount of money is invested preferentially in companies with a good CSR record, their cost of capital will fall. What constitutes a significant amount is, of course, debatable, but there is little evidence that the growth of SRI has significantly lowered the cost of capital for companies with a good CSR record (Vogel, 2005; Heal, 2005; Margolis and Walsh, 2003). There is, however, some growing evidence that CSR did have such an effect in the special case of environmental performance (Hamilton, 1995; Dowell, Hart, and Yeung, 2000).

One possible explanation (for example, Heal, 2005) for this finding is that capital markets treat good environmental performance as evidence for lower liability risks. This approach is very different from any of the strategic approaches discussed so far (that is, the idea that CSR policies serve as competitive strategies that can satisfy the demand for virtue). The common thread in all demand-based approaches is that the presence of nonfinancial values among customers, employees, or investors creates strategic opportunities for companies to compete on this new dimension. The goal of a CSR institution is therefore to differentiate itself from other competitors to be more attractive to value-based business partners. Note that in each case the interaction between these partners was based on contracts—whether for goods and services, for labor, or for capital. Nobody forced a company or fund to adopt CSR-based guidelines. Companies or funds did it voluntarily to better satisfy the goals of their customers or suppliers. (This is also a key distinction from the operational rationales discussed previously.)

An explanation for CSR that focuses on minimizing risks, however, provides an entirely different reason for companies to adopt CSR policies. This rationale has nothing to do with differentiation in the marketplace but is based on a conflict between markets and their social and political environments. The key actors here are not customers or suppliers, but social activists, the media, pressure groups, politicians, and the courts. (These actors are sometimes called nonmarket actors; for example, Baron, 2006a.) Companies that adopt CSR policies do not try to differentiate themselves but try to avoid being singled out for questionable business practices. The companies' objectives are not to create a competitive advantage but to avoid a competitive disadvantage due to increased risk or reputational damage. In short, these strategies are about defense, not offense.[2]

RISKS AND REGULATION

To understand this second motivation for CSR, it is important to recognize that in some cases there is a value conflict between companies and society. What is best for the company may lead to inefficiencies and/or may violate common standards of fairness or widely accepted rights. In some cases, the reasons for the conflict may be the lack of a proper regulatory or legal system. This is frequently true in the case of social inefficiencies caused by externalities. Global warming, acid rain, overfishing, and so on, are all examples of effects of business practices for which the social costs may not be properly reflected in the companies' private costs of operation. Yet there are (at this time) no political or legal institutions to force companies to internalize such costs.

A second source of conflict has to do with standards of fairness. In many poor countries, the market wage for unskilled labor is about a dollar a day. Note that there may be no inefficiencies here. But many observers would conclude that such miserly wages reflect a fundamental injustice and violate basic standards of fairness, especially if the companies involved create highly profitable luxury products. Similar issues arise in the context of working conditions (especially in poor countries), child labor, animal welfare, and so forth. Finally, certain business practices may be perceived as violating some basic rights. Examples include privacy rights, nondiscrimination, and many others.

This introduction is not the place to assess whether or to what extent such concerns are justified. The point is that they reflect moral judgments of both customers and noncustomers and that some subsegment of such stakeholders is willing to take action against a company to force it to comply with its moral stand. In other words, we can conceptualize these values and principles as constituting the formal and informal "rules of the game" of market competition. If there is a perception that the rules have been violated, external stakeholders may impose costs on companies to make them change their policies and practices.

It is important to note that these rules of the game go beyond current legally binding rules and regulations. In some countries, it may be perfectly legal for a company to hire twelve-year-olds in their manufacturing plants or to dump toxic waste into a river. Still, such behavior may violate widely held ethical standards. Also, the rules of the game usually vary significantly from country to country and market to market. Again, this is not only true of legal rules, but especially of ethical norms and values. Finally, the rules of the game are contested and ever changing. Ten years ago, concerns about animal rights did not play an important role for American business; today it is illegal to serve foie gras in the city of Chicago.

These three factors (informality, cross-country variation, change) are largely responsible for the emergence of crises when companies are confronted by an environment of hostile stakeholders. Consider the example of the 1995 confrontation between Royal Dutch/Shell and the environmental activist group Greenpeace over the issue of deepwater disposal of the Brent Spar oil buoy. After an acrimonious battle between activists and the company, during which sales in Germany and other European countries dropped by as much as 50 percent, Shell UK, which had operating responsibility for the Brent Spar, decided to abandon deepwater disposal and seek a license for onshore disposal (see Diermeier, 1995, for more details). Only one year later, Royal Dutch/Shell was targeted again, this time over human rights issues related to Shell Nigeria. Royal Dutch/Shell subsequently engaged in an extensive reorganization and value-based change process to avoid similar issues in the future.

In the case of the oil buoy disposal issue, all three factors were at play. Shell argued that it was acting within the law, but that did not stop motorists from boycotting it. The main backlash was in Germany, not in the United Kingdom, even though Shell Germany had played no role in the decision favoring deepwater disposal. Finally, Shell had missed the fact that its stakeholder environment was beginning to hold multinational oil companies accountable for their environmental performance. Note also that while the customers who participated in the boycott played an important role in this example, so did Greenpeace and the media that covered the issue. Also, Shell's change in business practices initially did not reflect a desire to differentiate itself as the socially responsible oil company but was an attempt to minimize damage to its reputation. This is, in effect, a cost-based strategy. To lower the long-term expected costs from reputational damage, the company "invests" in socially responsible business practices. Such an investment will improve the firm's competitive position if the costs of complying with such practices are on average smaller than the expected savings from the avoidance of reputational damage. Moreover, since reputations cannot be built overnight, the ability to simulate such a strategy in the short term is rather limited.

Of course, reputational damage is not the only cost that companies try to avoid. Corporate social responsibility strategies may be adopted to decrease the likelihood of regulatory or legal action. Self-regulation is one such example. Here companies may "voluntarily" adopt socially responsible business practices to preempt regulation by legislatures, agencies, or the courts. The rating systems used in the entertainment industry or advertising restrictions in the spirits industry are well-known examples.

We can now reconnect this rationale for CSR with the findings about capital markets discussed previously (Hamilton, 1995; Dasgupta et al., 2004; Dowell, Hart, and Yeung, 2000; see also Heal, 2005, for an overview). Using various methodologies borrowed from the empirical finance literature, these studies provide evidence that superior environmental performance leads to positive stock market valuation. Similarly, inferior performance leads to significant drops in stock price.[3] The common idea is that at some point firms will be held accountable if their actions violate the commonly accepted rules of the game, whether the negative consequences are legal, regulatory, or reputational. Investors recognize these risks and incorporate them in their valuation of companies. Good environmental performance then can be interpreted as an insurance policy against such risks.

Note that this argument differs greatly from the one that relied on socially responsible investors. Here investors are assumed to *only* care about financial rewards. Still, environmentally responsible companies are rewarded, not because investors care about their CSR activities per se, but because such companies are less likely to be penalized for having violated the implicit contract between companies and society of what is acceptable corporate behavior.

Although it is clearly an important driver of managerial decision making, our understanding of how to effectively manage reputational or regulatory risk is still quite limited. One problem is that a company's reputation on social issues is to a large extent mediated by third-party actors such as the media, activists, and public institutions. That is, in contrast to other kinds of corporate communications (such as direct-to-consumers advertising), companies have much less control over the messages that their current and potential customers will receive. Similarly, issues vary in how likely they are to lead to regulatory or legal consequences. These important areas for future investigation go beyond the scope of this essay.

In summary, our discussion of the business case for corporate social responsibility has led to some perhaps sobering conclusions.

- There is no general association between good CSR performance and financial performance.
- In the case of environmental performance, such an association exists. Companies with poor environmental records are penalized by capital markets; companies that excel are rewarded.
- The first of two distinct strategic reasons for companies to invest in CSR is based on the existence of some member of the company's value chain (customers, investors, employees) that cares about social or ethical outcomes that go beyond the firm's financial performance. Companies can then adopt competitive strategies to target this segment by differentiating themselves as the responsible alternative. In the current business environment, such strategies are most likely to succeed in niche markets for affluent consumer segments.
- The second strategic reason for investing in CSR focuses on risk avoidance. It is intended to avoid a competitive disadvantage and to limit damage due to regulatory, legal, or reputational risk. This risk is driven in large part by external actors that are not part of the company's value chain such as public institutions, NGOs, or the media. Corporate social responsibility serves as a risk-management strategy with respect to the external stakeholder environment.

COMPANIES AS CATALYSTS FOR CHANGE

So far, our discussion has been from the perspective of a profit-maximizing firm. This has been useful because it has allowed us to directly investigate the business case for CSR. Yet many existing businesses were not created with the sole goal of maximizing profits. Rather, they are the creation of visionary entrepreneurs with a clear social agenda. Examples include Ben & Jerry's, the Body Shop, Whole Foods, Patagonia, and many more. As discussed previously in the case of socially responsible investors, we would not necessarily expect these businesses to outperform profit-oriented competitors. But from the perspective of such "social entrepreneurs," these investments may be just fine, since they also care about the social performance of their businesses and therefore would be willing to accept some trade-offs.

Some commentators have argued that including social objectives in a for-profit business model violates the fiduciary duty to shareholders. The most famous case of this argument is Friedman's claim that the social responsibility of business is to maximize profits (Friedman, 1970). Yet this argument is flawed. First, in the case where such companies are privately held, this argument does not apply. Second, in publicly traded companies, shareholders may value the social dimension of the business. We have seen evidence of this effect in the case of sin stocks (Hong and Kacperczyk, 2006). Third, as David Baron (2006a) has shown recently, even when shareholders care only about financial performance, they will not bear the cost of a company with a non-profit-maximizing social orientation, as the lower relative profitability will be fully reflected in a lower share price. (The argument assumes that all CSR activities and their costs are properly disclosed to be reflected in company valuations.) The person who does bear the financial cost is the social entrepreneur. But if social entrepreneurs indeed establish companies to create social change, these trade-offs may be exactly what was intended.

Creating companies as instruments for (or catalysts of) social change is not entirely new, but it has certainly grown in recent years. Let us consider this motivation in more detail. Suppose we have a potential entrepreneur who is considering whether to create a socially responsible firm or a regular profit-maximizing firm. Suppose further that this entrepreneur is not only motivated by financial gains; he also wants to effect social change. Now, for this individual, creating a CSR-based company is one option, but certainly not the only one. He also could create a profit-maximizing business and then donate a share of the profits to a social cause, create a nonprofit, serve on a nonprofit board, and become active in the political process. In each case, the (assumed) added financial performance of a profit-maximizing venture could fund these (non-profit) ventures either by direct financial contributions or by subsidizing the entrepreneur's time to serve in a nonprofit capacity. So the question becomes, Why invest in a CSR-based for-profit venture as an instrument of social change rather than choosing more traditional forms of social activism?

Unless the reason is a specific "warm glow" from creating a socially responsible business, the answer must lie in the fact that for-profit entities are somehow superior to nonprofits and government as engines of social change. So from the perspective of social change, the right comparison is not between CSR-based ventures and standard, for-profit businesses, but between for-profit businesses as agents of change and nonprofit organizations. To answer this question, we need to understand what companies actually do to effect social change, what the social consequences of their actions are, and what the success factors are in designing and implementing CSR strategies. (See also Vogel, 2005, for detailed examples of CSR activities.)

This volume provides a rich kaleidoscope of how companies try to address various important social challenges and what explains their success and failure. Its focus is on global challenges in developing countries, because these are precisely the environments where companies more and more are asked to adopt responsibilities usually thought to be the domain of government. The need for today's business leaders to become more effective global corporate citizens is growing. The chapters in this volume assess how well these demands are met.

NOTES

1. Hong and Kacperczyk (2006) also carefully investigate an alternative hypothesis, that sin stocks have higher liability risks than other stocks of comparable value, but they find no evidence for this claim. This suggests that the depressed price of sin stocks indeed does reflect the choices of a segment of socially responsible investors rather than the sophisticated risk assessment of investors that care only about financial gains. We will return to the risk-based approach to investment.

2. In the conceptual framework suggested by the discipline of strategic management, such a defensive strategy focuses on creating a competitive advantage based on cost—for example, the cost of capital discussed previously.

3. Some of the studies (for example, Hamilton, 1995; Dasgupta et al., 2004) use an event-study approach. That is, firms take an action, and then the subsequent stock price reaction is measured. This rules out the possible objection that companies adopt CSR strategies because they can afford to do it (Vogel 2005).

References

Baron, David P. 2006a. *Business and its environment,* 5th edition. New York: Prentice Hall.

Baron, David P. 2006b. Wal-Mart: Nonmarket pressure and reputation risk (B): A new nonmarket strategy. Stanford, Calif.: Stanford University Graduate School of Business Case (draft).

Bonini, Sheila M. J., Mendonca, Lenny T., and Oppenheim, Jeremy M. 2006. When social issues become strategic. *McKinsey Quarterly, 2.*

Crook, Clive. 2005. The good company. *Economist,* January 20.

Dasgupta, S., Hong, J. H., Laplante, B., and Mamingi, N. 2004. *Disclosure of environmental violations and the stock market in the Republic of Korea.* Working paper 3344, World Bank Policy Research.

Diermeier, Daniel. 1996. Shell, Greenpeace, and Brent Spar. Harvard Business School Case P19, September 1. Reprinted in David Baron, *Business and its environment,* 5th edition. New York: Prentice Hall.

Dowell, G., Hart, S., and Yeung, B. 2000. Do corporate global environmental standards create or destroy market value? *Management Science, 46,* 1059–1074.

Feddersen, T. J., and Gilligan, T. W. 2001. Saints and markets: Activists and the supply of credence goods. *Journal of Economics and Management Strategy, 10*(1), 149–171.

Fisman, R., Heal, G., and Nair, V. 2006. *Corporate social responsibility: Doing well by doing good.* Working paper, Columbia University.

Friedman, Milton. 1970. The social responsibility for business is to increase its profits. *New York Times,* September 13, pp. 32–33.

Friedman, Stan. 2003. Corporate America's social conscience. *Fortune* magazine, special advertising section (May 16).

Geczy, Christopher C., Stambaugh, Robert F., and Levin, David. 2003. *Investing in socially responsible mutual funds*. Working paper, University of Pennsylvania.

Hamilton, J. 1995. Pollution as news: Media and stock market reactions to the toxic release inventory data. *Journal of Environmental Economics and Management, 28*, 98–113.

Heal, G. 2000. Environmental disaster—not all bad news. *Financial Times*, October 30.

Heal, G. 2005. Corporate social responsibility: An economic and financial framework. *Geneva Papers on Risk and Insurance Issues and Practice, 30*, 387–409. www.palgrave-journals.com/gpp.

Hong, Harrison, and Kacperczyk, Marcin. 2006. *The price of sin: The effects of social norms on markets*. Working paper.

Margolis, Joshua D., and Walsh, James P. 2003. Misery loves companies: Rethinking social initiatives by business. *Administrative Science Quarterly, 48* (June), 268–305.

Maslow, A. H. 1943. A theory of human motivation. *Psychological Review, 50*, 370–396.

Merton, Robert C. 1987. A simple model of capital market equilibrium with incomplete information. *Journal of Finance, 42*, 483–510.

Porter, M. E., and van der Linde, Claas. 1995. Green and competitive. *Harvard Business Review* (September/October), 120–134, 196.

Reinhardt, F. 2000. Global climate change and BP Amoco. Harvard Business School Case N9–700–106, April 7.

Simms, Jane. 2002. Business: Corporate social responsibility—you know it makes sense. *Accountancy, 130*(1311), 48–50.

Tirole, J. 2002. *The theory of industrial organization*. Cambridge, Mass.: MIT Press.

Vogel, David. 2005. *The market for virtue: The potential and limits of corporate social responsibility*. Washington, D.C.: Brookings Institution.

PART 1

ACCOUNTING, TRANSPARENCY, AND MONITORING

Chapter 2

LABOR STANDARDS IN THAILAND: THE PLAYERS AND THEIR IMPACTS

Julie Boris, Kaya Davis, Michael Gross,
Jessica Keintz, and Jami Totten

In recent years, televised images of young children working in unsafe conditions have touched viewers in the United States, causing an outcry against multinational corporations (MNCs) that manufacture their products abroad and sparking an international movement to implement minimum labor standards worldwide. This movement has had a particular effect in Southeast Asia. Here, we examine the labor-standards situation in Thailand, based on official documents, articles, and in-country interviews. We identify the groups driving improvements in current conditions, describing their recent efforts and the issues they must confront moving forward. In the process, we investigate the financial and social costs of their actions.

THE KEY PLAYERS

Four groups play key roles in advancing labor rights in Thailand: the Thai government, international and local nongovernmental organizations (NGOs), multinational corporations, and local companies.

THAI GOVERNMENT

Thailand has long been known as one of the Asian tigers. Underlying its economic success are the country's relatively abundant and inexpensive labor and natural resources and the government's fiscal conservatism, openness to foreign investment, and encouragement of the private sector. Throughout the 1980s and 1990s, Thailand's economy grew an average of 9 percent per year, making it a hub of business and development in Southeast Asia. Then came the Asian financial crisis of 1997. Currency speculation and devaluation of the baht created a financial disaster in Thailand that spread to its neighbors. Much of the infrastructure development in progress came to a halt, banks were unable to finance growth, and foreign direct investment dropped. In the aftermath, the Thai government focused its efforts on improving the economy and its citizens' living standards. Labor issues were a relatively low priority. Nevertheless, in 1998 the government passed the Labor Protection Act, which updated the 1975 legislation providing workers in the private sector with basic, internationally recognized rights. The laws in place today comply with norms promulgated by the International Labor Organization (ILO). Stipulations include:

1. A minimum working age of fifteen
2. A minimum daily wage of approximately US$4
3. A maximum workweek of eighty-four hours
4. Entitlement to severance pay
5. No termination because of pregnancy
6. Up to thirty days per year of compensated sick leave
7. Equal treatment of the sexes
8. No sexual harassment
9. Full-time, qualified, and accessible safety and health officers at companies with fifty or more employees
10. Establishment at companies with fifty or more employees of occupational safety and health (OSH) committees, to be composed of both workers and management and to hold regular meetings.

Despite these laws, Thailand has continued to be vulnerable to media charges of labor abuses. This is largely because of two weaknesses in its system of worker protections: ineffective implementation and enforcement of its laws and the lack of clear provisions to protect unions and their activities in the workplace.

A huge number of factories exist in Thailand, from basement workshops where a few people make T-shirts to sophisticated manufacturing centers employing several thousand. The Thai government has scarce resources to police all these facilities. Inspections therefore occur only when violations are reported. Even if these sporadic inspections are effective, the majority of local companies still operate without any government oversight of their labor-standards compliance.

As to the second area of vulnerability, multinationals operating in Thailand contract with manufacturers that permit organized labor unions in their factories. Rather than being affiliated with independent labor organizations, however, the unions are normally tied to the factories' owners. This association makes it difficult for the workers' representatives to handle problems effectively without bias or worrying about job security.

NONGOVERNMENTAL ORGANIZATIONS

As in many other developing countries, labor-rights issues in Thailand are the purview of numerous NGOs, ranging from international bodies such as the ILO to local groups like the Thai Labor Campaign. The activities of these groups vary from research, education, and advocacy to monitoring and enforcement. It is reported that a few of the groups specialize in creating controversy, hoping that the government will pay them to quell it. Although this behavior is not prevalent, reports that it occurs highlight the complicated role of NGOs in Thailand and the current stage of maturation of the NGO sector. In general, though, NGOs are not a significant force in Thailand.

The international organizations, however, have been able to wield considerable power by partnering with the media to bring worldwide attention to the country's labor-rights situation. The exposure and resulting outcry have impelled companies selling in U.S. and European Union (EU) markets to implement and enforce relatively aggressive labor standards in their factories in developing countries.

Some of the key international organizations, such as the United Nations (UN), have taken an active role in improving human rights around the world. In August 2003, the UN adopted the "UN Norms on the Responsibilities of Transnational Corporations and Other Business Enterprises with Regard to Human Rights," which mandates a set of workers' rights. Unfortunately, although the document provides for UN monitoring, it puts a great deal of responsibility on individual countries to create the legal framework for enforcing its stipulations.

Between 1930 and 1999, the ILO passed eight fundamental conventions to support human rights. Of 175 ILO member states, 70 have ratified or confirmed previous obligations regarding the conventions and are thus legally obligated to implement and enforce them. Thailand has not yet ratified four of the conventions, including the one on the right to organize and collectively bargain.

The role of the World Trade Organization (WTO) in promoting core labor standards is controversial. In much of the developing world (and in some of the developed world as well), the WTO's actions in this regard are seen as protectionism in another guise. Many officials in developing countries argue that economic growth produces better working conditions and stronger labor rights and that if core labor standards became enforceable under WTO rules, any sanctions imposed would merely perpetuate poverty and delay improvements in the workplace.

The U.S.-based nonprofit Social Accountability International (SAI) works to implement and monitor the SA8000, a set of rigorous, clear-cut, and easily auditable standards that it created and that are used by businesses and governments around the world. Its systems feature certification of compliance at the facility level and support for companies seeking to implement its standards. The organization leverages the power of responsible consumers and investors by identifying companies and other organizations that adopt its standards.

The AFL-CIO has been active in Thailand for many years, educating workers about union activities and effective ways to use unions to drive improvements in the workplace. It has been trying to organize employees to speak out for themselves and teaching them about collective bargaining. Amnesty International promotes human-rights education in the country. Human Rights Watch has helped spur labor improvements in multinational and local factories through its investigations into human rights abuses; its findings, published yearly in books and reports, generate extensive local and international media coverage. The International Confederation of Free Trade Unions (ICFTU) directs campaigns to ensure employees' right to free association, encourage workforce education, and improve working standards. The nonprofit Fair Labor Association (FLA), which combines the efforts of corporations, NGOs, and universities to promote adherence to international labor standards, attempts to fill the enforcement void many feel is left by the Thai government. It helps companies such as Adidas-Salomon, Eddie Bauer, Liz Claiborne, New Era Cap, Nordstrom, Nike, Patagonia, Puma, Reebok, and Phillips–Van Heusen to implement and enforce labor standards in their subcontracted manufacturing facilities, and it partners with universities to ensure that any apparel they buy is produced in FLA-approved factories.

Despite the proliferation of such agencies, the enforcing of standards or guidelines and the monitoring of compliance constitute a significant leap. Of foremost importance in establishing worker protections and rights is the formation of independent labor unions. As mentioned earlier, Thailand's labor unions are closely linked to factory owners and are considered inadequate advocates for the workers. In addition to international bodies like the AFL-CIO and the ICFTU, many local NGOs in the country have been trying to change this situation.

The Labor Congress of Thailand and Thai Trade Union Congress, along with government-related labor congresses, support ten unions in a broad range of industries. These organizations were involved in the February 2004 "Stop Trading Away Our Rights" campaign aimed at improving conditions for female workers and textile factory employees and at getting more ILO conventions ratified by the Thai government. The Thai Labor Campaign, which focuses on worker education, helped employees at the Thai Durable (Kreing) Factory win wage increases of one baht per day and supported striking members of the Light House Union, who were laid off by a local Samsonite factory and then reinstated with a 30 percent pay cut.

MULTINATIONAL CORPORATIONS

Under pressure from NGOs, the media, and public opinion, MNCs have played a central role in creating and implementing labor standards globally. This is particularly true of those that sell into U.S. and EU markets, where working conditions are an explosive issue and the potential damage from media exposure of abuses is extreme. In addition to protecting their businesses, these companies hope to use their codes of conduct as promotional tools.

The majority of MNCs in Thailand do not participate directly in the country's economy; rather, they contract with local factories to produce their goods. It is not uncommon for one factory to manufacture for several multinationals and for one multinational to subcontract with multiple factories in Thailand, throughout the Asian region, and in other international locations. Because they operate in many different locations having different labor standards, many MNCs put compliance stipulations in their contracts with manufacturers or implement labor codes of conduct in their foreign-owned factories.

The corporations we visited had codes of conduct or standards that were stricter than the Thai laws. Although the codes vary from company to company, they generally stipulate:

1. Adherence to applicable local laws and environmental regulations
2. Job selection based on ability to perform, not personal characteristics or beliefs
3. No forced labor
4. No child labor

5. Minimum wage
6. Maximum regular and overtime work hours
7. Compensation for overtime
8. Documentation of hours worked and wage rate
9. Provision for holiday and sick pay and for time off
10. Minimum health and safety requirements in the factory and company-provided housing
11. Freedom of association.

Because the government does not have the resources to enforce even its own labor regulations, the MNCs must take measures themselves to ensure compliance with their standards. These measures include education for workers and factory owners, audits, factory tours, and joint compliance initiatives. The larger facilities that manufacture for many MNCs are subject to numerous compliance inspections, whose stringency depends on the company involved.

To carry out their audits, MNCs must retain substantial compliance teams, a costly commitment. The Gap company has nearly seven hundred compliance personnel who, including audits and follow-ups, visit each of its 150 subcontractors, located all over the world, up to six times a year.

Hundreds of factories in Thailand now adhere to MNC-imposed labor standards, and the country's attitude toward the issue of working conditions has begun to change. The standards are not yet close to being universally accepted, but significant progress has been made in the past few years. Complying facilities boast human resources personnel and complete paperwork on all workers. The working conditions in these facilities have improved, as have the workers' wages and rights.

LOCAL COMPANIES

Most local manufacturing companies in Thailand are in the textile and apparel, agricultural products, rubber products, food processing, or tobacco industries. They fall into two groups: large factories that subcontract for MNCs and small mom-and-pop operations that often produce knockoffs of the major brand labels. The large facilities, out of a desire to retain their business, generally adopt the labor standards of the MNCs they contract with. The most successful typically obey the local laws as well. If violations occur, word can spread quickly through the MNCs' compliance teams. In contrast, the smaller factories, which are not audited by any governmental or regulatory body, have little motivation to create their own labor standards or to adhere to the government's standards. Many of these local companies do not have the human resources staff, personnel or payroll records, or other tools needed to determine if labor standards were being implemented. Clearly, many of these companies do not meet even the minimal Thai standards.

Even the larger facilities can have trouble implementing and supporting MNCs' labor standards. The task requires a substantial investment of capital they may not have and may have trouble accessing. The expenses involved present a significant challenge to companies already facing cost pressures from manufacturers in other Asian countries. The problem is aggravated for local companies that subcontract for more than one MNC, which are thus subject to multiple codes of conduct and must endure multiple audits. Moreover, some of the restrictions embodied in the MNCs' codes are unpopular with Thai workers. Many of them, for example, chafe at limits on their hours, preferring to work longer hours and make more money. As a result, manufacturers may collude with their employees, falsely reporting hours so that the company gets extra production and the workers extra wages.

ISSUES MOVING FORWARD

Clearly, there are sometimes complementary and sometimes conflicting roles played by government, NGOs, MCNs, and local companies in the formulation and implementation of labor standards in Thailand. We next explore how these roles and the relationships among the players might develop in the future.

Government

The Thai government, grappling with issues such as political stability and economic development, has few resources to allocate to improving labor standards. Under pressure from multinationals with strong brands, it is focusing much of its enforcement muscle on infringements of intellectual property rights, attempting to stem the flow of Louis Vuitton, Nike, and North Face imitations and knockoffs from local companies. Nevertheless, the Thai government has taken some small initiatives in improving labor standards, largely through collaboration with the multinationals. As noted, MNCs in Thailand have established their own international labor standards, which they themselves enforce. Now the government is using the companies' expertise to improve standards gradually on the national level. It is also teaming in similar efforts with selected NGOs, such as the Thai Manufacturing Association and representatives from labor-rights-related organizations.

One focus of these collaborations is working hours. In 2005, the Thai government reduced the maximum workweek from eighty-four hours to seventy-two, with plans to decrease it ultimately to sixty. A second focus is the exploitation of the approximately one million migrant workers in the country, especially those coming from Myanmar. Some factories have been paying local authorities to get around restrictions related to such labor. In October 2001, the government passed legislation offering an unlimited number of work permits to migrant workers, hoping in this way to eliminate the local corruption. The main challenge in ending exploitation, as in implementing other labor standards, is effective enforcement of the law.

A principal impetus driving the government to take these actions is the changing global business environment. Most significantly, in January 2005 the WTO's Agreement on Textiles and Clothing (ATC) quota expired. The ATC quota protected Thailand's second-largest export, textiles and clothing, which brought in $5.2 billion in 1999. Although it is risky for a company to manufacture in only one country, cost savings will likely entice many MNCs to move their production from Thailand to China.

The government recognizes that it needs to offer extra value to induce the companies to remain in the country. One inducement could be factories that have no compliance problems, provide on-time delivery, and respond more quickly to orders. The government is also reacting to the fact that fewer and fewer companies serving international markets will source from manufacturers that do not adhere to basic international labor standards.

NONGOVERNMENTAL ORGANIZATIONS

International NGOs are now well established in Thailand; the AFL-CIO, for instance, has been successful in setting up unions in the country and wants to focus future efforts on obtaining maternity leave and social security for workers. Local organizations, on the other hand, are still getting their bearings. Nevertheless, the Thai government, MNCs, and local companies have taken note of the presence and emerging power of NGOs. Both international and national NGOs will continue to keep the spotlight on Thai labor rights and to nudge the public and private sectors to create and enforce those rights.

MULTINATIONAL CORPORATIONS

As noted earlier, MNCs realize that creating and enforcing labor standards for their local subcontractors can help them avert incidents that might attract unwanted media or legal attention and also can help them handle incidents that do occur. In implementing this strategy, however, the companies have run into resistance from local factory owners, factory managers, and Thai workers.

The Thai people have decidedly mixed feelings about the labor standards imposed by MNCs. Although some appreciate the quality of the facilities and the relatively high wages, others feel such issues are irrelevant, given the country's current economic landscape. Many employees prefer to increase their earnings by working more hours than the maximum mandated by the new Thai laws and the MNC-imposed standards. Factory owners who are trying to live day to day cannot justify a capital investment, such as that required for improved labor conditions, that does not increase productivity.

Such sentiments cast doubt on the readiness of the Thai people and economy for labor standards. Accordingly, many MNCs view education as of primary importance in creating a system of standards and enforcement with which factory owners and the workforce will comply.

Local Companies

Issues of labor standards and intellectual property rights are seen very differently by the large factories producing for MNCs and the smaller ones producing for the black market. Although some smaller facilities are starting to adopt the same standards as the big ones, this is by no means widespread. The younger generation of factory owners is leading a drive for improved labor standards. Progress is slow, however, because many of the small companies lack the infrastructure for tracking employees' hours and safety information.

In Conclusion

When it comes to improving labor standards, the Thai government, nongovernmental organizations, local companies, and multinational corporations clearly have different incentives and must answer to different stakeholders. These differences lead to conflicts in how the groups approach the issue. Unless the key players can find common ground, only baby steps will be taken toward labor rights, and the Thai workers will suffer as a result.

The main incentive for the Thai government is to attract foreign direct investment. To do so, it must keep both MNCs and the Thai people satisfied. Those two constituencies, however, often have opposing needs and positions. Multinational corporations, for example, wish to cap working hours, while workers want to maximize their wages, regardless of the hours. The result is that the government continues to create labor laws without enforcing them.

Thai laborers' emphasis on high earnings over working conditions is also problematic for nongovernmental organizations struggling to gain traction on the issue of labor rights in Thailand. The differing interests and perspectives of their major stakeholders—international consumers, the international media, and the Thai government—further complicate their mission. As a result, NGOs continue to seek effective ways to advocate for the rights of the Thai worker.

Multinational corporations have one primary goal: profits. But they have many stakeholders: international media, international consumers, the Thai government, and NGOs, among others. To keep all these groups happy, MNCs have had to create and enforce their own labor standards.

Local Thai companies, like multinationals, are most concerned with profits. Unlike MNCs, however, they don't have multiple stakeholders to satisfy. Barring effective enforcement of labor regulations by the Thai government, therefore, these companies will do what it takes to maximize their bottom lines. The issue of workers' rights is largely irrelevant to them. That may change now that the ATC quota has expired and effective labor standards have become a major way for local Thai companies to distinguish themselves and influence corporations to keep production in Thailand, rather than moving it to China or some other nation with lower costs.

REFERENCES

Broadmoor, Tony, and Sot, Mae. 2002. Land of guile: Migrant workers in Thailand. *Irrawaddy, 10*(8) (October).

Brown, Earl V., Jr. 2003. Thailand: Labour and the law. *Asian Labour Update, 46* (January–March).

Bunnag, Pisut. 2004. Marketing director for Reebok and Wongpaitoon Footwear Public Co. Ltd., Thailand. Interview by authors, March.

Sumeth Srisangthaisuk, Sumeth. 2004. Compliance manager for Gap in Thailand. Interview by authors, March.

UN Commission on Human Rights. 2003. Economic, social, and cultural rights: Norms on the responsibilities of transnational corporations and other business enterprises with regard to human rights. www.unhchr

.ch/huridocda/huridoca.nsf/0/64155e7e8141b38cc1256d63002c55e8 ?OpenDocument.

U.S. Department of State. 1998. 1998 Country report on economic policy and trade practices: Thailand. www.state.gov/www/issues/economic/ trade_reports/eastasia98/thailand98.html.

U.S. Department of State. 2002. 2002 Human rights and labor report: Thailand. www.state.gov/g/drl/rls/hrrpt/2002/18265.htm.

Chapter 3

THE IMPACT OF LABOR
AUDITS IN VIETNAM

*Janice Farrel, Gregory Merchant,
Andrew Sofield,
and Mareike Willimsky*

The difference between a good and a bad economist
is that the bad economist considers only the
immediate, visible effects, whereas the good
economist is also aware of the secondary effects,
effects that are indirectly related to the initial policy
and whose influence might only be seen or felt with
the passage of time.
—*Frédéric Bastiat, Selected Essays
on Political Economy*

Vietnam has experienced remarkable economic growth since the
mid-1990s. As a result, poverty levels there have dropped dramatically, and the average citizen's standard of living has improved
significantly. At the same time, multinational corporations (MNCs)
operating in Vietnam have been criticized for the poor labor conditions in their facilities. Many of these companies have responded to
the criticism by adopting the Workplace Code of Conduct (WCOC),
a set of guiding principles aimed at defining "decent and humane
working conditions." This move raises an important question: Do
such Western-imposed fair-labor standards improve Vietnamese

living conditions, or do they in fact counteract the improvements achieved to date?

Our initial hypothesis is that the implementation of fair-labor standards may directly ameliorate the lives and working conditions of factory workers in Vietnam but may indirectly harm them by driving companies and foreign investment to nations with less expensive labor, thus slowing the country's economic growth. On the basis of existing research and data gathered through interviews with sources in private and nongovernmental organizations, the following sections analyze how fair-labor standards are currently audited in Vietnam and how foreign-owned companies' compliance with these standards directly and indirectly affects Vietnam's economic growth.

LABOR-STANDARDS AUDITS IN VIETNAM

Audits of labor standards have existed in Vietnam for several decades, but they did not gain a significant profile until the early 1980s. The first formal audits were conducted by public accounting firms against standards set by the companies being audited. A series of public relations fiascoes caused many MNCs operating in Vietnam to put more emphasis on, and assign more resources to, monitoring labor standards in their facilities. For example, Nike's contract factories came under harsh scrutiny by labor-rights groups after a worker at the Tae Kwang Vina Industrial Company (TKV) leaked the now-infamous Ernst & Young 1997 labor audit, which found that employees at TKV were exposed without protection to toxic chemicals and other workplace hazards, made to work illegal excess overtime, and limited to one trip to the toilet and two drinks of water per shift; one group of workers, moreover, was ordered to run around the perimeter of the factory for failing to wear regulation work shoes. Soon after these conditions were made public, Nike revamped its audit process to include independent external auditors such as the Center for Economic and Social Applications (CESAIS).

Publicity about labor outsourced to sweatshops resulted in the formation of the Apparel Industry Partnership (AIP), a Clinton administration initiative involving the participation of many U.S. apparel manufacturers. From the AIP was born the Fair Labor Association (FLA)—a consortium of consumer-, human-, and labor-rights groups as well as leading apparel and footwear manufacturers and retailers and more than 100 colleges and universities. The FLA created the WCOC. Audits are now often performed by such specialized FLA-accredited labor-monitoring groups as Global Standards and Verité rather than by public accounting firms, and they employ the WCOC or some closely related code of conduct for their standards.

Some MNCs operating in Vietnam have been quite successful at distancing themselves from the sweatshop scandal. Most—Adidas-Salomon, Levi Strauss, Nike, Reebok, and Timberland are good examples—have Web sites and other promotional materials describing the steps they have taken to improve and monitor working conditions. Close examination, however, reveals that the practice of labor-standards audits sometimes falls short of their promoted promise.

First, significant questions have been raised about the independence of labor-standards monitors. Global Standards, one of the most active monitors in Vietnam, is a coalition of foreign-owned apparel companies, including Adidas-Salomon, Eddie Bauer, Levi Strauss, Liz Claiborne, Nordstrom, Nike, Patagonia, Reebok, and Polo Ralph Lauren. David Boje, professor of management at the New Mexico State University business school, likens this to "asking a murderer to pick his own jury." Verité, which audits and monitors such companies as New Balance, Timberland, and Tommy Hilfiger, makes greater claims to independence, citing the fact that it is funded in equal measure by foundations, individual donors, fee for services, and research projects. Nevertheless, many critics wonder how independent the firm actually is.

Second, the FLA does not require audit results to be made public. We were not, for example, able to obtain results for several MNCs manufacturing in Vietnam. The audits' lack of transparency casts their legitimacy into question. What does a statement by Liz Claiborne that Global Standards has signed off on its audit signify if no details are revealed—if we don't even know what sorts of deviations from the standards are permitted?

The efficacy of audits is potentially compromised by other FLA policies. For instance, Nike employees we spoke with told us that audits were always scheduled. This practice gives management time to clean things up before the auditors arrive. The FLA also permits MNCs to designate a subset of their facilities to be monitored, enabling the companies to have different working conditions at different locations. Finally, the executive director of the FLA unilaterally decides which workers' complaints emerging from audits should be investigated, again without any type of disclosure.

Labor-standards audits in Vietnam thus have many deficiencies that call their effectiveness into question. Despite their shortcomings, however, the audits do have an impact, and this impact needs to be examined. In the next sections, we look at the WCOC in detail, extrapolating the expected direct and indirect effects of implementing the standards it sets and testing our predictions against actual economic and social developments.

WORKPLACE CODE OF CONDUCT

The WCOC consists of nine broad guidelines. The first guideline concerns forced labor. Two forms of forced labor are prevalent in Vietnam: trafficking in human beings, which primarily occurs in the sex trade, and compulsory work required for national infrastructure projects. Neither of these involves factory workers, so this guideline is not relevant for our study. Nor is the second provision, which stipulates the freedom to associate and bargain collectively. Labor unions in Vietnam are organized under the Vietnamese Communist Party, with party members serving as union leaders. Consequently, while FLA members may recognize and respect the right of employees to unionize and bargain collectively, workers' power in this regard is limited.

The third and fourth WCOC provisions, preventing harassment and discrimination, should, on their face, directly benefit Vietnamese factory workers. However, these abuses are likely to be as difficult to diagnose and prove in Vietnam as they have been in the United States. A U.S. Department of State report on human rights practices in Vietnam in 1997 stated that discrimination, especially against women and ethnic minorities, was pervasive in the Vietnamese workforce.

Provision five, which mandates a healthy and safe work environment, should have had a positive direct effect, since it has been argued that Vietnamese workers enjoy better health and experience fewer injuries than they did previously. Still, as with guidelines three and four, testing for this stipulation is difficult, since accurately recognizing violations requires specialized scientific knowledge.

The remaining guidelines all affect workers both directly and indirectly. The sixth limits work hours, thus enabling employees to pursue outside interests and to spend time with their families; the seventh stipulates that when these limits are exceeded, workers must be fairly compensated with overtime pay. Recently, the Vietnamese government reduced the standard workweek for civil servants from forty-eight to forty hours. Although it did not mandate limited hours for manufacturing or service employees, it has made an informal recommendation to that effect. The indirect effect of a shorter workweek should be job creation: When each employee puts in fewer hours, the work must be spread among more laborers. Government officials claim that the shorter workweek has indeed resulted in higher employment in the country.

Guideline eight states that, like overtime pay, the regular wage that participating companies pay must be at least the local minimum or the industry standard for the country, whichever is higher. In practice, many FLA members pay well in excess of the local minimum. Nike, for example, pays its Vietnamese workers an average of US$54 a month, compared with an industry average of $40 a month. Beyond the beneficial direct effect of raising workers' pay, however, this guideline can have the negative indirect effect of attracting people to factory jobs who might otherwise work in socially valuable but less financially rewarding professions such as medicine or education. Furthermore, higher wages can induce companies to move their operations to countries where manufacturing costs are even lower. How these potential indirect effects are manifested in Vietnam is examined in the next section.

The ninth WCOC guideline, concerning child labor, prevents FLA factories from employing any person under the age of fourteen. This encourages children to attend school and prevents them from being exposed to harmful environments that could restrict their physical and psychological development. Like the minimum-wage provision, however, this guideline can have a detrimental indirect effect: A child refused work by an FLA member may seek employment in a factory where conditions are worse and the pay lower. Many FLA members in Vietnam have sought to prevent this by instituting child-labor remediation programs. Nike, for example, pays for the education of any workers found to be too young (having lied about their age during the application process), continuing the payments until the children are old enough to work; the company then offers them positions. Such programs can be effective, but they benefit only the small number of underage children who manage to wangle their way into jobs at these companies.

In summary, although the efficacy of labor-standards audits remains uncertain, the WCOC appears to have improved the working conditions in factories where it is implemented. In the next section, we look at some of the indirect effects that the WCOC may have on both the Vietnamese economy and the country's society as a whole.

INDIRECT EFFECTS ON VIETNAM'S ECONOMY AND SOCIETY

In this section, we look at four areas where the implementation of fair-labor standards at factories might have deleterious effects: employment in socially important sectors, export competitiveness, income inequality, and employment in nonfarm household enterprises. In each case, we discuss the expected effects and then examine the data for the actual impacts.

Employment in Socially Important Sectors

In 1999, two years after Nike revamped its audit process to include independent external auditors, the company's five Taiwanese and South Korean subcontractors in Vietnam paid an average monthly salary that was more than twice the wage of a teacher and considerably above that of a young doctor practicing at a state-run hospital. Inflated salary and benefits packages like these could theoretically draw educated workers to factory assembly lines and away from socially beneficial careers as doctors, teachers, and bureaucrats. Such a drain would be devastating to Vietnam's economy.

That drain does not seem to have occurred. One reason is that most factories create jobs for the unemployed in rural areas. Although factories are located in all cities and provinces in Vietnam, the majority of those demanding large labor forces (footwear and apparel manufacturers, for instance) are concentrated in the industrial zones carved out of the agricultural areas of the south. The establishment of factories in the provinces of Ho Chi Minh, Dong Nai, and Binh Duong creates jobs for local inhabitants who would otherwise be planting rice or working part time in city jobs. In a 2000 survey of 2,220 factory workers in Vietnam conducted by external auditor CESAIS, a majority of the respondents reported difficulty in obtaining nonfactory jobs. Those surveyed didn't even consider farming, because factory work is more stable and generates higher income. Nearly 85 percent planned to continue at their current workplaces for the next three years.

A large portion of the factory workforce, moreover, is composed of women, who have the highest unemployment rate of any segment of the population. Nike, for example, reports that a staggering 85 percent of its factory employees are female. The reason for this is simple: The majority of jobs in apparel and footwear factories involve stitching and sewing, which in many Asian countries is traditionally women's work. Factories thus draw from populations comprising those who are not already gainfully employed—the rural labor force and women—and who would be unlikely to pursue employment within a socially important sector.

Another reason factories have not tapped out the educated labor force is that the government's centralized employment process prevents people from choosing where they work. Although some MNC facilities in Vietnam—such as Nike, Reebok, and Timberland—undergo independent labor-standards audits and have desirable salary and benefits packages, others conform to the Western stereotype of a sweatshop. Because they can't be sure which type of company they would be assigned to, Vietnamese citizens are less likely to gamble on a factory job if they have the ability to teach, practice medicine, or serve in some other public-sector profession.

EXPORT COMPETITIVENESS

Labor standards that result in higher wages raise factories' production costs, hurting a country's export competitiveness. This in turn may induce foreign-owned companies to leave and discourage new foreign investment. The final result is fewer MNC jobs in the country.

Such a chain of events can be particularly devastating to East Asian countries like Vietnam. Many foreign manufacturers made the decision to outsource labor-intensive operations to Vietnam primarily because of the availability of inexpensive labor. If the introduction of audits and enforcement of labor standards increase this cost, the manufacturers may move their operations to other Asian countries without similar labor audits, where many of them have affiliates. The competition between Vietnam and its regional rivals for foreign investment has drastically reduced the dollar cost of wages in the area. Vietnam's competitiveness has also been affected by its neighbors' initiatives to improve their infrastructure and legal climate, areas in which Vietnam lags behind.

In analyzing the impact of labor standards on Vietnam's export competitiveness, we looked at three economic variables: the volume of its garment/textile and footwear exports, the number of Vietnamese jobs provided by foreign-owned businesses, and the amount of foreign direct investment (FDI) in the country over time. Export figures are critical to an analysis of the impact of labor standards in Vietnam because they demonstrate the degree of manufacturers' satisfaction with the country as base of operations, in terms of its social and financial environment. Similarly, the quantity of jobs offered by foreign-owned businesses in Vietnam can reveal companies' decisions to relocate operations closer to cheaper labor sources. Finally, a comparison of FDI levels in Vietnam with those in other Southeast Asian countries both before and after the adoption of fair-labor standards can show if corporations have moved their investments to lower-cost markets that have fewer controls.

Although we examined aggregate levels of FDI in our analysis, we drew our export and job data principally from the garment/textile and footwear industries. We chose to focus on those industries because, first, they had the largest export growth of any segment in Vietnam from 1992 through 1997; second, they are labor intensive; and third, they have been the primary locus of efforts to reform labor standards in Vietnam.

As we had expected, our research showed that wages in Vietnam grew in concert with the imposition of labor standards and labor-standards audits. Real average hourly wages grew at 10.5 percent annually between 1993 and 1998, including a 14.5 percent spurt in 1997 that, interestingly, coincided with the leaking of the Nike labor-standards audit. Although this spurt occurred across the entire economy, the industrial sector was a prime driver: an 11.1 percent decrease in industrial real wages in 1996 was followed by a 15 percent increase in 1997. Significantly, the increase in wages from 1993 to 1998 outstripped the 6 percent annual growth in output per person over the same period. This fact, combined with the dramatic spike in wages between 1996 and 1997, suggests that earnings growth over the broader period was propelled by factors other than performance—among them adherence to labor standards. After 1998, growth of real wages stabilized somewhat, increasing 0.5 percent in 1999 and 2.7 percent in 2000.

When wages are artificially elevated above market levels, as occurred in Vietnam, export quantities, MNC jobs, and overall FDI might be expected to decrease. What actually happened in the country was quite different: From 1998 to 2002, garment/textile exports skyrocketed, MNC employment opportunities grew, and FDI was not damaged as badly in Vietnam as in some regional rival countries where labor was less expensive.

Export Volume

Rather than decreasing, Vietnamese garment and textile exports have increased enormously since 1997—from $1.50 billion that year to $5.48 billion in 2005. These exports are the country's second-largest earner of foreign exchange. In fact, the United States attempted to establish restrictive quotas on Vietnamese textile exports, partly to revitalize the U.S. textile industry and partly in response to a tenfold increase in U.S. imports of Vietnam-made garments over the eleven months ending in November 2002. Footwear exports have mirrored this impressive growth.

MNC Jobs

In 1998, businesses that are wholly foreign owned and joint ventures between foreign investors and local partners employed almost 1.2 million Vietnamese, accounting for about 1.5 percent of the total population. This percentage is significant, considering that nearly 80 percent of the country's citizens are self-employed, with 59 percent continuing to live as subsistence farmers. The numbers of MNC and joint-venture employees have risen since 1998, with textile jobs accounting for a major portion of this growth: The Vietnamese government estimated in 2003 that its textile export industry supplied approximately two million, or 2.5 percent, of the country's jobs.

Foreign Direct Investment

Since 1997, foreign direct investment has diminished in nearly all East Asian countries, excluding China. In Vietnam, however, it has remained fairly constant in recent years. Even though the country's 2001 net FDI inflow of $1.30 billion was barely half of 1997's $2.58 billion, it represents a slight increase from the $1.29 billion recorded in 2000, when global FDI levels dropped 45 percent. Moreover, Vietnam's 2000–2001 rise in foreign investment, though small, still compares favorably with the situation of its primary rivals for FDI. Malaysia, for instance, suffered an 85 percent decrease in net inflows in this period, and Indonesia merely managed to slow the flow of funds *leaving* the country, improving its FDI deficit from –$4.55 billion in 2000 to –$3.2 billion in 2001, according to the United Nations (UN) *World Investment Report 2002*. Vietnamese FDI continued to be sluggish in 2002, but the UN report nevertheless ranked the country twentieth in the world for the year in terms of the ratio of its share of global FDI flows to its share of global gross domestic product (GDP).

These figures imply that MNCs are willing to absorb the additional costs associated with labor-standards audits and to continue to invest in Vietnamese operations. This willingness was also reflected in our interviews with executives. Nike management, for example, indicated that it planned to continue expanding its substantial Vietnamese operations over the next five to ten years. This commitment by the largest private employer in Vietnam suggests that FDI will not necessarily decrease in the face of increased production costs.

The continued success of Vietnam in attracting foreign investment dollars, combined with evidence that textile exports have grown rapidly and that MNC employment opportunities have not withered, indicates that considerations other than labor costs play a role in determining where foreign companies deploy their investments in Southeast Asia. One such factor is a country's risk profile. In explaining its decision to invest in Vietnam rather than Indonesia, Nike specifically cited as a major concern the relative instability of the latter country's government. The Political Risk Services Group of the World Bank rates Vietnam above its regional competitors in terms not only of government stability but also rule of law, corruption, and quality of bureaucracy.

Another factor that plays into FDI decisions and the flow of investment funds and jobs from one country to another is the microregional impact of labor standards. For example, employee pay in Ho Chi Minh and Hanoi provinces, which together account for 25 percent of Vietnamese wage jobs, was approximately 50 percent higher than in other regions of the country. Any increase in these two provinces' pay levels would likely have a greater impact on future FDI decisions than a rise in one of Vietnam's medium-sized urban areas, where wages are approximately 15 percent lower.

The U.S. government's ongoing attempt to impose quotas on Vietnam's garment exports may also affect future investment in the country by reducing U.S. companies' ability to exploit economies of scale there. The U.S. Association of Importers of Textiles and Apparel warned U.S. trade representative Robert Zoellick that members already faced significant costs because of efforts to cut back Vietnam's trade with the United States and that the members were looking for other countries in which to do business.

In sum, the rise in wages associated with the implementation of fair-labor standards has not priced Vietnam out of the inexpensive-labor market, in part because of the weight given other considerations, such as the relative stability of the country's government. However, still other factors, such as trade restrictions, together with changes to different FDI drivers, could combine with higher labor costs in the future to the detriment of the Vietnamese economy.

INCOME INEQUALITY

The minimum wage for domestic companies in Vietnam is far lower than that for foreign enterprises. The rule mandating the minimum wage at Vietnamese-owned facilities, moreover, is often not enforced. As a result, there is a systematic income gap between employees of MNCs and the rest of the workforce. With more and more foreign companies establishing a presence in Vietnam, this inequality is expected to increase. With inadequate job growth and excess supply of labor, this is unlikely to change soon.

Between 1993 and 1998, overall income inequality in Vietnam increased. Since disparities are smaller among households engaged in agriculture than among those engaged in wage employment, the income gap may be expected to widen as more people shift from farming to factories.

Although within the wage segment overall, general inequality declined from 1993 to 1998, it rose quickly in medium-sized and large cities. Since most foreign enterprises are located around major cities, this increase could be at least partly due to the higher wages paid by companies implementing fair-labor standards. The exact role of the standards, however, is difficult to evaluate and is beyond the scope of this chapter.

Movement Away from Nonfarm Household Enterprises

Nonfarm household enterprises typically play an important role in economic development, providing a bridge between agricultural jobs and better-paying wage jobs. Their importance increases as a country's overall income level rises. Vietnam's continued growth depends on the success of nonfarm household enterprises and their ability to prosper and create jobs.

By increasing wages at factories, the implementation of fair-labor standards could accelerate the movement away from nonfarm household enterprises. Indeed, between 1993 and 1998, the percentage of adults working in these enterprises, although still substantial, declined. Surprisingly, the data imply that high local wages generally increase the probability of self-employment. This is not the case, however, in the richest region in Vietnam, Ho Chi Minh City. Nonfarm household enterprises are less likely to survive in this province than in other areas. One reason might be that implementation of fair-labor standards by MNCs there have given a particular boost to wages. The exact degree of influence is not known, however, and a more detailed analysis is again beyond the scope of this chapter.

In Conclusion

Although labor-standards audits need to be more effective, their direct effect on Vietnamese factory workers has been positive. Furthermore, their main indirect effects have not been as detrimental as feared: Jobs are not leaving socially important sectors, nor are they leaving the country, since the many benefits of operating in Vietnam offset the increase in labor costs caused by implementing the standards. Labor standards do appear to contribute to income inequality and the movement away from nonfarm household enterprises. In sum, however, the economic and social effects of their enforcement are currently beneficial.

References

Adidas. 2003. Standards of engagement. www.adidas-salomon.com/en /overview/corporate_governance/sea/default.asp.

Bastiat, Frédéric. 1848. *Selected essays on political economy,* ed. George B. de Huszar, trans. Seymour Cain. Irvington-on-Hudson, New York: Foundation for Economic Education, 1995.

Belser, Patrick. 1999. *Vietnam: On the road to labor-intensive growth?* World Bank Policy Research Working Paper 2389. Washington, D.C.: World Bank.

Boje, David. 1999. When is monitoring dependent and when is it independent? August 5. http://cbae.nmsu.edu/~dboje/AA/monitors.htm.

Edmonds, Erik, and Turk, Carrie. 2001. *Child labor in transition in Vietnam.* World Bank Policy Research Working Paper 2774. Washington, D.C.: World Bank.

Fair Labor Association. 2005. Workplace code of conduct. www.fairlabor .org/all/code/index.html.

Free Vietnam Alliance. 1997. The state of labor union[s] in Vietnam. www.fva.org/0597/labor.htm.

Gallup, John Luke. 2002. *The wage labor market and inequality in Vietnam in the 1990s.* World Bank Policy Research Working Paper 2896. Washington, D.C.: World Bank.

Glewwe, Paul. 2000, Summer. Are foreign-owned businesses in Vietnam really sweatshops? *University of Minnesota Extension Service, 701.* www .extension.umn.edu/newsletters/ageconomist/components/ag237-701a .html.

Global Alliance for Workers and Communities. 2000. Workers' voices: A study of the assets and needs of factory workers in Vietnam. Center for Economic and Social Applications, University of Ho Chi Minh City (June). www.theglobalalliance.org/uploads/vietnam1%5B1%5D.pdf.

Global Exchange. 1997. Labor abuse charge at Vietnam Nike plants refuted (March 28). www.globalexchange.org/economy/corporations/nike /vietnam.html#refuted.

Hammond, Keith. 1997. Leaked audit: Nike factory violated worker laws. *Mother Jones Archives* (November 7). www.motherjones.com/news _wire/nike.html.

International Country Risk Guide 1984–1997. 2003. *The World Bank Group, development topics, globalization, data and statistics.* www1 .worldbank.org/economicpolicy/globalization/documents/FDI.zip.

International Monetary Fund (IMF). 2002. *Vietnam: Selected issues and statistical appendix.* IMF Country Report 02/5. Washington, D.C.: IMF.

Lamb, David. 1999. Job opportunities or exploitation? *Los Angeles Times,* April 18.

Le, Hoang. 2001. The long and short week in Vietnam and Malaysia. *World Paper* (July). www.worldpaper.com/2001/july01/work4.html.

Levi Strauss. 2003. Social responsibility/sourcing guidelines. www.levistrauss .com/responsibility/conduct/index.htm.

Nike. 2003. Country profile: Vietnam. Nike information brochure, March 20.

Philliber, Kenten. 2003. Director of manufacturing operations for Nike's Southeast Asian operations. Interview by authors, March 20.

Reebok. 2003. The Reebok human rights production Standards. Our business practices. www.reebok.com/static/global/initiatives/rights/business/index.html.

Timberland. 2003. Global labor standards. www.timberland.com/timber landserve/content.jsp?pageName=timberlandserve_inform_global.

Types of forced labor. 2001. *USA Today,* June 19. www.usatoday.com/news/world/2001-05-25-labor-chart-usat.htm.

UN Conference on Trade and Development (UNCTAD). 2002. Benchmarking FDI performance and potential. In *World Investment Report 2002: Transnational corporations and export competitiveness.* New York: UNCTAD.

U.S. Department of State. 1998. Vietnam report on human rights practices for 1997. U.S. Department of State Bureau of Democracy, Human Rights, and Labor. www.fva.org/0298/story6.htm.

U.S. Vietnam Trade Council. 2003. A U.S.-Vietnam agreement on textiles likely by the end of the week. *U.S. Vietnam Trade Council, in the News* (April 17). www.usvietnam.com/publications.cfm?sid=1&pid=8584&x =1&z=30&print=1.

Vijverberg, Wim P. M., and Haughton, Jonathan. 2002. *Household enterprises in Vietnam: Survival, growth, and living standards.* World Bank Policy Research Working Paper 2773. Washington, D.C.: World Bank.

VinaTradeUSA. 2002. Vietnam's export success. www.vietnam-ustrade .org/Eng/major_exports.htm. Accessed 2003.

World investment prospects: On trends in and the role of FDI. 2003. *Economist Intelligence Unit.* http://store.eiu.com/index.asp?layout =product_home_page&product_id=460000246&country_id=.

Chapter 4

PREVENTING LABOR-STANDARDS "EXPLOSIONS" IN THAILAND AND VIETNAM

Jared Cluff, Andrew Knuckle, Carlo Libaridian, R. David Smith, and Wonita Williams

> In today's world, a TV exposé on working conditions can undo years of effort to build brand loyalty. Why squander your investment when with commitment, reputation problems can be avoided?
> —*Robert Hass, former CEO of Levi Strauss*

Developed nations are making a concerted effort to link fair labor standards to global integration and international trade. Nongovernmental organizations (NGOs) and labor unions are using media campaigns to create consumer pressure that will help them realize their goals. However, in less developed countries (LDCs), governments worry that behind the calls for uniform standards are protectionist policies and cultural imperialism.

Corporations operating internationally have been caught in the middle of this debate. Lee Swepston of the International Labor Organization (ILO) says corporations must perform a balancing act between those who see globalization as "the chance of developing countries to tap into the world economy and achieve the development they have been missing" and those who see it "as a license to exploit workers in developing economies and as a channel to export jobs from richer countries to poorer ones." Swepston is senior adviser for human rights to the executive director of the ILO's Standards and Fundamental Principles and Rights at Work Sector.

Companies that fail to take the concerns of the second group seriously are courting disaster. In the mid-1990s, when Nike suffered a labor-standards "explosion"—escalating negative media coverage of (correctly or incorrectly) perceived human-rights violations—the company's net income decreased 69 percent, its first decrease in thirteen years. Its stock price plummeted, and 1999 gross revenues fell, not returning to 1998 levels until 2002.

Here, we address the question of how multinational corporations (MNCs) can avoid costly public relations calamities like Nike's. Specifically, we examine how companies wishing to set up operations in Thailand and Vietnam can gauge their exposure to labor-standards violations and reduce the risk of explosions through best practices, industry choice, public relations campaigns, and other strategies. We take the view that the benefits of devising such strategies most often exceed the cost of implementing them.

THE EVOLUTION OF INTERNATIONAL STANDARDS

The concept of international labor standards dates back to the creation of the International Labor Organization under Part XIII of the 1919 Versailles Treaty, which ended World War I. This section of the treaty was a product of nineteenth-century labor and social movements that culminated in widespread demands for social justice and higher living standards for the world's workers. The ILO was assigned the task of drafting international labor standards, known as Conventions and Recommendations, to which all member states (45 at the organization's inception, more than 130 today) and the companies operating in these states would willingly adhere. Among other important stipulations, the Conventions and Recommendations contain guidelines on child labor, protection of women workers, work hours, paid rest time and holidays, and basic human rights. In the beginning, the ILO was more a symbol than a practical force, and companies did not take seriously the idea of minimum acceptable labor standards. But although the organization did not have the power or funding to monitor and enforce its mandates, it symbolized the growing importance of labor standards in the Western world.

The credibility of minimum labor standards received a huge boost when, in 1938, President Franklin Roosevelt signed the Fair Labor Standards Act (FLSA) into law. Although the act applied to industries that accounted for only 20 percent of U.S. employment at the time, in the thousands of corporations it did cover, it banned "oppressive" child labor, set the minimum wage at twenty-five cents per hour, and limited the maximum work week to forty-four hours. Thus were the concept of workers' rights and the idea that all laborers were entitled to certain minimal protections firmly established in the United States.

In the decades following FLSA, workers' rights in the United States and in Europe were more clearly delineated and expanded under the law. At the same time, the desirability of fair labor standards was becoming a part of the Western mind-set, not only among laborers but among companies, which found high standards a competitive advantage in attracting skilled workers in a labor-scarce post-Depression market. Meanwhile, in 1946, after the demise of the League of Nations, the ILO became the first specialized agency associated with the United Nations. In the next few decades and throughout the cold war, international labor standards remained in large part a Western ideal. That, however, was soon to change.

After the cold war, the rising prosperity of the United States, the growing interconnectedness of the global economy, and improved information about and travel to remote destinations led to the rise in the West of theme-based, mostly charitable non-governmental agencies. At first, NGOs mainly disseminated information. As their numbers grew, however, and competition for donations increased among them, the organizations became more vocal, often targeting MNCs for alleged labor-standards and environmental abuses. NGOs increasingly thought of themselves as counterbalances to the power of for-profit businesses. Today more than 25,000 NGOs operate around the world, half of them involved at least to some extent with working conditions. In the recent past, NGOs concerned with labor standards have had a more direct influence on global companies. As the demonstrations at the 1999 World Trade Organization (WTO) meeting in Seattle made clear, some formerly marginal organizations have been able to influence the way global corporations transact business, particularly in emerging markets. With small staffs and budgets and thus a limited focus, they have been able to influence acceptable standards of global behavior.

Labor standards are ratified and applied on the global level. However, what constitutes an appropriate labor standard in the international context is not always clear. It is, in fact, the subject of much disagreement among the various parties—governments, NGOs, international legislative bodies, companies, shareholders, and laborers—involved in the labor-standards debate.

There is broad consensus in the world community about core principles or primary standards. In fact, most democratic countries already have labor laws that go beyond these principles. Even members of the Association of South East Asian Nations (ASEAN), to which both Thailand and Vietnam belong and which has resisted linking labor standards and free trade, agree that there should be no forced labor and that workers should be granted freedom of association. Considerable disagreement does, however, exist over a second tier of "arguable primary standards." Some countries, for instance, worry that by banning child labor, they will force children into worse employment situations, including prostitution. Even the ILO favors flexibility with regard to this standard, to ensure that children actually benefit from its enforcement.

EFFECTS OF THE LABOR-STANDARDS
MOVEMENT ON COMPANIES

Nike was among the first casualties of the NGO revolution. In the mid-1990s, the company was charged with standing idly by as its shoe-assembly subcontractors in Southeast Asia permitted dangerous working conditions in Vietnam, imposed forced overtime in China, and drafted fourteen-year old laborers in Indonesia. Phil Knight, Nike's chief executive officer (CEO), insisted that these issues were being dramatized and that the company respected and cared for all its employees. He further argued that as a for-profit corporation, Nike could not legislate labor standards in the countries in which it had contracted labor. The mass media, informed by NGOs, were not, however, content to let the issue go. Consumer boycotts of Nike products followed. Finally, in 1998, the company began to take an active role in devising and enforcing the labor standards under which its subcontractors operated: It increased the minimum age and minimum wage of factory workers and decreased weekly work hours. But it was too late; the damage to the Nike brand had already been done.

Nike was not the only MNC to be damaged by NGOs' allegations of labor-standards violations. Kathie Lee Gifford's clothing label, for example, was also exposed, in 1996, for producing its clothing in Central American sweatshops. The brand damage to such companies was usually swift and significant.

To avoid similar fates, multinationals operating in countries with low labor costs have scrambled to address issues involving working conditions. In this effort, they have employed both detailed standards and a wide array of compliance tactics. The latter include devising codes of conduct, implementing such workplace programs as educational initiatives, forming labor unions, and allowing third-party monitoring. Some of the tactics are merely token gestures; others have been undertaken in earnest. Not surprisingly, the results have been mixed.

The correlation between the number of initiatives undertaken and improved labor standards, as measured by independent auditors, is weak. Companies that addressed labor standards before a labor-standards explosion seem to have been much more successful in actually improving working conditions and minimizing risks to their brands. One such company is Reebok. In 1992, the company instituted a formal worldwide code for contractors that barred child and compulsory labor, discrimination, and overtime without additional compensation and called for freedom of association, fair wages, and a safe working environment. In 1993, Reebok took the further step of sending independent auditors to its factories to ensure compliance with these standards.

IMPLEMENTING LABOR STANDARDS IN DEVELOPING COUNTRIES

Devising and implementing fair labor standards in less developed countries is inherently complex because of the numerous parties involved and the lack of a consensus among them on what constitutes "fair." For key stakeholders in the debate, the goals of each group may coincide with or diverge from those of the others. Although our analysis and proposed solutions are derived solely from our work in Vietnam and Thailand, they could be applicable to other emerging markets, such as those in Africa and Latin America.

Our research and interviews conducted in Thailand and Vietnam indicate that several key stakeholders are involved in the development, understanding, and enforcement of labor standards in the region. These are the multinational corporations, local governments, international lawmaking bodies, local workers, nongovernmental organizations, and end consumers.

Faced with slowing revenue, earnings, and market-share growth in the industrialized world, multinational corporations— mostly large U.S.-based companies—have increasingly turned to LDCs to boost their bottom lines. Their plan is to do this initially by exploiting the nations' low labor costs and eventually by developing additional consumer markets there. To realize the savings they hope for from outsourcing their production, however, MNCs must avoid incurring additional costs in the form of reduced revenues. They also must avoid the necessity of defensive marketing resulting from a perception among their mostly Western shareholders and customers of labor-standards abuses.

Local governments play a role by developing and enforcing labor laws in their countries. In part because of the influence of NGOs, these laws increasingly reflect internationally accepted— that is, Western—labor practices. Typically developed in partnership with international policy-making bodies such as the ILO and WTO, they may also be adapted to local conditions and local workers' concerns. Our interviews with low-skilled Vietnamese and Thai workers in the countries' various labor-intensive industries revealed that for them, fair standards mean a decent wage and a safe place to work, as well as the opportunity to work as much as they want.

NGOs, on the other hand, insist that fair standards include high minimum age limits, tight workweek restrictions, and broad worker benefits. Much of the funding for NGOs depends on these organizations' ability to expose "abuses," even those that do not technically violate any national labor law. Many MNCs view NGOs as rabble-rousers that seek to justify their existence through endless and costly third-party labor-standards audits. The intense scrutiny, MNCs believe, adds to the inherent risk of entering emerging markets and thus complicates their decisions to do so. It should be noted that in many cases, the jobs these companies create are a great boon for the developing countries in which they set up business. Western activists who condemn the working conditions at the MNCs' factories are less likely to recognize the benefits that would be lost if the companies were to leave the countries or not enter in the first place.

Through their purchasing power and thus their potential to stanch revenues by cutting spending, consumers of the MNCs' products and services, the great majority of whom are Western, can exert significant pressure on the companies. In general, this group wants the highest-quality product for the lowest possible price. A large segment, however, also wants to feel good about its purchases. According to a 1999 study conducted by the Marymount

University Center for Ethical Concerns, Americans would typically pay one dollar more for a twenty-dollar item if they were assured that it was not produced using sweatshop labor. Thai and Vietnamese consumers we interviewed were much less concerned about the conditions under which their products were produced, and most indicated that such information would not affect their purchasing decisions. In making their purchasing decisions, socially conscious Western consumers are likely to take into account a company's adherence to a verified code of conduct in its manufacturing. Nongovernmental organizations, which keep the public informed of labor-standards developments, exercise leverage over MNCs by threatening, in effect, to erode consumers' brand loyalties and thus the companies' profits.

CONFLICTING GOALS AND CONCERNS

In Vietnam and Thailand, workers,' governments,' and NGOs' concepts of "appropriate" creation and enforcement of labor standards differed widely. The extent of the variation poses a real problem for MNCs, which must try to please all parties while still making a profit.

The Vietnamese and Thai governments are focused on attracting and retaining long-term foreign direct investment (FDI) to their countries. They therefore see their role in the labor-standards debate as being extremely limited. Our discussions with government officials suggest that although they do require that factories be safe and sanitary, it is difficult to legislate a comprehensive suite of minimal labor standards as prescribed by organizations like the WTO. Nor do they have the funds to monitor compliance with such standards. Vietnam's government takes a somewhat more active role in legislating labor standards than does Thailand's. MNCs in Vietnam, for example, must provide social and health insurance for all employees. David Payne, director of the Vietnam Union of Friendship Organizations (VUFO)–NGO Resource Center in Hanoi, notes, however, that "the quality and enforcement of such benefits is weak and inconsistent."

The Thai and Vietnamese governments view actively enforced labor standards as barriers to FDI in their countries and so consider them luxuries they can ill afford as they seek to expand their economies and increase per capita gross domestic product. As they see it, MNCs are already undertaking significant risk in investing in emerging markets. They don't need the added disincentive of stringent labor standards that would eat directly into their bottom lines, particularly since cheap labor was their main reason for coming in the first place. To participate actively in the labor-standards debate is therefore seen by these governments as economically irresponsible.

The workers we interviewed appreciated the efforts MNCs made, whether on their own volition or through the urging of NGOs, to ensure that factories and dormitories were safe and sanitary. They expressed indignation, however, at the imposition of many of the labor standards developed by the Western world, which they regarded as restricting their ability to maximize their economic contributions to their families. The young mothers and fathers we spoke with from very rural areas of Vietnam were typical. The demand for jobs in their home regions far exceeded employment opportunities, so they had come to Hanoi or Saigon in search of work. This they found mainly in textile, assembly, and agricultural factories. Because they were not from the area and typically did not have relatives or friends there, they had to rely on the MNCs or their subcontractors not only for work but also for accommodations. To decrease their dependence on the MNCs and to maximize the money they earned for their families, these young people wanted to work as many hours as possible. They did not understand the need for regulations limiting their work hours. Many, in fact, resented having these rules imposed on them by Westerners without regard for the rules' appropriateness to the local situation. Workers believed they should be the ones to decide whether they worked seventy or fifty hours a week. They also felt that requiring extra pay for overtime, weekend, and public-holiday labor restricted their earning potential by discouraging employers from allowing this labor. Such restrictions on their earning potential made it difficult for them to justify economically the emotional turmoil of leaving their families for months at a time to work in urban factories and live in urban dorms. In fact, some chose to return to their local villages and surrounding areas and earn their living instead through prostitution or by selling drugs or black-market goods.

Those who stayed in the factories developed ingenious ways of working the system to meet their economic needs. If they had to take vacations or weekends off, they might fill the downtime by working elsewhere. Employees at a garment assembly plant just outside of Bangkok created a makeshift factory in one of their homes where they continued to work after reaching the mandated pre-overtime maximum of forty hours a week stipulated by the company's code of conduct. Management pretended not to notice the disappearance of essential factory equipment such as sewing machines and of raw materials like cloth, zippers, thread, and pins, as well as the huge increase in inventory. At first, only a few of the boldest workers used this makeshift factory; the others feared censure from the factory managers. After it became clear, however, that management desired greater productivity as much as the workers desired more work—and would in fact arrange covert compensation—many other workers joined in. The practice is now commonplace, and several after-work home factories are operating in and around Bangkok.

Factory workers in Hanoi described another, more daring solution: They convinced factory managers to keep two sets of books and punch cards—a fake one for the audits performed by the MNCs and third parties, and a real one for calculating the payroll. In the event of an unannounced inspection, managers might revise or destroy these documents, and all parties involved were sworn to secrecy.

Interestingly, we found that local NGOs in Vietnam and Thailand had significantly different opinions from international NGOs as to which measures they felt would most help laborers. In Vietnam, for example, almost all of the local NGOs were concerned not with the mechanics of labor laws but with ensuring that disabled or otherwise disadvantaged people had employment opportunities. The organizations avoided the more combative areas of labor policy, partly because they were closer to local workers and therefore more sensitive to workers' objections to labor standards perceived as too restrictive. When local NGOs did get involved in policy fights, it was for standards they believed directly and immediately benefited local workers. For instance, we noted previously that although the Vietnamese government requires MNCs to provide social and health insurance, the extent and enforcement of these services was often insufficient. It is also difficult for companies to substitute programs providing more suitable health-care benefits for the government-mandated schemes. Local NGOs have lobbied the government to change the mandated health benefits to better suit workers' needs, and they have lobbied MNCs to provide benefits in addition to or as alternatives to the federally required ones. They have also worked to make mechanisms for resolving health-benefits conflicts more transparent and objective.

International NGOs, in contrast, have been more concerned with monitoring the enforcement of labor standards and highlighting for the Western world the abuses they uncovered. Local factory and MNC managers recounted numerous examples of unannounced and extraordinarily thorough labor-standards audits by international NGOs and other third parties. It appears, therefore, that NGOs may actually provide a service not for the laborers in developing countries but for Western consumers, enabling them to buy the products they want while perceiving themselves as socially responsible.

A LABOR-STANDARDS PROGRAM STRATEGY

Corporations investing in LDCs might seem to be caught between a rock and a hard place, having to juggle the concerns of shareholders who want to see profits, workers who chafe at restrictive labor laws, and end customers who, egged on by NGO-informed media, worry about labor abuses. In fact, though, many MNCs have managed to perform this balancing act profitably. These companies see labor standards not as a human-rights issue but as a marketing opportunity. They find that the money, time, and effort they devote to developing stringent codes of conduct, screening subcontractors, and monitoring subcontractors for compliance with the codified labor standards is well spent. Gap in Thailand, for example, like Reebok after Nike, has actively used its excellent human-rights record in Thailand to build its brand in overseas markets, such as the United States, that are sensitive to strict enforcement of Western labor standards.

This is not to say that companies seeking to invest in LDCs have an easy task. They must design labor-standards programs that meet the needs of both their U.S. stakeholders (primarily trade unions, consumer activists, and NGOs) and their foreign ones (local governments, local NGOs, and the local workforce). And they must avoid tactics that appease one stakeholder while offending another. To be successful, their programs must be effective, transparent, and easy to communicate.

Effective labor-standards programs reduce the likelihood of explosions. They have both operational and strategic components. The operational component includes the creation of a code of acceptable working conditions, applicable to both the company itself and its suppliers, and the establishment of externally managed audits to ensure that the code is implemented. The strategic component includes partnering with local NGOs to create mechanisms through which employees can share their concerns and using the company's sensitivity toward workers' rights as a promotional tool to build brand, often at the expense of slower-moving peers.

To be *transparent*, a plan must avoid the appearance of conflict of interest. The corporation will never be fully trusted by stakeholders, so credibility is best obtained by transferring responsibility for labor-standards programs and policies to external players. One step in this process might be to adopt SA8000, an internationally recognized code of labor standards.

Finally, a company needs to *communicate* to all relevant stakeholders the steps it is taking to prevent abuses. Audits should be performed publicly and the associated reports made available to outside constituents. Codes of conduct should be displayed prominently within a firm's marketing material and touted to internal and external parties. Most important, U.S. stakeholders must be kept informed of the company's labor-standards agenda. Ducking the issue, the course often taken in the past, is without doubt the most injurious tactic in today's business climate. Companies that take the offensive against labor abuses enjoy minimal risk of reprisal and in many instances are able to use their approach to the issue to carve out profitable market niches in their industries.

An MNC wishing to enter an emerging market thus needs to create a labor-standards program that is effective, transparent, and easy to communicate. But what specific steps should it take to reach that goal? The following sections describe some recommended actions.

BUILD CREDIBILITY AMONG U.S. STAKEHOLDERS

U.S. consumers distrust corporations' own assertions of compliance with labor standards and tend to be skeptical of statements by third-party monitoring agencies the companies employ. As a result, these customers are susceptible to media reports and secondhand rumors of violations, which in turn reinforce their distrust of the company.

To establish credibility with its U.S. stakeholders, a company needs to build a reputation as a good corporate citizen and defender of workers' rights. One way to do this is to give workers a voice. Additionally, the company should arrange for labor-standards audits to be performed by teams pairing local NGOs with recognized third-party accreditation agencies. Then it should actively market its good citizenship to its socially concerned customers. In reality, this is a type of brand building. Just as some consumers choose products they feel are reliable, trendy, or classic, others select products based on the producer's reputation for social responsibility. It is much easier to establish this reputation from the beginning than to repair a tarnished one.

IDENTIFY AND SERVE THE NEEDS OF LOCAL WORKERS

Ironically, many labor laws designed to benefit local workers wind up alienating them. As noted earlier, although Vietnamese workers appreciate regulations that mandate safe and hygienic factory conditions, they resent those that limit work hours, viewing such protections as restricting their earning potential. They circumvent such rules through actions such as working from home and cooking the books. The parent company runs the risk of these circumventions being discovered and exposed as "abuses" in the Western media. To prevent this, companies entering an LDC should adopt labor standards that meet the needs of local laborers, rather than imposing regulations that serve the very different needs of U.S. workers.

COMMUNICATE THE REAL NEEDS OF LOCAL WORKERS TO U.S. STAKEHOLDERS

A large and persistent gap exists between the reality of Vietnamese working conditions and how U.S. stakeholders perceive them. Our research contradicted the view often expressed in the labor-standards debate that workers in developing countries are exploited, underpaid, and forced to work in dangerous conditions. Although worker protections in Vietnam have deficiencies, these primarily concern health insurance coverage and coherent legal mechanisms for conflict resolution in the workplace. Moreover, local NGOs strongly believe that the country's existing mechanisms for enforcing workers rights and labor standards are excellent, and in many cases far more progressive than those in the United States.

It is clearly in the interests of a multinational seeking to operate in a developing country to erase the gap between reality and perception. To do so, the company must stem the flow of misinformation by finding ways to articulate workers' true needs clearly and credibly to U.S. stakeholders, demonstrating that far from exploiting local workers, it actually offers them hope and opportunity.

GAIN A BETTER UNDERSTANDING OF END CUSTOMERS

Once a company has ensured that it is meeting all primary labor standards, it must establish how much further it should go. We've seen that even MNCs that exceed the primary standards may come under attack from NGOs. To reach a proper balance between the expenses it will incur preventing an explosion and the savings it realizes in production costs, the company should determine how sensitive its particular customers are to "outcry" about abuses.

PREEMPT THE NGOS BY MARKETING SOUND LABOR PRACTICES

Historically, large corporations have marketed their products, not their practices. Today, that approach leaves them vulnerable to attack. Companies that promote their labor efforts before NGO outcry begins can control their consumers' perceptions, preventing explosions that have no factual basis. A good example of the effectiveness of marketing one's practices is the success of tuna manufacturers in neutralizing environmental concerns by promoting their products as being dolphin safe.

MOBILIZE LOCAL WORKERS

Mobilizing the employees is the cornerstone of an integrated approach to preventing labor-standards explosions. MNCs entering Vietnam should support the formation of workers' unions and the election of labor spokespersons to close the information gap between local and U.S. stakeholders. Additionally, they should adopt codes of conduct tailored to the particular needs of local workers. These measures prevent covert operations such as after-work factories and create a credible vehicle for informing U.S. stakeholders of employees' real-world needs and actual working conditions. They establish the company as a champion of workers' rights, thus enhancing its credibility and forestalling criticisms by U.S. labor unions and activist communities.

Empowering employees to design the company's code of conduct and method of enforcement ensures that their needs are voiced and met, thus maximizing their satisfaction and encouraging their productivity. This approach also thwarts third-party allegations of ignoring or denying workers' needs, since the company can point to its employees as the source of the code that guides its policies and programs.

Beyond codifying its employees' needs, the company should enlist local NGOs to represent workers' interests to global participants. These organizations, as credible sources of local market knowledge, are in the best position to act in this capacity. They can thus bridge the communication gap between the factory floor and the often politically charged playing field of international workers'-rights organizations.

REFERENCES

Asian Development Bank (ADB). 2002. *Recommendations on occupational safety and health.* ADB Regional Workshop on Labor Standards, Manila (September 18–19).

Asian Development Bank (ADB). 2002. *SA8000: A systematic approach for pursuing a high road to development.* ADB Regional Workshop on Labor Standards, Manila (September 18–19).

Bornstein, David. 1999. A force in the new world, citizens flex social muscle. *New York Times,* July 10.

Buchanan, Paul, and Nicholls, Kate. 2003. *Labor politics in small open democracies: Australia, Chile, Ireland, New Zealand and Uruguay.* New York: Palgrave MacMillan.

Burnett, Erin, and Mahon, James. 2001. Monitoring compliance with international labor standards: Industry trend or event. *Challenge* magazine (March).

Elliott, Kimberly Ann, and Freeman, Richard B. 2003. *Can labor standards improve under globalization?* Washington, D.C.: Institute for International Economics.

Engerman, Stanley. 2003. The evolution of labor standards. In Kaushik Basu, Henrik Horn, Lisa Román, and Judith Shapiro (Eds.), *International Labor Standards.* Oxford, UK: Blackwell.

Finn, Ed. 2001. A new role for unions. *Briarpatch* magazine (October).

Freeman, Richard B. 1996. International labor standards and world trade: Friends or foes? In Jeffrey J. Schott (Ed.), *The world trading system: Challenges ahead.* Washington, D.C.: Peterson Institute for International Economics.

Frost, Stephen, and Wong, May. 2004. Monitoring Mattel in China. *Asia Monitor Resource Center* (February 20).

Hasan, Rana, and Mitra, Devashish (Eds.). 2003. *The impact of trade on labor: Issues, perspectives, and experiences from developing Asia.* Amsterdam: Elsevier Science (North Holland).

Hilton, Margaret (Ed.) 2001. *Monitoring international labor standards.* Washington, D.C.: National Academic Press.

Kantor, Harry S. 1958. Two decades of the Fair Labor Standards Act. *Monthly Labor Review* (October).

Levine, Marvin J. 1997. *Worker rights and labor standards in Asia's four new tigers: A comparative perspective.* New York: Plenum Press.

Longworth, R.C. 1999. Activist groups gain influence in global body. *Chicago Tribune,* December 1.

Marymount University Center for Ethical Concerns. 1999. The consumer and sweatshops. www.marymount/edu/news/garmentstudy/overview.html.

Mitchell, R., and O'Neal, M. 1996. Managing by values. *Business Week* (September 12).

Onishi, Norimitsu. 2002. Nongovernmental organizations show their growing power. *New York Times,* March 22.

Payne, David. 2004. Director of VUFO-NGO Resource Center, Hanoi. Interview by authors, April 1.

Shepard, Ed. 2004. Credibility gap between codes and conduct: A smokescreen for poor labor standards. *Asia Monitor Resource Center* (February 20).

Siebert, Horst. 1999. *Globalization and labor.* Tübingen, Germany: Elsevier Science.

Singh, Nirvikar. 2003. The impact of international labor standards: A survey of economic theory. In Kaushik Basu, Henrik Horn, Lisa Román, and Judith Shapiro (Eds.), *International Labor Standards.* Oxford, UK: Blackwell.

Singh, Sumeth. 2004. Marketing manager for the Gap in Thailand. Interview by authors, March.

Spar, Debora L., and Burns, Jennifer. 2002. Hitting the wall: Nike and international labor practices. Harvard Business School Case 700-047, September 6.

Staiger, Robert. 2003. The international organization and enforcement of labor standards. In Kaushik Basu, Henrik Horn, Lisa Román, and Judith Shapiro (Eds.), *International Labor Standards.* Oxford, UK: Blackwell.

Swepston, Lee. 2002. *Globalization and international labor standards: Countering the Seattle syndrome.* Address presented at Raoul Wallenberg Institute Seminar Series in Human Rights, Lund, Sweden (October 14).

Swinnerton, Ken. 1996. *An essay on economic efficiency and core labor standards.* Washington, D.C.: U.S. Department of Labor, Bureau of International Affairs.

Vijaya, Ramya. 2002. *An empirical evaluation of the economic determinants and impacts of labor standards.* Doctoral dissertation, American University.

Yimprasert, Junya, and Candland, Christopher. 2000. Can corporate codes of conduct promote labor standards? Evidence from the Thai footwear and apparel industries. Thai Labor Campaign. www.thailabour.org/docs/CodesReport/index.html.

Yimprasert, Junya, and Candland, Christopher. 2000. Corporate codes of conduct: A follow-up study. Thai Labor Campaign. www.thailabour.org/docs/CodesReport/followup.html.

PART 2

ECONOMIC EMPOWERMENT AND GLOBAL CITIZENSHIP

Chapter 5

THE IMPACT OF FOREIGN
DIRECT INVESTMENT ON
CHINESE WOMEN

*Alison Curd, Amelia Julian,
Adam Sabow, and Leigh Seligman*

The twentieth century witnessed a marked improvement in the
financial and social status of Chinese women. Capitalist industrialization, communism, and government laws and policies all contributed to this amelioration. We explore the impact of another
major factor: the foreign direct investment (FDI) in China of multinational corporations (MNCs). Specifically, we look at how FDI
has affected women's lives in the country and evaluate whether this
effect will continue into the future.

After describing women's evolving economic role in China
during the twentieth century, we examine the tendency of foreign
companies investing there to actively target women. We next investigate whether such targeting has increased the number of women
in the workforce and what effect it has had on wages. In answering
these questions, we draw on evidence from China itself as well as
from studies conducted in other developing countries, since
Chinese data on this topic are limited and potentially suspect.
Finally, we look at the impact of FDI on women's social status, both
on a macro level and, by examining the lives of several women who
have been affected by FDI, on a micro level.

In addition to consulting secondary sources and government
surveys, we interviewed management and workers at several of the

"best-in-class" MCNs operating in China. However, for reasons of confidentiality, we have not identified the companies for which they work.

THE EVOLVING ECONOMIC ROLE OF WOMEN IN CHINA

Chinese women have been largely dependent on their families and spouses for survival. During the twentieth century, however, several economic and political developments improved women's social and financial status. One of these was the introduction of capitalist industrialization. At the beginning of the twentieth century, the introduction of modern factory production in many Chinese towns and cities caused the workforce to become disproportionately female. When factories were initially established, management had difficulty controlling male workers and preventing them from engaging in political activity. In addition, female labor tended to be cheaper. As a result, employers hired women workers. This development advanced most quickly in Shanghai, China's largest industrialized city. According to a study by sociologists Norman Bonney, Norman Stockman, and Sheng Xuewen, "As early as 1929, 61 percent of the workers in Shanghai's industries were women, and in the largest industry, the cotton industry, 76 percent were women."

Like their male counterparts, many of the new female workers lived in factory dormitories and were given clothing and food. In the Shanghai cotton mills, women recruited as contract labor were restricted by the terms of those contracts to living where their employers told them to, eating what the employers provided, and leaving their living quarters only with their employers' permission. In contrast, many women who were not recruited under contracts used their wages to contribute to the maintenance of private family households whose members performed the necessary domestic labor.

Ironically, the communist revolution in China furthered the improvement in women's financial and social status begun by capitalist industrialization. One of the primary goals of the revolution was to engage the entire population, both men and women, in the economic reconstruction of the nation. Consequently, the government sought to liberate women and involve them directly in the labor force, considered the only road to gender equality.

Toward the end of the century, especially from the 1980s onward, a series of laws and government policies—including the Marriage Law of 1980, the Inheritance Law of 1985, and the Law on the Protection of Rights and Interests of Women of 1992—expanded the legal rights of women and broadened the scope of their economic activities. These developments, in turn, increased opportunities and helped improve women's earning potential.

An example of the government's efforts to ameliorate women's financial status is the nationwide Double Learning and Double Competing initiative, which targets rural women. This program has been run since 1989 by the official All-China Women's Federation (ACWF) in collaboration with a dozen government ministries and organizations and helps women overcome illiteracy and receive technical training. The initiative has had a positive impact on women in numerous small towns throughout China. In 1994, for example, in the town of Dongdatum, many young village women worked in three garment factories run by the town government and a textile factory run by the national government. At the village level, a dozen privately and collectively owned small-scale enterprises—including a brickworks; a vegetable-processing factory; a small ironworks; a stone yard; factories making ink, canned food, and bottle caps; and a flour mill—employed local women.

TARGETING WOMEN WORKERS IN CHINA

Existing research suggests that companies involved in FDI actively seek out Chinese women as employees. Magazines and news articles often publish pictures of women on the assembly line. Women are targeted for two main reasons. First, they are perceived to be more productive in light-assembly roles, such as those in the electronics and apparel industries. Elissa Braustein, an economist who conducted the study "Gender, FDI, and Women's Autonomy," noted that employers cited "women's putative nimble fingers, their obedience and being less prone to worker unrest, their being suited to tedious work, and their reliability and trainability relative to men."

The second reason for hiring women is the gender wage gap existing in China. Even today, the average income of working women in cities is roughly 70 percent that of men. Since many companies investing in China have located their facilities there to lower their costs, it is logical that they would target women, who are often willing to accept lower wages than men. Early studies indicate that women were earning less than men when FDI started flowing into China. A 1989 study prepared for the U.S. Department of Labor by the Starnberg Institute, an economic research institute, also found that women tended to be concentrated in electronics, textile, and garment manufacturing, "where low labor costs are a crucial part of international competitiveness."

Just as foreign companies actively target women, many women, for their part, target assembly jobs with MNCs. Since these jobs are often easy to obtain and require a short time commitment, they allow young women to participate in the labor force while maintaining the flexibility to leave for full-time motherhood. The head of a small foreign chip manufacturer we interviewed put it this way: "We provide these women with a whole set of opportunities that they never had before. They come from small towns and now get a new sense of freedom—they live on their own and retain discretionary income that they can spend as they choose."

FDI AND ITS IMPACT ON THE FINANCIAL STATUS OF WOMEN

Multinational companies engaging in direct investment in China potentially affect women's financial status there in two ways: through increasing their participation in the workforce and by narrowing their wage gap with men. In the next two sections, we examine the evidence for these two developments.

CHANGING PARTICIPATION IN THE WORKFORCE

Since MNCs and women actively target each other, foreign companies in China should have a high percentage of female workers. Indeed, evidence in China suggests that women do participate disproportionately in the MNC labor force. However, the precise impact of FDI investment on China's overall female labor participation is difficult to determine, because the exact size of the workforce in these companies and the percentage of women in it are uncertain. The Trade Union Advisory Committee in 2002 estimated the number of employees in China's five special economic zones and fourteen open cities—which together provide attractive incentives for foreign companies and are thus where the majority of them are located—at more than sixty million. The committee further stated that "around 80 percent of special economic zone workers [were] women, mostly between the ages of sixteen and twenty-five." These figures are consistent with the statistics cited by a large multinational retail manufacturer we interviewed in China, which put the percentage of women in its total workforce at 70 percent and the percentage in line positions at 74 percent. Multiplying the Trade Union Advisory Committee estimate of the FDI labor force by the estimated percentage of female workers suggests that approximately fifty million female laborers are involved in FDI labor of some kind.

The next question is whether the introduction of FDI in China increased female participation in the country's workforce. A 2002 World Bank study provides some hints. According to the World Bank, when FDI began in 1980, women accounted for 43 percent of a labor force of 539 million, for a total of 232 million female workers. In 2000, female participation rose only slightly, to 45 percent, but the total labor force increased dramatically to 757 million workers, resulting in 341 million female laborers. Therefore, the number of female laborers grew by 109 million over this twenty-year period.

To arrive at an estimate of the contribution of FDI to the over-all growth in female labor participation, we could simply divide the fifty million female FDI workers (the change from 1980 to 2000) by the economywide increase of 109 million laborers. This calcula-tion, however, entails the potentially unwarranted assumption that women workers in MNCs would not have otherwise participated in the labor force. Evidence cited in a 2000 report by Delia Davin, emeritus professor of Chinese studies at the University of Leeds, does suggest that "most women working in export-oriented indus-tries came from villages where they had little or no entitlement to social welfare." Assuming that the "most" in this statement means 80 percent, then approximately 40 million of the 109 million increase in the overall number of female labors can be attributed to FDI. This, in turn, would imply that FDI was responsible for more than 35 percent of the growth in China's female labor participation from 1980 to 2000.

Other developing countries show a similar pattern. Braustein's study of semi-industrialized nations from 1975 to 1999 found a clear link between the level of FDI and female participation in the labor force. She looked at the share of women in the labor force (feminization) versus the average net FDI (inflows minus outflows) as a percentage of gross fixed-capital formation for twenty develop-ing countries during the period studied. Braustein notes that the "positive correlation between the two data series . . . suggest[s] that high net FDI flows are associated with relative employment gains for women." She warns, however, that before conclusions about causation can be drawn, more detailed econometric analysis is nec-essary, since it "could be that the same factors driving feminization also drive FDI."

THE IMPACT OF FDI ON WAGES

Like labor participation, the amount of women's wages relative to men's is an indicator of women's financial status. Here, though, the relationship with FDI is more hotly debated. On one side of the debate, Braustein finds a marked relationship between the level of

FDI and an improvement in women's relative earnings. Using data from a set of twenty countries similar to those she found in an earlier study, she looks at the annual average gender wage gap (female earnings/male earnings) in manufacturing versus the annual average net FDI as a percent of gross fixed-capital formation. Again, there is a positive correlation, which Braustein suggests shows "that in countries with higher levels of net FDI, the gender wage gap is lower." This relationship may appear to clash with the argument that companies target women because they accept lower wages, but the two propositions aren't necessarily inconsistent: Multinationals may prefer to hire women because of their more modest salary demands but still pay them higher wages than local companies in similar industries.

On the other side of the debate, some empirical studies find that FDI actually leads to a drop in women's average wages, and the tendency of foreign companies to seek out low-cost labor is cited as the culprit. Stephanie Seguino, associate professor of economics at the University of Vermont, contends that "gender inequality, measured as the gender wage gap, has been a stimulus to growth in Asia via its positive effects on exports and its impact on investment, where women are crowded into export sectors, lowering their wages and increasing profit for investors."

MNCs in China side with Braustein in this argument. In an interview, the head of the women's task force for a large multinational company told us that the firm's male and female employees received equal pay and that the wages of both groups were higher than wages they would receive in the local economy. In the same vein, a senior executive at a large telecommunications firm stated that "Chinese women target U.S. companies because they not only know they can receive higher pay but also because they receive better respect and a healthier work environment."

In summary, even if the evidence that FDI has narrowed the gender wage gap is equivocal, that regarding the link between FDI and increased female labor participation is not. Consequently, it seems fair to say that FDI has had a generally positive effect on Chinese women's financial status.

The Impact of FDI on Women's Social Status

Whether the social impact of FDI on women is seen as beneficial or not depends in part on whether it is looked at in relative or absolute terms. In the former case, according to Braustein, FDI jobs are viewed favorably, as "superior to [women's] current options"; in the latter case, they are criticized for falling below "absolute standards of human fulfillment and well-being." Our visits in Beijing and Shanghai suggest that both perspectives are correct: While FDI has had a positive impact on the social status of Chinese women, improvements are necessary—among them, more women in management positions and less disparity between wages for men and women holding similar positions, if not full wage equality.

The actual experiences of individual female MCN employees vary considerably, according to their needs and the particular companies they work for. For many women, the opportunities provided through FDI translate to a different and better life with new freedoms.

In a 1988 survey by Emily Honig and Gail Hershatter of 200 women working in nine occupations in Beijing, Tianjin, and Shanghai, 76 percent said they preferred remaining at the FDI factory where they were working—although they were often hundreds of miles away from their families—to returning home. More surprisingly, of fifty men Honig and Hershatter interviewed, only six were interested in having their wives devote full time to managing the household, and then only if their own wages were increased to compensate for the loss of income. The remaining forty-four didn't want their wives at home no matter how much more they themselves earned. This is remarkable evidence of the broader societal impact and paradigm shift resulting from women's integration into the workforce.

Our own research supports the view that MCNs have had a positive impact on the lives of the tens of thousands of women they employ. Female workers we interviewed praised the freedom they attained through employment as well as the agreeable working conditions at MCNs. This may be partly a function of the companies where we did our research, many of which are well-known multi-nationals. Among the amenities these companies provide are buses that transport workers to and from their housing units, on-site medical checkups and service, and free education. One corporation had dorms on its premises that employees could live in free of charge. Women employees were also allowed to allocate some of their wages toward apartments, enabling them to take ownership of their own places if they stayed with the company long enough.

Not all women working in MCNs, however, have pleasant experiences. Conditions vary widely across companies, even across factories owned by the same company. Ching Lee, author of *Gender and the South China Miracle,* comments that "China has become the world's new global factory . . . with millions of women workers toiling in sweatshops and modern factories, churning out Mickey Mouse toys, Barbie dolls, [and] Nike sports shoes. . . . These mass-produced commodities may be highly standardized, but the factory regimes that produce them are not." For many women working in these factories, the benefits of employment do not appear to out-weigh the challenges.

Even in factories that have good working conditions, women still do not have the same upward mobility that men do. Female employees who talked to Honig and Hershatter explained that men with families needed and wanted promotions, but that women in the same position could not be managers.

In Conclusion

Our research provides three insights into the impact of FDI on Chinese women. First, foreign investment has significantly improved their financial and social status. Women in China today are following a path reminiscent of that followed by women in the United States during their breakthrough into the labor force: From 1890 to 1930, American women's education levels and labor-force participation rose, significantly diminishing the gender wage gap. This progress continued into the post–World War II decades. In the 1980s and early 1990s, the earnings gap between men and women narrowed even further. The same pattern is occurring in China today, only at a much slower pace.

Second, despite the progress realized so far, much room for improvement remains in the areas of wage equality and upward mobility. Women must have greater opportunities to choose better working conditions. As more of them enter the workforce and realize the economic and social benefits of earning wages, it can be hoped that they will gain a stronger sense of independence. This, in turn, may lead to greater cohesion among female workers, resulting in demands for wage equality and management roles. Of course, as in America, the transformation will take years, but it is already beginning, and FDI has provided a major spark for it. Our study focused on employment opportunities and wages associated with assembly jobs in MNCs, but as women become better educated, we may see more progress toward wage equality in higher-level positions.

Third, several large companies—including Motorola, ICC, Mattel, Intel, and Nike—seem to be driving the improvements we have noted in Chinese women's situation through their exemplary corporate policies. Among these policies are providing educational programs, setting corporate goals for female promotions, and teaching women about savings and owning their own property. Motorola even has a women's task-force director for China, a progressive step for a company in that country. The company also aspires to have women occupy 40 percent of its management positions by 2006, a 27 percent increase from today's numbers. Motorola and the other companies mentioned are not afraid to challenge the status quo with their social principles and so are helping transform Chinese society into one that understands the benefits of having women participate at all levels of the workforce.

In sum, MNCs have benefited women in China in ways that have strong implications for the future. As an executive at a large retail manufacturer we visited put it: "I have been in China for five years now. One thing I have observed is that if you give a young woman, age eighteen to twenty-five, the ability to earn money or an education before she has a baby, you have significantly changed her life. You have given her the best thing you could have, because this will help her to better navigate a future for herself and gain increased independence and self-worth."

REFERENCES

Asian Development Bank (ADB). 2002. *The 2020 Project: Policy support in the People's Republic of China.* www.adb.org/Documents/Reports/2020_Project/prelims.pdf.

Bonney, Norman, Stockman, Norman, and Xuewen, Sheng. 1995. *Women's work in East and West: The dual burden of employment and family life.* London: UCL Press.

Braustein, Elissa. 2002. Gender, FDI and women's autonomy: A research note on empirical analysis. University of Massachusetts Amherst (April 1). www.umass.edu/peri/pdfs/WP49.pdf.

Davin, Delia. 2000. Impact of employment of women in export-oriented industries to their access to health and social welfare. United Nations Research Institute for Social Development.

Elson, Diane, and Pearson, Ruth. 1981. Nimble fingers make cheap workers: An analysis of women's employment in third world export manufacturing. *Feminist Review 7,* 87–107.

Jenkins, Rhys, Pearson, Ruth, and Seyfang, Gill. 2002. *Corporate responsibility and labour rights.* London: Earthscan Publications.

Joekes, Susan, and Weston, Ann. 1994. *Women and the new trade agenda.* New York: United Nations Development Fund for Women.

Honig, Emily. 1986. *Sisters and strangers: Women in the Shanghai cotton mills, 1919–1949.* Stanford, Calif.: Stanford University Press.

Honig, Emily, and Hershatter, Gail. 1988. *Personal voices: Chinese women in the 1980s.* Stanford, Calif.: Stanford University Press.

Kurian, George, and Ghosh, Ratna. 1981. *Women in the family and the economy—An international comparative survey.* Westport, Conn.: Greenwood Press.

Kynge, James. 2002. Doing overtime in the workshop of the world—part one: Migrant workers power a vibrant economy. *Financial Times,* October 29, p. 11.

Lee, Ching Kwan. 1998. *Gender and the South China miracle: Two worlds of factory women.* Berkeley: University of California Press.

Lim, Linda C. 1990. *Persistent inequalities: Women and world development.* Oxford, UK: Oxford University Press.

Min, Tang. 2002. Women in workplace on the slide. *China Daily,* December 17.

Minghua, Zhao, West, Jackie, Xiangqun, Chang, and Yuan, Cheng. 1999. *Women of China: Economic and social transformation.* New York: St. Martin's Press.

Seguino, Stephanie. 2000. Accounting for gender in Asian economic growth. *Feminist Economics* 6(3), 27–58.

Starnberger Institute. 1989. Working conditions in export processing zones in selected developing countries. Prepared by Starnberger Institut zur Erforschung Strukturen, Entwicklung und Krisen E.V., Otto Kreye and Folker Frobel, for U.S. Department of Labor. Washington D.C.

Trade Union Advisory Committee. 2002. Foreign direct investment and labour standards. www.tuac.org/statemen/communiq/fdicim.htm# begin.

World Bank. 2002a. *China: Country gender review.* Washington, D.C.: World Bank. http//genderstats.worldbank.org/genderRpt_asp?rpt=profile& cty-EAP.East Asia Pacific&hm-home4.

World Bank. 2002b. China: Summary gender profile. http://devdata .worldbank.org/genderstats/genderRpt.asp?rpt=profile&cty=CHN ,China&hm=home.

Yao, Esther S. Lee. 1983. *Chinese women: Past and present.* Mesquite, Texas: Ide House.

Chapter 6

AVON IN BRAZIL: DIRECT SELLING AND ECONOMIC EMPOWERMENT

*Helen Cha, Polly Cline, Lilly Liu,
Carrie Meek, and Michelle Villagomez*

Although many multinational consumer companies have strug-
gled in Brazil's turbulent economy, cosmetics retailers have
prospered. Beauty and health products are among the few non-
necessities that Brazilian consumers in all socioeconomic classes
purchase. Consequently, international cosmetics leaders such as
Avon, L'Oréal, and Unilever, as well as domestic players such as
Natura, have been launching new products, experimenting with
new brands, and embarking on targeted advertising campaigns.

Avon, in particular, has been very successful in Brazil. This success is largely because the company's direct-selling method suits the
culture, especially that of the lower socioeconomic classes. It has
been a mutually beneficial relationship, with Avon establishing a
loyal customer base and lower-class Brazilian women realizing a
measure of economic empowerment as the company's sales representatives in their communities. The company, however, now wish-
es to capture more of the upper-class market, which is less receptive
to the sole-distributor sales paradigm. Here we examine how Avon
is tailoring its marketing strategy to higher income brackets while
attempting to retain its existing consumer base.

Brazilians are the leading Latin American consumers of both mass and prestige cosmetics. By 2010, they are expected to be the second-largest market for these products in the world. Brazilian women, whatever their income and wherever they live, purchase beauty products to feel good about themselves and to be accepted by society. It is not surprising, then, that the personal-care industry, which includes cosmetics, is a significant component of the country's economy. The industry's net revenue in 2005 was US$6.3 billion, and its workforce numbered two million in 2005, double the size of its workforce in 1994. Although cosmetics accounted for only 5 percent of the personal-care sector's sales volume, they generated more than 20 percent of its revenue. According to the Brazilian Association of Personal Hygiene and Cosmetics Industry, the cosmetics sector grew 15.8 percent in 2005.

Despite being South America's leading economic power, Brazil has the most skewed distribution of wealth in the world. The population can be divided into five socioeconomic classes, designated by letters of the alphabet, based on employment, education, and personal possessions. At the top are the A and B classes, which make up 2.6 percent and 16 percent, respectively, of Brazil's urban population. Members of the A class have high incomes and advanced degrees and are the most sophisticated consumers with respect to travel, technology, homes, and other similar discretionary spending choices. The B class consists of middle- to high-income professionals, with either college or high school educations. The C group, which makes up nearly 30 percent of the urban population, comprises middle-income individuals such as skilled craftsmen. The D and E groups, composed of workers and the poor, represent more than 50 percent of the urban population.

The richest 20 percent of Brazilians control 61.7 percent of the country's wealth; the poorest 40 percent control only 8.8 percent. The poorest 10 percent earn just 1 percent of Brazil's total income, the richest 10 percent earn almost 50 percent, and the middle 20 percent earn 14.5 percent. By comparison, in the United States the poorest 10 percent receives nearly 2 percent of total income and the richest 10 percent less than one-third.

As might be expected, members of classes C, D, and E make few purchases of sophisticated consumer goods or big-ticket items. They are, however, willing to spend what little disposable income they have on personal-care and cosmetic products. Because of this, most manufacturers of these items compete in the mass as well as the prestige markets. For example, L'Oréal caters to lower classes with its L'Oréal and Maybelline brands and to the elite with Helena Rubinstein, Guy Laroche, and Lancôme.

DIRECT SELLING AND AVON'S SUCCESS IN BRAZIL

THE BRAZILIAN MARKET FOR DIRECT COSMETICS SALES

Avon entered Brazil in 1959, recognizing the country as a market well suited to the company's strategy of direct distribution. Several social and economic factors make Brazilians particularly receptive to door-to-door sales. First, the average household comprises 4.2 individuals, almost double the size of the average American household; thus, in Brazil someone is usually home to open the door for an Avon representative. Second, many remote towns and villages lack retail stores, making Avon's representative the sole cosmetics source for many consumers. Another reason the direct-sales method works well in Brazil is that the culture allows for the mixing of business with social affairs. Many consumers would rather spend more to buy from someone they know than make the same purchase in a retail store. Accordingly, in Brazil today, approximately 60 percent of perfume sales, 75 percent of eye-makeup sales, and 80 percent of lipstick sales occur face to face. Direct sales are also the leading channel for purchases of foundations, blushers, and bronzers.

AVON'S CONSUMER BASE AND SALES STAFF

When Avon opened a sales office in the northeastern state of Bahia in 1970, analysts warned that the citizens earned too little to afford cosmetics. They were wrong. Women living in mud shacks quickly bought up crystal bottles of perfume and other products that Avon sent to the area by the truckload.

Despite the fact that the top 20 percent of the population in Brazil earns more than 60 percent of the income, Avon's steadiest customers come from relatively poor, blue-collar households. In very rural areas, such as Patrocinio near the Amazon Basin, a woman must travel hours by boat to reach the nearest doctor or dentist, but one of the town's six Avon representatives is likely to come to her door each week peddling the latest facial cream or mosquito repellent, often in return for barter such as eggs or gold.

With more than 800,000 representatives in Brazil as of 2002 (compared with 500,000 in the United States), Avon has a staff four times as large as the country's army and a distribution network said to be more efficient than its national postal system. Most of the representatives, like their customers, are women from the lower socioeconomic classes. Avon saleswomen in Brazil are largely attracted by the 30 percent commission, which can generate a monthly income from $250 to $700, well above the national average of $260.

But the benefits Brazilian Avon representatives derive from their work go well beyond purely financial ones. Avon is often the only source of earnings for lower-income women, especially in rural areas, enabling them to support their families; this undoubtedly elevates their levels of self-confidence and respect. Thus Avon has had at least three positive effects on low-income women in Brazil: (1) The company's beauty products are cherished by this segment; (2) those women who become Avon representatives are afforded immediate economic empowerment via their relatively high earnings; (3) Avon saleswomen, because of their respected, nonmenial positions, are more likely to develop greater levels of satisfaction and efficacy.

DEVELOPING A NEW BRAND IMAGE (WHILE RETAINING A SUCCESSFUL SALES MODEL)

Now Avon faces a new challenge in Brazil: capturing a share of the higher-income segments while retaining direct-sales-based success with the established lower-income markets.

TARGETING BRAZIL'S UPMARKET SEGMENTS

When Andrea Jung took over as Avon's chief executive officer (CEO) in November 1999, she invested more than $200 million in taking the company upmarket globally, attracting new customers and building brand awareness. As part of this initiative, the company decided it had to reposition itself in Brazil, targeting consumers in the A and B classes. That required projecting a more upscale, international, and youthful image. So, together with media-marketing specialist Synapsys, Avon created a robust plan that promoted premium products through infomercials, advertorials, and product placement.

The cornerstone of the campaign was TudoAVON, a thirty-minute infomercial posing as a personal care show. TudoAVON airs Saturday mornings and is hosted by a well-known television personality. In the print media, meanwhile, Avon placed advertorials such as a two-page spread in *Nova*—the Brazilian equivalent of *Cosmopolitan* magazine—that featured top Brazilian model Daniela Cicarelli describing the Avon products she uses in her skin-care regimen and why. Finally, the company worked to place its products in *telenovelas* (the country's televised daytime serials), which are extremely popular with Brazilians across socioeconomic segments.

CHALLENGES TO OVERCOME

Avon's ambitious upmarket-focused campaign faces significant challenges, chief among them that it must attract customers from higher socioeconomic levels without alienating the company's lower socioeconomic consumer base. To accomplish this, the company has to find different communication methods and distribution channels to serve socioeconomic segments separated not only by geography but also by shopping habits and other consumer behavior. Women from the A and B classes, for example, are less willing to bring Avon sales representatives into their homes. Thus the company might try to reach them through their preferred distribution channels such as kiosks in luxury malls, where Avon products are currently unavailable. At the same time, the company would retain the successful direct-sales model for its strong lower-class customer base. In this way, Avon can change higher-income customers' perceptions of its products' quality while keeping existing sales representatives satisfied, because kiosks in upscale malls will not cannibalize their sales.

A subtler and more difficult challenge involves Avon's appealing to all target consumers on an emotional level. Emotional connection is the most powerful route to higher brand equity, especially with a new market. In this effort, unlike in those aimed at specific segments, it is important to have one—and only one—higher-order brand image, to minimize consumer confusion about what Avon represents. Empowerment, health, and self-respect are good examples of higher-order benefits to which the company can point in bridging the financial and cultural gaps among Brazilian women of different socioeconomic classes. Specifically, use of the company's beauty products—or employment as an Avon sales representative—is intended to promote these positive qualities among all customers, regardless of social status.

One way Avon has already implemented this bridging strategy is through social outreach. The company has launched an aggressive campaign in Brazil to promote a caring, health-conscious image. In February 2003, it announced plans to establish Instituto Avon, aimed at developing and supporting projects concerned with women's health issues. The institute builds on successful programs the company already has in place, such as *Um Beijo pela Vida* ("A Kiss for Life"), which educates women about breast cancer. Avon has also donated half a million U.S. dollars' worth of mammography equipment to São Paulo hospitals and clinics. The health benefits associated with these tactics are intended for all target segments.

In addition, Avon has brought its famous Walk for Breast Cancer to Brazil. This move not only demonstrates the company's commitment to helping the community, particularly women, but reinforces its image as an international brand, because the walk also takes place in cities such as New York, Chicago, Los Angeles, and San Francisco. Magazine advertorials show flags of countries all over the world where Avon is sponsoring the event, thus making customers and representatives aware that it is helping women globally, uniting them under an umbrella of beauty-enhancing products, female empowerment, and optimal health.

In Conclusion

Avon has taken advantage of the widespread consumption of cosmetics in Brazil and established a strong customer base among the country's lower socioeconomic classes. This has had the trifold benefit of bringing (1) beauty products to underserved regions, (2) economic power to Avon's saleswomen, and (3) sizable revenues and profits to the company. Recently Avon launched a campaign to expand its market into Brazil's upper socioeconomic classes. At the same time, however, it has sought to maintain its existing lower-income segments, ongoing sources of customers and representatives. To do so, the company has employed branding and channel strategies, which promote higher-end products under different brand names and via retailers rather than direct sales. It has also used bridging tactics, forging emotional connections to Avon's products across all income brackets based on advertising messages and community events focused on women's empowerment, health, and positive self-image.

References

Alvarenga, Denise F. 2002. Brazil cosmetics and personal care industry synopsis. *Lafis Company Report* (August 5).

Bernhoeft, Renata. 2003. Strategy consultant. Interview by Carrie Meek, March 21, in São Paulo, Brazil.

Brazilian Institute of Geography and Statistics National Household Survey (IBGE/PNAD). 1999. *Introduction to Brazil* (October).

Business Wire. 2003. Avon launches Women's Health Institute (March 21). www.businesswire.com.

Da Matta, Roberto, and Hess, David (Eds.). 1995. *The Brazilian puzzle: Culture on the borderlands of the Western world.* New York: Columbia University Press.

Datamonitor. 2001. Brazil: Face Make-Up. www.datamonitor.com.

Etchenique, Rodrigo. 2003. Chief operating officer and general director at Synapsys. Interview by authors, March 20, in Rio de Janeiro, Brazil.

Euromonitor. 2000. Consumer lifestyles in Brazil. April. www.euromonitor .com.

Euromonitor. 2001. The world market for cosmetics and toiletries. April. www.euromonitor.com.

Jordan, Miriam. 2003. An army of underemployed goes door-to-door. *Wall Street Journal,* February 19.

Lemes, Jose Clovis. 1997. *Industry sector analysis: Brazil cosmetics and toiletries.* Washington, D.C.: U.S. Department of State.

Liu, Jianguo. 2003. Effects of household dynamics on resource consumption and biodiversity. *Nature, 421,* 530–533.

Male vanity might up sales by 15 percent in Brazil. 2003. *Panorama Brasil,* February 13.

River-to-river saleswomen—Avon is selling its cosmetics in the Amazon. 1993, May. *Financial Times.*

Shizen represented Brazil in the world's biggest cosmetics event. 2003, March 26. Shizen Company. www.cosmoprof.it/comunicati/it/comunic ati-elenco.asp?E=6.

Teicholz, Nina. 1996. The Avon ladies of the Amazon. *National Public Radio* (June 20).

Travel Industry of America. 2001. Brazil travel view 2001: Attitudes and trends. www.tia.org/ivis/Brazilportal.asp.

Chapter 7

CORPORATE SOCIAL RESPONSIBILITY: A CASE STUDY OF MULTINATIONAL CORPORATIONS INVESTING IN INDIA

Scott Benigni, Brandon Davito, Adam Kaufman, Andy Noble, and Risa Sparks

Multinational corporations (MNCs) entering emerging markets must integrate effective programs promoting corporate social responsibility (CSR). Such programs may not always improve their bottom lines, but they can be of great utility in helping the companies protect their brand equity, navigate the nonmarket environment, and benefit the societies the resources and people of which they employ. Here, we present a road map for establishing CSR initiatives in developing markets based on an analysis of the successful ones operated in India by two large MNCs: General Electric (GE) and Ford Motor Company. In studying these two programs, we seek to answer the following questions:

- How does a company's strategy for operating in a developing market like India affect how it plans and implements its CSR program?

- What roles do the government and the nongovernmental organizations (NGOs) play in a company's program?
- How does a company decide which social and environmental issues to address?
- Should a company promote CSR primarily in its day-to-day operations or in areas beyond its core business?
- Should donations or volunteerism constitute the main channel for CSR?

FOREIGN INVESTMENT AND SOCIAL RESPONSIBILITY IN INDIA

In 1991, the government of India began a series of reforms aimed at liberalizing its economy, including the privatization of state companies. The reforms have spurred economic growth—gross domestic product (GDP) has expanded by nearly 7 percent since 2003—especially in the services and manufacturing sectors. The country has also attracted increased multinational corporate investment: Foreign funds flowing into the country surged from US$150 million in 1991 to about $10 billion in 2005.

From the MNCs' point of view, India's potential is enormous. With a population of more than a billion, it represents a tremendous market for their products. Additionally, its strong education system for the middle and upper classes, focused on engineering and the sciences, has created a highly trained yet relatively low-cost workforce. Many of these workers, moreover, speak English, a particular plus for American companies that have come up against communication obstacles with other low-cost labor pools. Finally, the Indian government is relatively stable.

At the same time, however, the country presents severe challenges. India suffers from widespread poverty, an overburdened urban infrastructure, and government corruption (it was ranked the sixty-ninth most corrupt country in the world in 2000). Despite a government-instituted affirmative action program, a huge wealth gap separates the upper and lower castes. Many Indian children need to work to help their families survive, making it impossible for them to attend school. This contributes to the cycle of poverty. In addition, India does not have a government welfare system that can provide support for citizens living below the poverty line.

Most Indian cities do not have the infrastructure to handle large increases in population. As more people migrate to cities from rural areas, they stress an already overloaded system, resulting in sprawling shantytowns, families living on the streets, increased pollution, and congestion. Without improvements to roads, water and sanitation systems, and power distribution, foreign investment and economic growth will be limited.

It is essential for MNCs investing in India to understand the wide range of social issues that affect the country. Such an understanding can help them construct effective CSR programs that, together with job creation and infrastructure development, will not only alleviate poverty in the country and build a middle class of consumers, but will also create a more attractive working environment.

The CSR activities discussed here are those of companies that go above and beyond normal business practice. For instance, attention to consumer demand does not by itself constitute CSR, nor does fostering mutual commitment between a company and its employees. Nor do actions forced on a company by its environment. Instead, we specifically address CSR initiatives that are motivated not by short-term profit maximization but by the long-term benefits they offer to society. Such actions have the most impact on the local communities and provide the clearest insight into a company's core beliefs about CSR.

FORD IN INDIA

Ford Motor Company entered India in 1995. It was attracted both by the tremendous opportunities presented by the local market—

Ford India estimated in 2002 that the Asia-Pacific region would account for more than 60 percent of global auto-industry growth by 2011—and by the country's potential as a site for manufacturing vehicles and components for export. With an initial investment of $260 million, Ford established a joint venture with Mahindra & Mahindra to assemble and distribute the European model Ford Escort. In 1999, through a change in the venture's equity structure, the American company gained a majority stake and made it part of Ford Asia Pacific.

At first, Ford's performance in the Indian market was disappointing. This was largely because the vehicles it was distributing were not specifically designed for the country's unique conditions. India's roads were in various stages of disrepair, and the gasoline available was of inconsistent quality. In addition, the Escort's carrying capacity was insufficient for most Indian drivers' needs. The company learned from the Escort experience, and its next release was the first automobile launched by a multinational car manufacturer to be tailored to Indian consumers. With enormous ground clearance and a huge trunk, the Ikon captured almost 25 percent of India's burgeoning "affordable luxury" segment, which accounts for about 10 percent of the country's auto market.

Ford India has continued to grow its business, introducing new vehicles specific to India and modifying global platforms to fit local customer demands. As of 2003, it employed almost 1,150 people, primarily in its Chennai production facilities. The company is well on its way to achieving its fiscal goals: becoming profitable from an accounting standpoint by the end of 2004 and profitable on a cumulative basis by 2008. Not all has been smooth sailing, however: The company's costs have increased both for raw materials, because of the tremendous demands of the Chinese economy, and for European-sourced parts, because of the strengthening of the euro. Moreover, the Indian market has not grown as fast as was predicted in the 1990s due to multiparty coalition governments, poor infrastructure, and government corruption.

CSR Philosophy

> Business must be run at a profit, else it will die. But
> when anyone attempts to run a business solely for
> profit and thinks not at all of the service to the
> community, then also the business must die, for it no
> longer has a reason for existence.
>
> *—Henry Ford*

As evidenced by this quote by its founder, Ford has a long history of giving back to the community. The company demonstrates its social responsibility not only in its core business practices—investing in low-emission vehicles, recycling programs, environmentally friendly plants, and hybrid-engine technology—but also through its contributions to Henry Ford Health Systems and by its encouragement of employee donations to the United Way. In India the company has made CSR a high priority, investing in the local infrastructure, supporting employee volunteer programs, and setting high standards for employee safety and supplier behavior.

Monitoring and Evaluating CSR

The key to Ford's philosophy of maintaining ethical standards globally is its program of monitoring its CSR activities. Worldwide, it prepares annual reports in accordance with the guidelines established by the independent Global Reporting Initiative (GRI). In March 2002, Ford India published its first assessment of itself as a corporate citizen. Although this review does not have the depth of detail required by the GRI, it does follow many of its guidelines. The report documents the ways in which the company has served shareholders, employees, consumers, suppliers, dealers, the environment, the government, local communities, and greater society.

CSR in Daily Business

Ford India complies with Ford Motor Company's global ethical standards, which are embodied in company policies on honesty and integrity, harassment, open communication, smoking, alcohol and drugs, and empowerment. In a country where corruption is still prevalent and bribery often determines contract winners, Ford India claims not to have offered any bribes or to have engaged in any accounting fraud.

All Ford plants worldwide maintain the same health and safety standards. Ford India's vice president for finance, George Graham, noted that his company currently operates the facility with the lowest accident rate in the entire Ford network. The 2002 report states that the company's average annual wages are higher than those at comparable facilities in the country. It also notes that women, who are actively recruited, make up 20 percent of Ford India's workforce, compared with an industry average in India of 5 percent. The company provides health benefits to employees and dependents, as well as subsidized meals and transport (the latter being common practice in India). However, according to the report, some areas with regard to workloads, stress levels, and training and development need to be addressed.

Ford sets high standards for its suppliers, monitoring their product quality, social responsibility, and treatment of the environment. This policy may prevent Ford India from dealing with the lowest-cost providers, but it should improve the country's business practices in the long term.

The company requires that all its primary suppliers be ISO 14001 certified as of 2003. Certification entails achieving conformity with environmental-management standards promulgated by the International Organization for Standardization. An independent survey in October 2001 by the Centre for Science and Environment ranked Ford India eighth out of twenty-seven Indian auto manufacturers in environmental management. In response, the company put in place a plan to improve emissions and fuel efficiency. It also introduced initiatives to eliminate, recycle, or treat waste products.

A wastewater treatment facility treats and recycles all water discharged from its own plant and from the surrounding supplier park. The company's Pollution Control Board is authorized to buy and recycle waste solvent that previously could only be stored at the plant. And it requires that all suppliers within a radius of one hundred kilometers pack goods in reusable plastic containers, which are returned to the suppliers by Ford after use. The policy so far has saved an equivalent of sixty-two mature trees, and plans are in place to extend it to a supplier radius of three hundred kilometers.

Ford India also helps the environment through innovations in its products. The Ikon uses rare-earth catalysts, which reduce usage of precious metals, and the company has developed a model fueled with liquefied petroleum gas that will go into production when the filling-station infrastructure is in place.

COMMUNITY INVESTMENT

Mirroring the types of investments that it makes in the rest of the world, Ford contributed approximately $1 million from 2000 to 2001 to community-development projects in India, of which approximately 75 percent went to health-related projects. In 1999, it constructed the Sanjeevi Health Centre, which provides free care for the local community; it has donated two ambulances for the Trauma Care Consortium in Chennai. The company provided disaster relief to earthquake victims in Gujarat and flood victims in Orissa and Tamil Nedu.

To advance environmental preservation, Ford India in 2000 initiated the Conservation and Environment Grant Programme. It has also donated emissions-testing equipment to the Automotive Research Association of India at Pune and constructed a state-of-the-art wastewater treatment plant. The company has supported local education by creating scholarships and donating books and schoolbags to two schools in the Maraimalai Negar area. It created the Ford Academy of Manufacturing Sciences (which prepares students for future Ford employment) and established the Henry Ford Research Chair (for the study of vehicle emissions, biomechanics, and transportation safety) at the prestigious Indian Institutes of Technology (IIT) in Madras and Delhi, respectively.

The local communities have noted the improvements in health care and education that these initiatives have produced. Some residents, however, have told the company that it could be an even better corporate citizen by pushing for cleaner fuels and encouraging more employee involvement in the community.

Ford is relatively new to India. It is still trying to boost both its share of the Indian market and the social benefits it brings to Indian communities. The company has had its greatest social impact on health care. It is planning to build on its successes in this area with an HIV/AIDS program in India similar to the one it runs in South Africa (South Africa and India rank first and second in the world in terms of HIV infections). Like every company, Ford India could improve its social responsibility, but by measuring itself on its ability to serve its complex web of stakeholders, it is off to a good start.

GENERAL ELECTRIC IN INDIA

General Electric (GE) was one of the pioneers of corporate investment in India. In the late 1980s, led by Raman Roy, who had earlier persuaded American Express to make a similar bet on the country's workforce, GE set up data-entry centers in Delhi. Other divisions quickly followed: GE Plastics in 1991, GE Lighting in 1992, and GE Capital in 1993. GE Capital expanded into the country's credit card market in 1998 through a joint venture with the State Bank of India. Also in 1998, GE started moving some of its back-office operations to India, helping to spark the trend in outsourcing business processes to the country. The number of employees performing back-office functions for GE in India grew from 600 in 1998 to 12,000 in 2002, and the company has made strategic alliances with such Indian information technology companies as Birlasoft, Mascot Systems, Satyam Computer Services, and Tata Consulting Services. In 1999, GE established its media presence in the country by striking a deal to broadcast CNBC in India in conjunction with TV18. On September 17, 2000, it inaugurated the John F. Welch Technology Center in Bangalore, an indication of its belief that India would become a global leader in high-tech services and innovation.

Today, all thirteen of GE's operating divisions are present in India, some producing for the domestic market, others for export to the United States or China. GE Motors, for example, sends 80 percent of its products to the United States, while 100 percent of the output of GE Plastics is sold in India. Overall, GE has revenues of more than $1 billion in India and employs more than 17,000 people. Still, the business its Indian divisions transact is small by GE standards. Many are strategic bets, expected to grow with Indian industry. As Scott R. Bayman, president and chief executive officer (CEO) of GE India, says, "We will invest for the local market as opportunities present themselves. Recreating GE in India continues as our vision." In pursuing this vision, the company invests about $400 million annually in the country.

CSR PHILOSOPHY

GE takes a very structured approach to corporate social responsibility, expressing it as a pyramid of corporate citizenship. The pyramid's base consists of the company's core business values, including constant evaluation, Six Sigma, and stringent personnel review. From this foundation it builds up, through engagements with suppliers, NGOs, and the public, to the peak of volunteerism and philanthropy.

Most of the CSR activities associated with the pyramid are part of the company's day-to-day work. The pinnacle of volunteerism and philanthropy, however, is managed through Elfun (short for Electrical Funds), the international volunteer arm of GE. Elfun originated in 1928 as an association of key GE leaders whose mission was to further the interests of GE and its affiliates, promote the welfare of Elfun members, serve the communities in which they work and live, and encourage cooperation, commonality, and friendship. In the 1980s, its mission was expanded to include all the company's employees. Today it has more than 52,000 members in forty-four countries. With 3,086 volunteers, GE India's Elfun organization is second only to that of GE in the United States. GE provides Elfun with financial and other support—use of employee time and office space, for instance—and partners with it through the company's philanthropic arm, the GE Fund.

GE's Corporate Citizenship Council sets the priorities for Elfun. In India, the council is made up of the most senior managers of each division in the country. This strong backing at the highest level contributes to Elfun's success in India. Another contributing factor is the evaluation of employees on their citizenship, including participation in Elfun activities.

CSR in Daily Business

Venu Venugopal, CEO of GE Plastics, said that GE is "not interested in getting business by any means." That is a significant stand in a country where corruption is still common. It is company policy not to engage in bribery or any corrupt activities. To this end, GE has strict guidelines on what sorts of meetings with government officials are appropriate. It also monitors its suppliers to ensure that they obey all applicable laws, including those involving taxes, and will do business only with companies that can certify that they pay overtime, enforce hygiene and workplace-safety programs, and do not hire children. In this way, GE spreads its corporate values through hundreds of its suppliers in the country, many of which display the GE stamp of approval to show that they meet the program's rigorous standards.

Such policies put GE at a cost disadvantage to many of its competitors. Contracting with higher-quality suppliers translates into higher operating expenses. There are, in addition, administrative costs involved in tracking suppliers' performance and performing due diligence on them.

Also expensive is GE's commitment to sound environmental practices. In a country of lax regulations, the company sets its own standards far higher. Unlike most lighting manufacturers in India, for instance, GE prohibits filaments made of mercury, which is toxic, especially to children; it searches out less harmful, but more expensive, alternatives for its bulbs. Those hazardous materials that it does use are stored or properly disposed of at a high cost rather than being dumped, as is common among many Indian companies.

In terms of its personnel policies, GE strives to create a productive, satisfying work environment and an inclusive, socially committed workforce. The company has a large percentage of female employees, which is relatively rare in this traditional country. Its review policy has a citizenship component, which, among other things, measures the degree of participation in team building and Elfun events.

COMMUNITY INVESTMENT

In 2004, GE spent $1 million on Elfun and community-investment projects in India. Of that sum, $38,000 went to Vidya Integrated Development for Youth and Adults, which runs educational programs across India; the remainder funded other education projects, including $400,000 for seventy-two scholarships and more than $100,000 for the Healthy Futures program. The company, however, does not believe that monetary investments on their own can have a significant impact on a developing country like India. GE Plastics CEO Venugopal commented that "with all the NGOs in India, funding is no longer a big issue. We encourage hours, not money." Following this vision, Elfun's chapters in Bangalore, Chennai, Delhi, Hyderabad, Jaipur, and Mumbai coordinate projects and volunteers across the country. Last year, 1,600 GE employees staffed projects for thirty-four NGO partners, logging 30,000 volunteer hours in the community.

On top of the GE Fund donation to the organization, Elfun contributes volunteer hours to Vidya, an NGO for underprivileged women and children, mentoring the children over the summer break, for instance, and providing vocational training to older students. Of Vidya's many projects, the most innovative is the Comfort School in Gurgaon, outside of Delhi, which gives children from nearby slums intensive training in subjects such as English and hygiene (soap is a new concept for many of the students). Where typical public schools in India have fifty to as many as seventy-five pupils per teacher, the Vidya program currently has five teachers teaching seventy-five children. The goal is to send one of these to an IIT university—a high aspiration, considering that none of the students' parents graduated from high school and that much of the early teaching focuses on personal hygiene.

Elfun staff helps out at the Comfort School by mentoring students over the summer break and putting together events like sports days, parent-teacher fairs, and a theater show on Elfun's seventy-fifth anniversary. When we visited the school, all of the Vidya staff knew the volunteers by name and asked about upcoming birthdays. This familiarity was evidence of a degree of support and dedication that is crucial to making corporate/NGO initiatives successful.

GE volunteers have been working on several additional educational initiatives. Elfun-Delhi assists Balsudha, another organization that focuses on children from slums. In Bangalore, the employees of the JF Welch Technology Center have developed a relationship with the Nallurahalli Literacy Initiative, raising funds to cover the cost of books and uniforms, to set up special learning days like the global visitors day, and to staff a weekly Wednesday mentoring session at the school with fifteen Eflun volunteers. One of the mentored students, Prema, who is from a low-income family, was ranked fifteenth in the All India Science Talent examination.

Elfun volunteers have provided hours of service to all kinds of community projects, which include support to local hospitals and schools. They also go beyond education, organizing activities for underprivileged children such as a swimming pool outing and a plane ride.

LESSONS LEARNED

General Electric and Ford have each created CSR programs at their factories in India that have contributed to the success of their operations in that country. The following sections examine the lessons that can be drawn from the GE and Ford examples, as well as from the sometimes less happy experiences of other multinationals, to create a model for structuring CSR programs in India and similar developing countries. "Anyone can write checks," said Mike Reisinger, a retired Ford employee with extensive experience in emerging markets, "but the important thing is getting people involved. CSR needs to be a part of your core business responsibility, because you are going into a nation to leverage their labor and resources."

MAKING CSR INTEGRAL TO ENTRY PLANNING

A multinational about to enter an emerging market like India's should incorporate CSR in its planning from the beginning. In this way, the company can assure the country's government that it will be a good corporate citizen and can avoid the often costly missteps that may result from delaying such considerations.

The Indian government, focused on attracting multinationals to the country, has not yet dictated requirements for corporate citizenship. Officials of Tamil Nadu, for example, provided Ford with tax incentives to locate operations near Chennai without asking for any specific CSR programs in return. Given the company's global reputation, they just assumed—correctly—that it would be a good corporate citizen. Many governments in the developing world seem to make similar assumptions about multinationals operating in their territories. This does not mean, however, that they are disinterested in these companies' CSR plans. Ford, for one, says it is often questioned by governments of countries where it is beginning operations about how it intends to contribute to society as part of its market entry. It is thus good policy for a company to have a CSR plan in hand when beginning operations in a less developed country.

If a global reputation eases entry into an emerging market, it also imposes an obligation on the company to maintain its image. A mistake can become a public relations disaster that is immediately broadcast around the globe. Coca-Cola learned this the hard way. Coke has invested $1 billion in India since 1993. It has also aided the community by funding programs to prevent polio and hiring cancer patients to sells its products. All this was dwarfed, however, by accusations in 2004 that its plant in Plachimada had drained and significantly degraded the water in the villagers' wells. Local protests against the plant drew international attention and calls for a global boycott of the brand.

Multinational companies must realize that they will be judged more strictly than local ones, held to the higher standard set by international business and political communities and by themselves through internal value statements. Hence, in India Ford cannot sell cars without airbags, GE cannot dump mercury, and Coke cannot pump wells dry, even if domestic companies engage in similar practices. High international standards basically make it impossible for a U.S. or European company to be the lowest-cost provider in a developing country. Instead, MNCs should aim at the middle and upper market tiers. Luckily, through effective CSR, they can help build these markets and drive demand for their higher-value, more expensive products.

ALIGNING CSR WITH CORPORATE STRATEGY

The design of a CSR program that an MNC entering into India adopts should reflect its business industry and its goals in the country. It should look at issues such as to whom it primarily sells its goods and whether or not it views India as a market for selling its goods and services or just as a low-cost venue for production. These considerations will help align a solid CSR program.

The CSR program of a business that sells to consumers should function as an outgrowth of its marketing efforts. Studies of consumers in developed countries have found that 94 percent select the product of a company associated with a charitable cause over that of one without such an association. A properly structured CSR program can enhance a multinational's image in the community and help brand it as a local company. Ford's programs in India, for instance, distinguish it from Mahindra & Mahindra and enable it to emphasize its commitment to the country. A company that sells to other companies (a business-to-business, or B2B, operation), on the other hand, should gear its CSR program not toward mollifying its market, but toward its employees—fostering teamwork and furthering their desires to help the community. Businesses that use India mainly as a site for outsourcing back-office procedures would follow the business-to-business model.

Focusing CSR Activities

Effective CSR programs blend global initiatives—Ford's involvement in health care, for instance, and GE's in education—with ones that address local needs. The latter can take many forms, as evidenced by the range of projects these two companies have undertaken in India.

It might be expected that a multinational corporation would evaluate prospective CSR activities based on how they related to its core business—that Ford, for instance, would invest in India's infrastructure, improving roads and building highways to help develop the car and truck market there. This does not seem to be the case. Although, as described in the previous section, the CSR activities of a successful program generally align with the company's overall strategy, several criteria not directly related to business go into their selection. Ford uses the metrics developed by the Global Reporting Initiative to measure the social benefits of prospective CSR efforts and picks those with the greatest potential. GRI would give higher marks to building a new health-care center than to constructing roads, installing traffic lights, and creating traffic safety programs. It is also possible, of course, to be a little creative and forge projects, like Wells Fargo's financial literacy program in California, that serve both the community and the bottom line.

Companies should select programs and alliances that produce quick wins and tangible results. Activities that involve face-to-face interactions—whether with needy children, the mentally challenged, the disabled, or the destitute—build satisfying relationships between employees and the community. Programs that deal with controversial issues, including sex education and women's rights (in some parts of the world), should be carefully considered and sometimes avoided.

CSR Governance

CSR activities can be carried out through NGOs funded by the company or by in-house manpower. The GE and Ford experiences suggest that combining these two options works best. NGOs may be most effective in identifying needy groups or areas and selecting projects that send the right message, while employee volunteerism can strengthen the relationship between the company and the organizations and create the personal bonds that are necessary if the activities are to have an impact in the community.

At many multinationals, investment and volunteer decisions are made at different organizational levels. Large corporations typically have charitable foundations—for example, the GE Fund and the Henry J. Ford Foundation—that control their giving; volunteer activities and the small-scale fund-raising efforts are typically overseen at a much lower level, such as the individual office or region. It is important not to delegate large projects to too low a level, such as a local branch, since that may put too much reliance on the motivation and skill of a single volunteer coordinator to be sustainable. In addition, it may make it difficult to mobilize the numbers required to have an impact on the community and could result in ad hoc projects rather than ones chosen to mesh with a corporate strategy.

In a successful program, the foundations support local initiatives, as the GE Fund does Vidya, through both grants and volunteer hours. This enables the company to implement a cohesive global strategy while still responding to the unique needs of a local community and to mobilize quickly to respond to urgent needs. One potential downside of this structure is that due diligence and coordination may be repeated at multiple levels. However, we did not see this in these two companies.

CSR programs are most effective when publicly supported by senior management and reinforced in the company culture. Executive involvement—such as GE's staffing of its Corporate Citizenship Council with the CEOs of its business units—makes it clear that CSR programs are truly important to the company. It has the side benefit of exposing many tiers of employees to the leadership team. Senior executives should set the overall strategy, choosing activities that, as suggested in the previous section, fit with the company's global goals while taking into account unique local needs. Involvement of the lower ranks ensures that projects can be implemented. Reinforcing volunteerism and good citizenship in the corporate culture involves establishing, monitoring, and enforcing ethical business practices and rewarding community involvement through both personnel evaluations and public recognition. Even something as simple as posting the names of the most active volunteers on a lunchroom bulletin board emphasizes that socially active employees are highly regarded.

Finally, the links between the company and community groups must be strong. If the company chooses to partner with an NGO, expectations should be articulated clearly and commitments should be followed through. Companies should track the results of NGO partnerships as they do the relative worth of financial investments. Actual accomplishments should be measured against stated goals, and scorecards of both the project and the NGO should be developed. In tandem with monitoring individual projects, the company should evaluate its overall CSR program against its goal of improving public relations, encouraging teamwork, or retaining employees. In sum, it should treat CSR as a critical facet of its business strategy in the country.

SOCIALLY RESPONSIBLE BUSINESS STANDARDS

As important as implementing volunteer and community outreach efforts is, it may have less of an impact on a community than imbuing day-to-day operations with the values of corporate citizenship. Because of the sheer volume of dollars that flow through a multinational and its vast web of suppliers and partners, the influence of its socially responsible business practices can be enormous. By certifying that their suppliers proscribe child labor, dispose of hazardous materials properly, and pay overtime, MNCs can dramatically improve the working conditions of thousands, if not hundreds of thousands, of Indian employees. GE's and Ford's strong certification programs exemplify this. The two companies are seeking ways to motivate suppliers to take on the added costs of aligning their operations with the requirements for certification. In the future, perhaps, multinationals can encourage compliance by developing and sharing lists of qualified suppliers.

Interacting with Social Organizations

As noted previously, the governments of developing nations tend to be more interested in attracting foreign investment than in promoting corporate citizenship. Nevertheless, they should be included as partners in developing CSR programs. In Malaysia, for example, Ford was careful to seek the government's cultural approval of a video on women's issues before releasing it to the public.

Nongovernmental organizations generally play a more direct and vital role than the government in the definition and long-term success of CSR programs. GE and Ford have worked with more than forty NGOs in India through volunteer hours and donations. This arrangement allows the companies to focus on their core businesses while the nonprofits, which have deeper connections to the community, target groups for assistance and recommend how that assistance should be supplied. It is important for companies to ally with NGOs that mesh with their CSR goals and strategies. An effective mechanism for finding such organizations is a corporate group like GE's Corporate Citizenship Council.

In Conclusion

The importance to an MNC of creating an effective CSR program in a developing country cannot be overstated. Such a program enhances public perception of the company's brand and reinforces its market leadership. Ford and GE, as leaders in their industries, have defined what a global company is and established a model for corporate aspirants to the world stage. The decision by India's Infosys to donate 1 percent of its post-tax revenue to charitable causes, for instance, clearly signals companies' realization that contributing to communities is a prerequisite for being a global player.

CSR activities should be consistent, supported, and effective. Ford's and GE's examples suggest that this can be achieved by taking the following steps:

- Develop a CSR strategy that embodies the corporate culture and combines socially responsible business practices with philanthropic initiatives.
- Elect a local executive council to support, tailor, and implement CSR activities.
- Ensure that the moral and ethical standards at plants and among subcontractors operating in a developing country are consistent with corporate values.
- Support philanthropic CSR efforts with both funding and volunteer hours.
- Work through NGOs whose goals align with those of the CSR program developed by the executive council.
- Create a system for evaluating CSR programs to ensure that the most effective ones are supported.

These measures will help multinationals build effective CSR programs that function as cornerstones of their efforts to define their images, reputation, and corporate cultures in developing countries.

REFERENCES

Baron, David P. 2003. *Business and its social environment.* Englewood Cliffs, N.J.: Prentice Hall.

Basu, Indrajit. 2002. Coke's Indian divestment plans under fire. *Online Asia Times* (August 28). www.atimes.com/atimes/South_Asia/DH28Df06 .html.

Christian Aid. 2001. Living its values: Coca-Cola in India (April). www .christianaid.org.uk/indepth/0401csr/csr_casestudy3india.pdf.

Corporate citizenship—GE India. 2004. Presentation to research group in Delhi, India, March 24.

Diermeier, Daniel. 2004. Global corporate social responsibility. Lecture, Kellogg School of Management, Evanston, Ill. (January 21).

Economist. 2004. AIDs in India: When silence is not golden (April 15). www .economist.com/printedition/displayStory.cfm?Story_ID=2603788.

Economist Intelligence Unit. 2003. Country profile 2003: India. www .eiu.com.

Economist Intelligence Unit. 2003. India: Economic growth prospects (May 14). www.eiu.com.

Ford India. 2002. A review of Ford's economic, social, and environmental performance in India. www.ford.com/NR/fordcom/microsites/sustain ability/2004–05.

Ford India. 2004. Indian NGOs. www.indianngos.com/corporate/indianex amples/fordindia.htm. February.

Ford Motor Company. 2002. Experiences of Ford in India. www.ciionline .org/Services/74/Images/Ford_India.pdf.

Ford Motor Company. 2004. The challenge of HIV/AIDS. www.ford .com/en/company/about/corporateCitizenship/principlesProgressPerfo rmance/our-actions/challenge-hiv.htm.

Friedman, Milton. 1970. The social responsibility of business is to increase its profits. *New York Times Magazine,* September 13.

General Electric. GE India, www.ge.com/in/Businessesworld.htm#capital.

Gifford, Carol. 2004. Corporate philanthropy and social marketing. Proceedings of the Beyond Brand Event at the Kellogg School of Management, Evanston, Ill., March 31.

Global Reporting Initiative. 2003. A common framework for sustainability reporting. www.globalreporting.org.

Graham, George. 2004. Vice president of finance, Ford India, Mumbai, India. Interview by authors, March 17.

Hopkins, Michael. 1998. *The planetary bargain: Corporate social responsibility comes of age.* New York: Palgrave Macmillan.

Lobe, Jim. 2001. Bangladesh: The most corrupt country in the world. *Online Asia Times* (June 30). www.atimes.com/ind-pak/CF30Df03 .html.

Messick, David. 2004. Defining the social sector: What is socially responsible business? Lecture delivered at Kellogg School of Management, Evanston, Ill., April 21.

Newcome, Jim. 2004. Corporate philanthropy and social marketing. Proceedings of the Beyond Brand Event at the Kellogg School of Management, Evanston, Ill., March 31.

Prakash, Siddhartha. 1998. Trade and development centre: A joint venture of the World Bank and the World Trade Organization. Trade and Development Centre. www.itd.org.

Reisinger, Mike. 2004. Former Ford executive. Discussion with authors, April 27, Dearborn, Mich.

Srivastav, Harsh. 1998. Coca-Cola India page. Indian NGOs. http:// indianngos.com/1/vikaskochar/.

UK Trade and Investment. 2003. Automotive industry market in India. www.tradepartners.gov.uk/automotive/india/profile/overview.shtml.

Venugopal, K. 2004. GE Plastics CEO. Discussion with authors, March 24, New Delhi, India.

Verma, Shweta. 2002. A Goliath called GE. *Dataquest,* October 17. http://dataquest.ciol.com/content/top_stories/102101702.asp.

Vittal, Nagarajan. 2001. Corruption and the state: India. *Harvard International Review, 23* (Fall).

Wells Fargo Foundation. 2003. 2003 report of giving and volunteerism: California and border banking regions. www.wellsfargo.com/pdf/about/charitable/2003_Annual_Report.pdf.

Young, Gayle. 1995. India's preference for boys tips the sex ratio. *CNN,* September 17. www-cgi.cnn.com/WORLD/9509/india_sex_ratios/index.html.

PART 3

PARTNERING FOR CHANGE IN SOUTH AFRICA

Chapter 8

EDUCATION FOR CHANGE IN SOUTH AFRICA'S AUTO INDUSTRY

*Kannan Arumugam, Akeshia Craven,
and Jackie Statum*

Since the end of apartheid in 1994, education in South Africa has improved significantly. Today, the country's system compares favorably with those of its African neighbors in both performance and spending—in 2006, education accounted for roughly 20 percent of the government's budget. Even this funding, however, has been insufficient to compensate for decades of apartheid during which white schools received generous infusions of money and black schools almost none. Adult black South Africans thus find themselves relegated to jobs that require few skills and offer little means for self-improvement and promotion. Although blacks make up 75 percent of the population, they occupy only 25 percent of the middle management positions and the same percentage of the senior management positions. The majority population's inferior education is an obstacle to national development, because it deters investment by foreign companies seeking to establish offices in countries with a known base of intellectual capital.

The government and companies in South Africa are striving to correct the situation by improving basic adult education and training, especially in poor rural areas. Here, we examine the contribution made by the automobile companies in improving basic adult education. The automotive industry is the country's third-largest industry (accounting for nearly 6 percent of its gross domestic product) and is a major consumer of unskilled labor. The industry can thus have a major impact by furthering the education and skill-development training of its workers. We examine the training programs at the BMW, Nissan, and Ford plants in Pretoria, analyzing their differences and the key success factors that will allow for the advancement of South African employees' education.

TWO TRAINING GROUPS: MERSETA AND AIDC

Two South African interest groups, the Manufacturing and Engineering Related Sector's Education and Training Authority (Merseta) and the Automotive Industry Development Center (AIDC), attempt to tailor workers' training to the skills required by the seven original equipment manufacturers (OEMs) that assemble vehicles in the country. Merseta, composed of representatives of every OEM in South Africa, sets education and training standards for these manufacturers and their suppliers and they, in turn, support the group's efforts through a tax of 1 percent of their total annual revenues. AIDC—which comprises both a nonprofit training branch and a for-profit branch that offers business services to companies—helps the industry meet its educational goals. For example, the OEMs are large and generally capable of supporting and managing training programs, but the smaller suppliers typically do not have the requisite resources for their programs. AIDC redresses this disparity by matching the suppliers' monetary contributions to human resources development initiatives.

THE OEM's CERTIFICATION PROGRAM

During a 1996 national bargaining forum in South Africa, automobile-manufacturing employees and employers agreed to develop a multiskill training program for hourly workers that would be used by the entire industry, thus serving as a nationally recognized qualification system. The end product was Merseta's Automobile Manufacturing Industry Certificate (AMIC) program. This consists of four levels associated with four progressively higher minimum hourly wages. Each level has three modules: basic education, which is concerned with mathematical and literacy skills; core competency, which covers subjects such as occupational health and safety, employee/employer relations, communications, and manufacturing concepts; and technical knowledge and skills related to activities specific to automobile manufacture, such as body construction, vehicle assembly, and warehousing. Employees start at the entry level, accumulating credits as they complete each course and prove proficiency in the relevant skill. When they have earned eight credits in each of the modules of one level, they are promoted to the next. On completion of the fourth level, they get an AMIC certification. The promotion opportunities available to an employee who has a certificate vary according to employer.

INDUSTRY LEARNERSHIPS

AIDC is in the process of creating a set of focused yearlong programs in auto manufacturing theory and practice. Participants in these "learnerships," as they are called, earn certification on eight levels: level three is equivalent to grade twelve; six, to graduating from one the country's technical-training institutes; seven, to a university degree; and eight, to a PhD. As of 2006, the center focused on the following training areas: development and basic training, shop-floor training, technical training, managerial skills training, and automotive engineering.

Companies receive reimbursement of eight thousand rands for each employee they put through a learnership and an even greater sum if they register a nonemployee. They also get tax refunds and can be refunded up to 75 percent of the money they pay to Merseta. Companies do not have to hire nonemployee students after they graduate, although most will, nor do students have to work for the company that sponsored them. Graduates who don't sign up with their sponsors become part of a pool of educated workers available to all auto companies, and the sponsors receive twelve thousand rands.

The programs, still in their pilot phases, face significant challenges, according to Jan Grobbelaar, manager of AIDC human resources development. Among them are overcoming employee skepticism and acquiring talented teachers. Nevertheless, the AIDC has had an effect. In 1968, BMW brought in one hundred German workers to establish its plant in Rosslyn, north of Pretoria. In contrast, the company planned to import only forty German workers to Rosslyn in 1998 to make the modifications and do the training necessary to prepare the plant for manufacturing a new 3 Series automobile. AIDC provided the support and made arrangements with educational institutions to provide the South African BMW workers with the requisite skills, these individuals in effect taking the place of sixty German trainers.

We turn next to the implementation of AMIC programs at the three major auto employers.

AMIC PROGRAMS AT BMW, NISSAN, AND FORD

BMW, Nissan, and Ford all provide adult education and training. Their programs differ, however, in how they are implemented and the amount of attention given to them. The next sections describe the three companies' programs and then compare them with respect to four measures: competence of management, sustainability, impact on employees and on the community, and employee motivation.

BMW

Plant Rosslyn, the first BMW plant established outside Germany, produces all of the company's E46 3 Series four-door vehicles, 80 percent of which are exported. In 2002, it received the J. D. Power and Associates European Gold Plant Quality award for outperforming all automobile factories in Europe.

Annually, 10 percent of the Rosslyn payroll goes toward train-ing that meets the requirements of the AMIC program. Management actively encourages participation: In 2005, 1,470 (49 percent) of the plant's 3,000 employees actively participated in the training program, and 500 (17 percent) of the employee participants have attained level four accreditation through the AMIC program.

NISSAN

Nissan recognizes that as education improves in South Africa, the unemployment rate will decrease. It thus regards its training program as a way to compete against other auto manufacturers for talented employees. At its plant in Pretoria, the company offers a variety of education options to employees and their families. In addition to the instruction in technical skills provided in the AMIC program, the company also offers education in "soft skills." Participants, who work full time and attend school part time, are taught about South Africa's economy and government and learn valuable life skills, such as how to create a budget based on their family's income and needs. According to Christopher Songwane, Nissan's training coordinator, mastering these subjects enables employees to contribute not just to Nissan but to their communi-ties as well.

Nissan encourages its employees to take two AMIC modules each year. Although participation in this and the other Nissan pro-grams is voluntary, management often asks individuals who per-form at a high level to sign up, so they can develop their skills and earn promotions. In recent years, however, enrollment in the AMIC program has decreased by 91 percent. This is partly attributable to the 1997 downsizing at the plant, in which many employees were offered early retirement and severance packages, reducing the pool of potential participants. Also contributing to the decline is the increase in South Africa's literacy rate since 1995: As new hires' edu-cation level increases, the need for the programs decreases. Nissan has recognized the increasing literacy of its South African workforce by introducing tuition assistance for employees interested in educa-tion that goes beyond the company's offerings.

FORD MOTOR COMPANY

Ford's adult education program goes far beyond the AMIC requirements, according to Anthony Mandi, the company's senior technical-training associate. First, Ford has formed a partnership with the Mamelodi College of Education, a technical-training institute near the plant. A branch of the college recently opened in the factory compound, just steps away from where the operators work. Ford employees are allowed to leave at 4:00 in the afternoon to take AMIC courses there. (They are also compensated for job-related training received elsewhere.) Nonemployees who are enrolled at Mamelodi are permitted to attend the Ford branch, too, taking advantage not only of its facilities but of its special technically oriented Ford Academy of Manufacturing Science (FAMS) curriculum as well.

Second, Ford has added its own fifth level to Merseta's four-level certification program. Based on the FAMS curriculum, it trains operators to become team leaders, thus advancing the company's goal of promoting from within. The fifth level takes an average of eighteen months to complete, compared with nine for the lower levels; about half the program is devoted to theory and half to specialized vocational skills. Employees who have attained AMIC level four may apply for the level-five curriculum as long as there is a team-leader vacancy. Candidates are evaluated on previous appraisals, merit, and psychometric and psychological tests.

Third, Ford offers a two-year in-house technician-training program for employees and outsiders. Students are paid during their training and are not required to work for Ford afterward. Ford's incentive for this program is to enlarge the pool of qualified technicians it can employ. Finally, the company has developed a "hard skills" program to introduce all new employees to the basics of automobile assembly, such as use of hand tools and operator safety. The hope is that this will reduce the amount of on-the-job training that must be done.

COMPETENCE OF PROGRAM MANAGEMENT

In assessing competency, three factors must be considered. The first is whether designated people are directly responsible for the everyday management of the program; dedicated managers serve as program advocates, thus assuring that it remains a priority. The second consideration is whether audits are done regularly to measure performance against a set of predetermined benchmarks; audits can keep programs from becoming stale and, further, can provide documentation of their value, without which they could be dropped from companies' budgets. The third factor is the amount of executive support and funding in the program itself.

The adult education programs at BMW's Plant Rosslyn are the purview of the communications manager. This person's primary job is to serve as liaison with suppliers and other external groups and ensure that messages from the company's corporate and executive levels are disseminated throughout the plant. Monitoring employees' activities and their participation in adult education is a secondary responsibility. In contrast, Nissan and Ford have both designated managers whose primary responsibility is to coordinate the companies' training programs, ensuring that they are running properly and documenting annual employee participation and progress. Ford also coordinates with the AIDC through one of its education managers. It also takes advantage of its relationship with the Mamelodi school, having it oversee and audit the company's programs.

SUSTAINABILITY

Companies do not fund programs without a future. To be sustainable, a program must have competent management. This, however, is not sufficient. There must also be an effective mechanism for disseminating information about the program, to ensure that it will continue once the current managers are gone. The program needs to be flexible, as well, to address employees' changing needs and find new ways of challenging employees.

For instance, BMW's adult education programs focus on basic literacy and mathematical skills. As South Africa's labor force evolves, these programs may need to change. Nissan, as noted earlier, in response to increasing literacy in the workforce has moved toward tuition assistance for education that goes beyond the company's offerings. It also documents the programs it offers and their effectiveness as measured by the number of employees participating.

Ford's relationships with AIDC and Mamelodi give it an advantage over the other companies. Its ties to AIDC enable it to model its programs, to some extent, on learnerships and provide it with information about overall trends in the industry and what technical-training institutes and universities are doing in response to them. Its partnership with Mamelodi allows Ford, whose core competency is not education, to be innovative in its programming, since the school has the resources to implement new ideas in the classroom.

IMPACT ON EMPLOYEES AND THE COMMUNITY

Workplace adult education programs enhance participants' job options, giving them the skills to move upward within the company or outward into other occupations. To qualify as true corporate social investments (CSI), however, the education provided must go beyond human resources development that directly benefits the employer with the side effect of aiding the employee; it must also provide intangible benefits to both the participants and the community at large.

BMW's programs give employees who are too old to attend public school an equivalent education and enable them to develop study skills that undoubtedly help them in their jobs and increase their pay. Since the training contributes primarily to improved job performance, which directly benefits BMW, the CSI contribution is diminished.

Nissan's and Ford's programs provide talented employees with opportunities to achieve the highest levels of education. Nissan identifies employees who can serve as team leaders and positions them for promotion through on-the-job training in complex skills.

Ford enrolls employees who have completed the company's level-five classes in training that prepares them for management positions on the plant floor. Both companies' programs contribute to upward mobility for employees who would otherwise find it impossible.

Nissan's programs are a mixture of human resources development and CSI activities. While much of its training is devoted to developing technical skills that benefit the company, it also provides education that serves employees and the community in areas and in ways that don't directly contribute to the bottom line. Nissan's soft-skills programs, for example, teach the fundamentals of budgeting and promote economic and government awareness, knowledge that enriches the employees, not the company alone. Extending its adult education programs to employees' family members without stipulating that they eventually work for Nissan similarly benefits the community more than the company.

Ford's programs also combine human resources development with CSI activities. However, a larger portion of its programs can be considered corporate social investment, particularly its partnership with the Mamelodi school, to whose budget the company contributes annually.

EMPLOYEE MOTIVATION

Individuals are motivated by the perceived links among performance, outcome, ability, and effort, according to organizational change experts David Nadler and David Lawler. An incentive exists to behave in a certain way if the outcome of that behavior, the reward, is perceived to be of sufficient value. The reward can be the external approbation of peers or supervisors or the internal, personal satisfaction of achievement. Effort and ability jointly determine the level of performance and thus motivation. If the amount of effort and level of ability required are perceived as too high, motivation declines. In other words, as Nadler and Lawler point out, individuals have the most incentive "to behave in that way which, [given their level of ability], seems to have the best chance of producing positive, desired outcomes."

The AMIC programs implemented at BMW, Nissan, and Ford appear to provide appropriate worker incentives. The standard program has several explicit outcomes, of which the most salient is salary increases. AMIC guidelines clearly spell out the wage increases associated with progress through the program's four levels. Since virtually all employees strongly value salary growth, this outcome is effective in encouraging the kinds of performance the companies need.

In addition to wage increases, the AMIC program results in improved literacy and more important roles for the participants in plant operations. For workers who value them, these outcomes augment the universal motivation of salary increases. The effect is enhanced by the fact that the program specifies the performance needed to achieve the outcomes and the methods used to assess them. The link between performance and outcome is further strengthened by the improvements in workers' abilities—in terms of both core competencies and specialized skills—achieved through the program.

Ford has significantly strengthened the motivational linkages by adding three outcomes and improving its workers' abilities. Employees who complete the company's level-five training achieve the South African equivalent of a general equivalency diploma, which certain individuals value highly. In addition, since the curriculum was designed to train team leaders, successful completion of level-five training increases employees' promotion potential. Second, Ford provides its team leaders with red jackets, which are significant status markers in the plant. BMW's program also awards status symbols—T-shirts proudly worn by those who have completed an AMIC level and photographs of these achievers displayed in a common area of the plant—but Ford's extension of the AMIC plan gives workers greater access to such rewards. Finally, Ford has increased its workers' skills with additional training adapted from the FAMS curriculum and with materials from the Mamelodi faculty. Its employee motivation seems to be borne out by the increase in the proportion of the company's operators at AMIC levels three and four—from 63 and 4 percent, respectively, in 2003, to 73 and 15 percent in 2004.

In Conclusion

Despite the strides that the South African automotive industry and some of its constituents have made in worker training in recent years, automobile manufacturers could take several steps to add value to their programs for themselves, their employees, and the country's economy. These steps involve the AMIC program and partnerships with organizations such as AIDC.

First, the AMIC program could be enhanced if other companies followed Ford's lead in augmenting its curriculum to make it more meaningful. By adding a level and instituting multiskill and technical-training programs, Ford created a smoother segue from operator to entry-level plant manager and, at the same time, countered the program's declining applicability. It is possible to go still further, extending Ford's model to provide a career path beyond plant supervisor for employees who meet performance requirements.

Second, companies should institute an evaluation system to measure the effectiveness of their training programs, including objective goals and progress indicators. This would help them justify the resources devoted to education and avoid ill-advised or counterproductive reductions.

Third, by increasing and strengthening their partnerships with outside organizations, companies can tailor their education programs so that they focus on the knowledge and skills needed in their plants. For example, the learnerships that AIDC is pioneering could extend the AMIC plan beyond primary-school equivalency.

Finally, there is significant value in partnering with consultancies that understand CSI and related matters. Trialogue, for instance, has expertise in strategic marketing and communication activities related to development and philanthropy, all of which improve companies' brand equity and public images.

Implementing these recommendations will not only enhance the value of training programs for employers and employees; it will also help South Africa as a whole. Improvements in education and skills training will further economic development and improve the life of all the country's citizens.

REFERENCES

Garson, Phillipa. 2003. Education in South Africa. South Africa Info. www
.safrica.info/ess_info/sa_glance/education/.

Hutton, Barbara. 1992. *Adult basic education in South Africa.* Cape Town,
South Africa: Oxford University Press.

Kerfoot, Caroline. 2001. *ABET and development in the Northern Cape
Province.* Bellville, South Africa: University of the Western Cape Centre
for Adult and Continuing Education.

Long learning curve ahead for South Africa's troubled education policy.
1999. *Financial Times,* July 22.

Mandi, Anthony. 2003. Ford senior technical-training associate. Interview
by authors, Pretoria, South Africa, March 20.

Merseta. 1996. AMIC standards. South Africa, 1996. www.merseta.org.za.

Nadler, David A., and Lawler, David E. 1983. Motivation: A diagnostic
approach. In Ruth Person (Ed.), *The management process: A selection of
readings for librarians,* pp. 315–326. Chicago: American Library
Association.

Rockey, Vanessa. 2002. *The CSI Handbook,* 5th edition. Cape Town, South
Africa: Trialogue.

Roodt, Marius. 2002. Automotive focus group responds to industry's human
resource needs. *Engineering News* (August).

Skills shortage impeding equity. 2002. *Business Day South Africa,* November
26.

South Africa Info. 2002. Motor industry set for more growth. www.safrica
.info/doing_business/businesstoday/businessnews/194353.htm.

Wallenborn, Manfred. 1989. *Vocational training strategies to promote employment and self-help in the third world.* Federal Republic of Germany:
Mannheim.

Chapter 9

BLACK ECONOMIC EMPOWERMENT IN THE SOUTH AFRICAN WINE INDUSTRY

Liliahn Johnson, Laura Koepke, and Amie Wang

Just north of Cape Town lie the beautiful peaks and valleys of South Africa's wine country. The vineyards here produce 3 percent of the world's wine, placing South Africa's wine industry in the top ten globally in terms of production and making it one of the country's leading export engines. In the decade since the end of apartheid, wine exports grew by almost 1,000 percent. The country's 4,500 commercial wine producers employ 350,000 farm workers, and this figure has been growing at 5 percent annually, in comparison to an average of 3 percent for other South African industries. About 40 percent of these employees are from disadvantaged groups. As South Africa struggles to reenergize its economy after years of sanctions imposed by apartheid opponents, it sees in the wine industry its key opportunity to becoming a major player in the global marketplace.

Wine production's vital role in South Africa's economy makes it central to the country's plans to redress the inequities that are apartheid's legacy. Historically, whites have owned the land on which the vines are grown and managed the production and marketing of the wine, while blacks and colored people have provided the labor. Even today, 90 percent of middle and senior managers at cooperative cellars are white, with the figure at 80 percent for private cellars. Guidelines issued by the Broad-Based Black Economic Empowerment Act required that both land ownership and production management be transferred to the disadvantaged majority. We examine how black economic empowerment (BEE) has been implemented in this industry through the prism of six successful initiatives. Despite successes, problems remain, and we look at how these could be addressed.

Land Reform

In its 1997 White Paper on Land Policy, the government articulated three goals: to restore land to individuals from whom it was taken under apartheid, to give blacks access to land for commercial and residential use, and to ensure that they had secure tenure on their land. The African National Congress (ANC) has attempted to achieve these goals by reclaiming land from distressed white farmers, transferring ownership of state-owned property, and giving low-income "willing buyers" 16,000 rands to purchase land from "willing sellers."

The program has not been entirely successful. The shortcomings are partly the result of budgetary constraints. Although it has increased in recent budgets, the funding given the Department of Land Affairs (DLA) still amounts to less than 1 percent of the national budget, with 79 percent of that allocated to land reform. This allotment has not gone far, since owners have insisted on receiving market value for their land. In consequence, by 1999 less than 1 percent of the country's agricultural land had been redistributed, and much of that was unsuitable for cultivation. The government has thus had to push back its deadline for a 30 percent reallocation to 2014.

Over the past ten years, both government agencies and private vineyard owners have pursued initiatives aimed at assisting black workers and disadvantaged communities to become vine growers and wine producers. Progress at first was slow. The industry took notice, however, when individual vineyard owners who had taken active roles in empowering their workers began realizing significant financial returns. In 1998, these vineyards started bringing out quality wines that were well received by wine enthusiasts domestically and internationally and in the press. Such successes spurred action by the wider industry, which drew lessons from the individual projects to create models of black empowerment in wine production.

SIX PIONEERING PROJECTS

The successful wine-producing projects all had the same goal: furthering black empowerment. They differed, however, in how they attempted to reach it. The vineyards described in the following sections illustrate some of the paths taken.

NEW BEGINNINGS WINERY

New Beginnings is a spin-off of Nelson's Creek Winery, which was founded by lawyer Alan Nelson in 1987. Nelson bought what was then a run-down vineyard with the ambitious goal of turning it into an award-winning wine estate. His first act as owner was to eliminate the centuries-old "dop" or "tot" system, in which workers are paid in wine instead of money. Banned officially in 1983, this arrangement continues to be used by an estimated 20 percent of South African winemakers. The dop system has been criticized not only for being economically unfair to black workers but also for promoting health and social problems including alcoholism, fetal alcohol syndrome, illiteracy, and domestic violence.

In addition, Nelson increased his employees' wages and promised rewards for hard work. In 1994, he announced to his senior workers that if they helped him produce an award-winning vintage, he would give them twenty-five acres on which to produce their own wine. It was a risky offer: It was not legal at the time to give land to black farmworkers. In 1996, when the winery won the trophy for Champion South African Wooded Chardonnay at the

South African National Young Wine Show, Nelson made good on his promise. He not only donated the land but also offered the workers the use of his farming implements and equipment for three years and committed to buy the grapes they produced. Finally, he agreed that if they decided in the future to make wine, he would make his high-tech cellar available.

The DLA adopted New Beginnings as a land-reform project and named as facilitator Victor Titus, a black headmaster whom Nelson had hired to coordinate the project. In 2000, with the winery fully operational, Titus attended the London Wine and Food Fair, where he marketed the vineyard's wine as the first "ever to be produced by people of color in South Africa with grapes grown on their own land."

With the money from the first sales of their wine, the New Beginnings farm workers bought another portion of the land offered by Nelson. On this they planned to build their own cellar, bottling plant, and housing and community facilities. Of the remaining funds, a small portion went toward daily living expenses, and the rest was put into the bank.

Nelson's initiative has been successful both financially—for the vintner himself as well as for the workers—and socially. "Under apartheid, my dad was paid in kind, wine in most cases," says Arthur Jacobs, one of the shareholders. "For that the whites made him work from dawn till dusk. New Beginnings allows me to start all over again in a new South Africa. I'm very proud because I now have access to my own land. We're mostly investing the profits in education, such as a child-care center for our children. We're providing burial insurance and life insurance for the first time. Most importantly, we're buying land so we can build our own houses."

Jacobs's words reflect a situation that is a far cry from the days when South African winemaking was synonymous with forced, unpaid spouse and child labor (in return for living on the vineyard) that precluded educational opportunities. Initiatives such as Nelson's can only help in an industry where 70 percent of employees still have less than a seventh grade education.

Titus, who today is the main force behind Nelson Creek's black empowerment initiative, adds: "The New Beginnings experience was an attempt to show to the rest of South African farm owners that have-nots could become haves, and that white and black could work together to make a success—that cooperation among government, private enterprise, and community was possible."

BOUWLAND WINES

Bouwland Wines was spun off from the vineyard Beyerskloof, established by Beyers Truter in Stellenbosch in 1988. For Beyerskloof, Truter hired a team of farmers from the surrounding area, many of whom had worked in the wine industry their whole lives; he viewed them as specialized employees who shared his vision of success, rather than manual laborers. Consistent with this view, Truter ensured that his farmers worked in safe conditions and were not subject to the dop system.

With the release of his 1991 Kanonkop Pinotage, Truter single-handedly restored the Pinotage grape to the international spotlight, winning several awards and accolades including the Robert Mondavi Trophy—the first time a South African winemaker had received this distinction. Truter leveraged this success to earn the reputation as the "King of Pinotage," consistently turning out well-received wines and growing revenues. And he has passed on this success to his employees, continuing to maintain safe working conditions and even offering overtime pay, a virtually nonexistent practice in the industry.

But Truter's benevolence extended beyond these offerings: In 2003, he gave sixty of his workers a property known as Bouwland, fifty-six hectares (138 acres) of prime Stellenbosch soil to use for their own winemaking efforts. In a press release on the transfer, Truter suggested, "[The workers] now have a vested interest in the estate and a real chance to create a better future for themselves and their children." Many of the employees work at Truter's wineries during the week and tend to their vines at Bouwland on weekends. All workers are free to sell their shares of Bouwland; so far, none has, planning instead to pass them down as inheritances. To nurture Bouwland's efforts, Truter has pledged to support the winery in its initial stages, leading wine-development efforts and including Bouwland's products in Beyerskloof's marketing.

In addition to the gift of Bouwland, Truter has made the education of workers a top priority. For example, he encourages employees to take classes at the Vineyard Academy, a public/private institution; those who enroll are subsidized by Truter. At the academy, students hone skills in business and viticulture (grapevine growing) while also receiving training in life skills such as literacy, personal budgeting, and health care (for example, dealing with HIV and substance abuse). Worker education continues in the form of Truter's mentorship: He has committed to teaching two Bouwland trustees the intricacies of wine production, including his secrets to consistently turning out top-quality products.

It is hoped that Truter's and his employees' efforts will pay off. Bouwland's first wines—a cabernet/merlot blend and a chenin blanc—entered the marketplace in 2004. Sales have already exceeded expectations, with more than 10,000 cases sold in the first year. By year five, Bouwland owners hope to be producing 25,000 cases annually. But with the growth have come production challenges. To meet demand, the winery must purchase grapes from other local vineyards. And production costs are an ongoing concern: Currently Bouwland must outsource the processing, storing, bottling, and labeling of its wines, sharing the costs of these services with Beyerskloof. Only with significant sales growth will the fledgling enterprise be able to invest in production capability.

THE THANDI INITIATIVE

Thandi—Xhosa for "nurturing love"—was born in 1995. It was a partnership among local winegrower Paul Clüver, a group of black forestry and farmworkers, an Anglican social-development body led by Father Austin Jackson, and the South Africa Forestry Company (Safcol). Clüver contributed 250 uncultivated acres of his family's 5,000-acre farm in the Elgin Valley, and Safcol chipped in some more land. The stakeholders formed a trust in which each group was equally represented and all future profits were to be equally divided. The original goal was to use fruit farming and forestry to generate wealth for the partners and develop the workers' skills. By 1997, however, forestry was no longer profitable, and wine production was added to the mix.

Both Safcol and the Clüver family committed to remain as mentors for the farm workers and to transfer their shares in the project to the community when it was able to stand on its own. In January 2000, the 120 participating families received their 16,000-rand family grants from the South African government and invested the money in the project. On July 19, 2004, Safcol announced the handover of its shares.

In addition to skills transfer, the project also promotes the establishment of health, welfare, educational, and recreational services for the local community. It has, for instance, given three young men from the Elgin area scholarships to study at the Elsenburg Agricultural College. The hope is that they will join the Thandi initiative after completing their studies, but they are under no obligation to do so.

FAIR VALLEY

In 1997, Charles Back, owner of the famous Fairview winery in Paarl, bought a nearby farm for his 140 workers. This became Fair Valley. The project is funded partly by Back and partly by the government, with the money going for workers' housing and to provide financial security until the business can sustain itself. Income from sales of Fair Valley wine goes to the communal property association. The wine is currently produced using grapes grown elsewhere, but the workers have planted vines so that eventually it will be made from grapes grown on site.

SPICE ROUTE COMPANY

The Spice Route Company in Malemsbury is another project of Charles Back's, this one in partnership with three others: wine writer John Platter, Thelema Vineyards owner Gyles Webb, and Jabulani Ntshangase, South Africa's first Zulu owner of a commercial winery. The winery's inaugural vintage is Andrews Hope, named for Ntshangase's home.

WINDS OF CHANGE

In 1999, the Swiss-owned wine company African Terroir launched Winds of Change to further the social welfare of its workers and to contribute to black economic empowerment in the wine industry at large. In pursuing this goal, it sold, at below-market prices, 173 acres of the Sonop vineyard, a property near Paarl that the company had bought in 1991, to twenty-eight of its grape pickers and their families, who used government grants to make the purchase. Today, these workers toil on their own land, producing grapes that African Terroir buys to produce Winds of Change wine. A portion of the proceeds from sales of this wine goes into community projects related to health, education, and home improvement. Another portion is invested in the vineyard. Although the winery is still in its infancy, more than a million bottles of Winds of Change have been sold, generating revenue in excess of 650,000 rands for the Sonop community.

GOVERNMENT AND INDUSTRY INITIATIVES

The BEE programs of individual vintners like those just described set an example that has been taken up and expanded on by the entire sector. In 2000, the industry's controlling body, the Co-operative Wine Growers' Association (KWV), contributed 363 million rands to the South African Wine Industry Trust (Sawit), a public/private partnership founded in 1987 to promote black economic empowerment and industrywide improvements. Devco, Sawit's industry development arm, has responsibility for the organization's social development efforts; these include the provision of legal advice, educational initiatives, and health-related services. Meanwhile, the country's wine producers established the South African Wine and Brandy Company (SAWB) to oversee and coordinate their policies. Sawit and SAWB—together, singly, and with other public and private bodies—have engaged in several projects aimed at promoting black participation in the wine industry and enhancing the industry's profile in the world market. In 2003, for example, Sawit and SAWB organized the two-day Black Economic Empowerment Consultation Conference, held in Cape Town, to align the wine industry with government efforts to deliver tangible empowerment results. This conference launched the Wine Industry Plan, whose goals are economic and social transformation, human resources development and training, technology innovation and transfer, the development of business knowledge and intelligence, and market development and promotion.

Another organization linked to BEE is WIETA, the Wine Industry Ethical Trade Association, a UK-based program established in 2002. WIETA is a not-for-profit voluntary association of industry stakeholders including farmers, producers, and distributors committed to improving the livelihoods of industry workers. The organization is working to promote its formal code of employment principles to wineries in South Africa, auditing and accrediting vineyards based on criteria including hours worked and overtime record keeping, wage levels, safety/health risks, discrimination, and trends in alcoholism.

The government and industry initiatives have focused on four areas: equity, incentives, funding, and education. We next look at how far these programs have succeeded in advancing black economic empowerment.

EQUITY

In February 2004, VinPro, South African wine producers' representative body, held a meeting to present its blueprint for a coordinated program to increase the equity of blacks in the industry. The idea was to incorporate all the best ideas from existing initiatives like those described earlier in a plan that vineyard owners could implement with modifications to suit their particular circumstances. The event was attended by key stakeholders in the industry, including winery owners, winemakers, and government officials.

Based on its research, the VinPro team that created the blueprint defined a successful program as one that provided all participants with positive returns on the capital invested, was sustainable both commercially and environmentally, and led to tangible results for black workers (such as ownership, management, and control over the business).

The VinPro team found that to accomplish these goals, a plan had to meet several criteria. First, it needed a financing structure that did not require newly empowered black farmers to invest so much of their own capital (including loans and government grants) in land acquisition where the long-term viability of the business was endangered. Implied as a corollary was that land ownership should not be the only means for blacks to enter the wine industry. Second, the plan must make provision for transferring the necessary technical knowledge and skills to new farmers, incorporating rewards both for acquiring the skills and for transmitting them. Third, it needed to offer an exit strategy that would allow new farmers to liquidate assets should they decide they want to leave the industry. And fourth, the black farmers had to see both financial returns and positive effects on their lives quickly, with the understanding that wealth accumulation needs to be stressed over immediate consumption.

The VinPro team defined six models meeting these criteria. The models differ in such elements as whether the ownership of property is transferred to workers, or just a portion of the profits from their labor, and whether wine production remains in the hands of the vineyard owner or is taken over by the community. They are not mutually exclusive. Rather, some models may be more appropriate for a project in its beginning stages and others when it matures.

INCENTIVES

The success of programs like those outlined in VinPro's blueprint depends on the support of landowners. Currently, wine producers show varying degrees of enthusiasm for BEE. Some are apathetic. Others have tried empowerment projects and made mistakes and

has led to many cases of poisoning. Additionally, reports of children drowning in farm ponds, which are often inadequately fenced, if at all, are frequent.

LACK OF COORDINATION AND STRUCTURE

The government has not published any official guidelines for assessing the quality of land-grant applications. Currently, all South Africans who apply are entitled to governmental funding on a first-come, first-served basis. As a result, a request that does little to advance BEE efforts and has a low probability of success may be funded before one that is superior on both of these counts, simply because it came in first. The lack of guidelines also leads to confusion about what constitutes a good proposal that is worthy of funding.

VinPro's six models (see previous section "Equity") were introduced to add some clarity to the process. Because they were designed to be applicable to as many farmers as possible, however, the models are subject to wide interpretation. This flexibility allows programs to be tailored to specific situations, but it also means that some factors critical to a project's success may be unwittingly omitted. It should also be noted that models giving workers a share in the land they till cannot truly empower them until a market exists in which they can trade their equity.

Confusion also abounds in the wine industry. The various associations have overlapping responsibilities, and a lack of coordination among KWV, Sawit, and SAWB sometimes results in the public receiving conflicting messages. Disagreements also exist in each organization regarding funding decisions and objectives. This lack of organization has also led to delays in important measures such as a formal BEE charter for the wine industry.

ADMINISTRATIVE SHORTCOMINGS

Staffing shortages have impeded both the government's and the private sector's BEE efforts, particularly with regard to disbursing funds. Just two employees, for example, oversee Sawit's fund, a bare-bones staffing level that is largely responsible for the fact that only 2 million of the 363 million rands available have been distributed to BEE projects in the wine industry. Lack of personnel has also led to long delays at the DLA in processing land grants. These delays do have a bright side, however, giving the government and private agencies an opportunity to improve current empowerment models so that money is not spent on imperfect designs.

INADEQUATE EDUCATION

For BEE initiatives in the wine industry to succeed, workers must be educated not only in viticulture and oenology (the study of wine and wine making) but also in marketing, distribution, exporting, and product design. This has proved to be more difficult than anticipated. The fault lies largely with the unequal school system inherited from the old apartheid government. Current government and private-sector initiatives to support students through school have made only a small dent in the problem. Just compare the twenty-one young people the industry has sent to the University of Stellenbosch with the approximately 350,000 individuals involved in the wine industry.

IN CONCLUSION

The challenges described here are significant but not insurmountable. Clearly, the government needs to allocate more money to BEE efforts in the wine industry, particularly to land grants. It should also find more creative ways to involve the private sector. For instance, it might offer incentives such as trade agreements and export licenses to encourage wineries to contribute to a cooperative fund on which smaller wineries with limited resources could draw so they could implement projects to empower their workers. The government needs to find ways to attract commercial banks and venture capitalists to empowerment projects, as well. And since South African wine is in a global market, aspiring wine growers should look to foreign banks and venture capitalists, too.

The government should define clearly what it considers a worthy BEE project for the wine industry, and it should make this definition widely known. The Black Economic Empowerment Commission is in the process of developing a scorecard for evaluating projects' merit and long-term viability and determining how well they align with the commission's empowerment goals. Adopting this scorecard for land-grant applications should help speed up their processing and ensure that funding goes to projects that have the greatest prospects for success. Applications that do not meet the standards established in the scorecards should not merely be turned down; rather, the government should counsel the applicants on how to improve their projects.

Since its funds are limited, the government needs to develop a system for prioritizing the projects selected through the application process. One element to consider is whether a proposal involves a major player in the wine industry. Having funding go to these first will bring greater publicity to the program, raising awareness and encouraging lesser-known wineries to participate and so "keep up with the Joneses."

The VinPro models provide a good framework for evaluating successful projects and prioritization. Companies should consider implementing a similar blueprint with fewer models and more stringent definitions. This will enable the government to streamline the programs necessary to support their implementation. It will also be less confusing for prospective farmers, allowing them to focus on the quality of their projects rather than the choice of model.

Formalizing the government system for evaluating and prioritizing projects might also help Sawit and SAWB allocate their funds in a timely fashion and loosen the logjam impeding the flow of private funds. As noted earlier, several banks have already set aside 130 million rands for BEE projects and are most likely awaiting government direction on how to use the money. The scorecard would provide the needed direction.

To ensure that scarce public and private funds go where they will do the most good, both the execution and the funding of projects selected through the process just discussed should be designed to take place in phases. At the end of each phase, a project would be evaluated, using the scorecard, to determine if it is achieving its social and financial goals and whether its long-term impact is still aligned with the objectives of the Black Economic Empowerment Commission. If the evaluation is satisfactory, the project will receive its next funding installment. Initiatives that do not meet their goals would be counseled on how to get back on track before receiving additional funds. The process thus would have the additional benefit of fostering a true partnership between donors and recipients.

Sawit and SAWB should be brought together into one organization having a single strategy for furthering BEE in the industry and a coordinated plan for executing this strategy. In particular, SAWB needs to work with Sawit to develop a plan for allocating the trust's remaining 361.8 million rands to BEE initiatives. This would require hiring at least one more employee dedicated to reviewing project applications. The combined structure would also greatly reduce the current confusion about overlapping areas of responsibility and increase the two organizations' leverage with the government, ensuring the success of their empowerment projects.

The South African government should enforce a consistent system of financial rewards and sanctions to encourage winery participation in BEE initiatives. For example, it could make implementation of BEE projects a prerequisite for awarding trade and export licenses, as well as granting access to vital assets that it controls, such as water. Vineyard owners might also be motivated to get on board by the prospect of greater unionization if they do not.

In addition, wineries' BEE efforts should be publicized, so that they can reap the public relations benefits. For example, U.S. and UK consumers have reacted negatively to reports of worker exploitation and lingering use of the dop system. Positive publicity for the wine industry could spill over to other South African industries, including those providing goods (for example, gold and diamonds) and services (for example, tourism). In this regard, the government might take as its model the National Association for the Advancement of Colored People's Economic Reciprocity initiative. The NAACP rated hotel companies on their diversity practices and published the results. Low-scoring companies soon realized that people were choosing lodgings based on these ratings and worked hard to improve their practices. To accomplish something similar in the wine industry, the South African government could place labels indicating vineyards' BEE ratings on their bottles as they are exported.

Finally, the wine industry and the government must manage people's expectations to avoid future frustration. The current time frame for achieving BEE goals seems unrealistic, given the United States' experience with school desegregation. It has been more than fifty years since *Brown Versus Board of Education,* yet huge gaps still exist between U.S. blacks and whites in terms of education, salaries, and types of employment. South Africa has a much larger percentage of disadvantaged blacks than the United States and so may take longer to reach its goals than it expected.

REFERENCES

African Terroir. 2002. www.african-terroir.co.za/. Accessed 2004.

All Africa.Com. 2004 (accessed). South Africa: Land won't belong to all by 2005. http://allafrica.com/stories/200402200563.html.

Berry Bros. & Rudd. 2003. Black "empowerment" in South Africa. www.bbr .com/GB/db/news-item/530?ID=null&first_news_F=21 (September 17).

Erlich, Reese. 2004. Exploring South Africa's wine country. *Savvy Traveler.* http://savvytraveler.publicradio.org/show/features/1999/19990213/ s-africa.shtml.

Fourie, Clarissa. 2000. Land and the cadastre in South Africa: Its history and present government policy. Paper presented at the International Institute of Aerospace Survey and Earth Sciences, Enschede, the Netherlands (November 1). http://users.iafrica.com/a/au/augusart/ online_itcsa.html.

Golen, Frederic, Heitz, Shawn, O'Neill, Matthew, and Tomback, Dave. 2005. Social responsibility in the South African wine industry: A case study of Bouwland Wines. Global Initiatives in Management Program, 2005 Research Report. Evanston, Ill.: Northwestern University Kellogg School of Management.

Jacobs, Arthur. 2004. New Beginnings Winery. Personal interview, March, South Africa.

Johnston, Yvonne. 2004. Chief executive officer, International Marketing Council. Personal interview, March, Johannesburg, South Africa.

Kabunda, Mbuyi. 2001. South Africa in black and white. *Crisis Watch.* June 26. http://observatori.barcelona2004.0rg/observatorio/mostrarDossier _i.htm?num_dossier=268.

Karaan, Mohammad. 2004. Professor at the University of Stellenbosch. Personal interview, March, Stellenbosch, South Africa.

Mail and Guardian Online. 2003. Wine industry tackles black empowerment (September 17). www.mg.co.za/articledirect.aspx?area=%2fbreaking _news%2fbreaking_news__business&articleid=29026.

May, Peter. 2000. Unusual wines (May 10). www.winelabels.org/wines.htm.

Owen, Danielle. 2004 (accessed). Land reform—Running out of time. *Progress Report.* www.progress.org/archive/land16.htm.

Parliamentary Monitoring Group. 2003. A strategic plan for a vibrant, united, non-racial and prosperous South African wine industry (July). www.pmg.org.za/docs/2003/appendices/030610sawbdraft.htm.

Port of Harlem. 2004 (accessed). www.portofharlem.net.

Schadomsky, Ludger. 2003. Cape to Cairo—1. *Deutsche Welle* (November 7). www.dw-world.de/english/0,3367,3083_A_1035430,00.html.

Sibanda, Sipho. 2001. *Land reform and poverty alleviation in South Africa.* Presented at SARPN conference on Land Reform and Poverty Alleviation in Southern Africa. www.oxfamgb.or.tz/what_we_do/ issues/livelihoods/landrights/downloads/sastudy.rtf.

Small Enterprise Development Agency. 2004 (accessed). www.brain .org.za/SUPPORT/black_empowerment.html.

South African Wine Industry Trust News. 2003. Land reform initiative for SA wine industry announced (October 31). www.mbendi.co .za/a_sndmsg/news_view.asp?PG=196&I=54601&M=0.

South African Wine Industry Trust News. 2003. Strategic plan to transform the SA wine industry {October 31). www.mbendi.co.za/a_sndmsg/ news_view.asp?PG=196&I=54599&M=0.

Stanford University Computer Science Department. 2004. The history of apartheid in South Africa. www-cs-students.stanford.edu/~cale/ cs201/apartheid.hist.html.

Titus, Victor. 2004. Facilitator of Department of Land Affairs land reform projects at Nelson's Creek and New Beginnings Winery. Personal interview, March 24, Paarl, South Africa.

van Zyl, Nelda. 2004. Manager of Delaire Winery. Personal interview, March 24, Stellenbosch, South Africa.

VinPro. 2004. Land Reform in the Wine Industry (February 27). www.wdi .umich.edu/files/Publications/PolicyBriefs/2006/PB44.pdf.

Wines of South Africa. 2004 (accessed). www.wosa.co.za/transformation2 .asp.

Chapter 10

VENTURE CAPITAL AND BLACK ECONOMIC EMPOWERMENT IN SOUTH AFRICA

*Stephanie Davis, Marene Jennings,
Srikanth Reddy, Yuji Sadaoka, and
Guhan Selvaretnam*

The development of a robust small-business sector can play a critical role in the economic and social development of a country. Unfortunately, the passing of the apartheid laws in 1948, which legalized racial segregation, severely disadvantaged black entrepreneurs in South Africa. By depriving blacks of quality education and vocational training, apartheid severely limited their opportunities to build a robust, sustainable small and medium enterprise (SME) sector. It is also extremely difficult for black-run SMEs to obtain funding.

Apartheid officially ended in 1990, the year that F. W. de Klerk was elected South Africa's new president and that he released African National Congress (ANC) leader Nelson Mandela from prison. From 1994, when Mandela became president, to 1998, the government focused on transferring equity ownership of large corporations to BEE entities. (South Africa's Black Economic Empowerment Commission defines BEE as a strategy to increase the participation of blacks—the majority population—in financial and economic pursuits at levels proportional to their numbers in the population.) Because BEE entities were controlled by a small, politically connected elite, the nation's accumulated wealth failed to trickle down very far. The Asian financial crisis of 1997 exacerbated matters by causing many of these transactions to unravel. As a result, by 1998 little had been accomplished in terms of economic empowerment, and the government changed tactics, switching emphasis from the transfer of corporate ownership to fostering black-run SMEs. It has attempted to facilitate the emergence of black-owned small businesses through government agencies such as the National Empowerment Fund (NEF) and Khula Enterprise Finance (Khula). These organizations' failure to allocate funds effectively, however, has weakened their credibility. Banks and other private lending institutions, meanwhile, have neither the appetite for risk nor the expertise necessary for funding black SMEs. Venture capital (VC) firms specialize in funding start-ups and could bring further benefits to black entrepreneurs in the form of flexible transaction structures and ongoing involvement in the business, but returns need to compensate for the related risks.

One possible solution is a public/private partnership (PPP) that balances the profit-maximizing objective of the private sector with the social agenda of the government. A partnership between the government and private VC firms integrates and exploits the talents and resources of each entity to generate an outcome that is closer to the optimum. Various funding vehicles have, in fact, emerged, such as venture capital and hybrid PPPs, which enable some progress and allow black entrepreneurs to overcome these obstacles. We examine in this chapter the role these vehicles can play and the challenges they face.

SMEs AND ECONOMIC DEVELOPMENT

Of the many legacies of apartheid, two in particular dim South Africa's prospects for economic development. The first is the significant financial and educational disparity between the minority whites and majority nonwhites, who comprise 89 percent of the population. In 2001, the country's Gini coefficient—which measures income inequality on a scale of 0 (denoting perfect equality) to 1 (denoting perfect inequality)—was 0.635, compared with 0.42 and 0.41 for Cameroon and Senegal, respectively. Sixty-five percent of whites over twenty years of age have a high school or higher degree, compared with 14 percent of blacks and 17 percent of coloreds. The second legacy is an economy dominated by large conglomerates that were built up during years of sanctions that stifled job creation, skill development, competition, and innovation.

A sustainable small business sector can play a critical role in a country's economic and social development. A 2001 survey of thirty-seven emerging economies conducted by Global Entrepreneurship Monitor (GEM) demonstrates a consistent and strong correlation between projected economic growth and the rate of new business formation. SMEs' impact on economic growth and development stems largely from their ability to create and sustain employment opportunities, provide training, and pay wages. Job creation and training act directly to reduce the unemployment rate and income disparities and indirectly to lower the crime rate and increase government tax revenues. According to the GEM survey, between January 1999 and July 2002, SMEs created 1.14 million jobs in South Africa.

To date, black SMEs have made disappointing progress in South Africa. A 1999 World Bank survey of 800 small businesses in Johannesburg put the share of black owners at just 7 percent, compared with 56 percent for whites. Even among the 30 percent of enterprises started after apartheid, only 13 percent were owned by blacks. Sixty-four percent of the black SMEs were in service industries requiring low skill levels.

Obstacles to Black SMEs

One challenge SMEs in South Africa face is the economic domination of large companies. Sanctions during the apartheid era forced domestic corporations to be self-sufficient, and most South African corporations became conglomerates. Conglomerates still control 80 to 90 percent of the economy, crowding out smaller start-ups.

Overshadowed by their larger competitors, black SMEs are unable to grow enough and compete in the marketplace.

Significant cultural barriers to black entrepreneurship exist as well. Starting a new business requires technical skills and a level of educational sophistication that most blacks, because of the insufficient funding given to their schools during apartheid, have been unable to attain. The few blacks with good educations tend to take positions at corporations, where they are much sought after and richly compensated, rather than run the high risk of failure associated with small enterprises.

Black entrepreneurs also struggle to obtain adequate funding. Many lenders in the financial services sector require borrowers to have prior business experience or significant capital to collateralize a new venture, both of which were difficult if not impossible for blacks to accumulate during apartheid. Even in well-developed markets such as that in the United States, it is more difficult for SMEs than for large publicly traded corporations to obtain financing. This is largely because of the relative informational opacity of small private businesses. Large corporations operating under regulations requiring disclosure of up-to-date, audited information can access the public equity and debt markets to fund their business. Small enterprises, in contrast, typically enter into informal or private contracts, and many do not have audited financial statements. This is an even greater problem for black SMEs in South Africa, many of which do not meet minimum standards of record keeping, let alone possess audited financial statements. Lenders require higher returns to compensate for the higher risk of loans to businesses for which they do not have good data. The high cost of funding discourages entrepreneurs who have sound business plans, often leaving only those who intend to flee with the money. That raises risks and increases the cost of funding even further.

In businesses of any size, the interests of management often diverge from those of investors and lenders. Financing institutions must monitor companies to ensure that their investment value is being maximized. Monitoring of SMEs is harder to accomplish because of the lack of verifiable information about their operations, and its cost typically represents a higher proportion of the lenders' original investment. The necessity for monitoring and its expense both increase when entrepreneurs have relatively small equity in their businesses. In that case, they may be tempted to use their external capital to enrich themselves rather than grow their companies. Black entrepreneurs are often further shackled by the racist mind-sets of private investors and bank loan officers who previously supported apartheid.

FUNDING SMEs

A small enterprise may be financed solely by its principal owner or by some combination of external funding from friends and family, the government, banks, and venture capitalists. As evidenced in the survey by GEM, different SMEs chose different funding options, each having advantages and disadvantages in terms of how it addresses the risks posed by the business's opacity and what it brings to the enterprise beyond financing.

Self-financing brings black entrepreneurs no additional support or advice in running their enterprises. The 2001 GEM survey found the owners' own capital, used by approximately 45 percent of the surveyed businesses, was the most common source of funding for black start-ups in South Africa. Few black South Africans, however, have enough savings to start a venture, thereby depressing the rate of new business formation among blacks. And, again because of lack of capital, the businesses they do start are mostly microenterprises having small or no staffs and making limited contributions to economic development.

Approximately 40 percent of black entrepreneurs received funding from friends and relatives, according to the GEM survey. This is significantly higher than the percentage of SMEs receiving similar help in the United States, possibly reflecting cultural differences. The small pool of savings accumulated in the black community limits the amount of funding available for enterprises from this source. Family and friends, moreover, have scant understanding of how the business owner is using their money and can bring little to the enterprise beyond their meager capital.

Only 5 percent of black entrepreneurs reported receiving government funding, according to the GEM survey. Yet, the government sponsors several funding institutions: the NEF, Khula, Ntsika Enterprise Promotion Agency, Umsobomvu Youth Fund (UYF), and the Industrial Development Corporation. That such a small percentage of black entrepreneurs receives funding is due to poor coordination among the institutions and low awareness of their services. The organizations do not do much in-depth due diligence, but they do add value to the enterprises they fund in the form of access to procurement contracts and subsidized business services. Unfortunately, their effectiveness is restricted by limited resources and lack of private-sector expertise.

Only 15 percent of black entrepreneurs received bank financing, according the 2001 survey. The number is relatively small at least partly because funding institutions impose certain conditions to hedge their risks: a pledge of collateral—that is, assets owned either by the enterprise (machinery, land, or buildings, for example) or by the entrepreneur (car or house)—and restrictive covenants requiring the business to meet certain financial ratios calculated at regular intervals. For most black entrepreneurs in South Africa, these conditions represent insurmountable obstacles; they have few assets and cannot meet banks' record-keeping standards. Khula, the government funding institution, offers credit guarantees for small businesses, but only 9 percent of entrepreneurs who received bank loans had taken advantage of this service. Those entrepreneurs who do get bank financing reap the added benefit of having a one-stop cash-management resource.

In the early post-apartheid era, banks seemed a promising source. After 1994, commercial institutions rushed enthusiastically into microlending. The banks, however, were accustomed to dealing with large corporations having stable cash flows. They had little expertise at evaluating small-business loans and a lower tolerance for risk than is required in SME financing. The situation worsened in the late 1990s when the ANC government tried to encourage microlending by allowing banks to deduct interest directly from the salaries of government workers who had loans. The banks subsequently boosted interest rates to approximately 35 percent, leaving borrowers with little take-home pay. People protested, and the government reversed course, revoking the ability to deduct interest and setting a cap on permissible interest rates. In consequence, commercial banks lost large sums on their microloans and reimposed strict collateral, credit, and reporting requirements. Since most SMEs can not meet these requirements, bank microlending has languished.

The 2001 GEM survey reported that only 0.4 percent of black entrepreneurs sought out VC financing. This is unfortunate, since venture capital has several advantages as a funding vehicle for businesses. Venture capitalism is a form of private-equity funding typically targeting enterprises at the early stages of development. To handle the risks involved in this kind of investing, venture capitalists do extensive due diligence, ensuring that the start-ups have feasible business plans, sustainable markets, and dedicated management and that they can further demonstrate the potential for satisfactory returns on investment and hedging opportunities. The investors also draw up clear exit strategies and structure their investments defensively—funding in stages and requiring voting control, for example. In return, entrepreneurs receive not only funding but also hands-on help with strategic planning and, occasionally, operational decision making. Venture capitalists provide instruction in best business practices and legal, tax, and information technology (IT) services, reducing their fixed costs for each company by aggregating demand across their entire portfolios.

Venture capitalism avoids many of the problems inherent in bank financing. Unlike with banks, VC firms specialize in providing capital to risky early-stage ventures, and they therefore have a much higher tolerance for risk. In addition, they are more involved in the strategic direction and operations of the businesses in which they invest, and they are better positioned to foster the entrepreneurs' management skills. The key advantage of this type of funding, though, is its flexibility. Unlike banks, VC firms have no rigid credit guidelines, replacing strict collateral requirements with close monitoring.

VC firms seem to be perfect matches for black SMEs, which makes it surprising that so few of these enterprises take advantage of this form of funding. According to the 2001 KPMG South Africa VC and Private Equity Survey, the average size of a private-equity investment in 2001 was 9 million rands. Most SMEs require funding of between 100,000 and 5 million rands.

The primary reason that venture capital, despite its suitability, plays such an insignificant role in financing small black-run businesses is that investments in these enterprises generate insufficient returns relative to their level of risk. Funding SMEs requires relatively little capital, but the associated costs—for analysis, legal documentation, and so on—are the same as for much larger transactions. Costs thus represent a very high proportion of the initial investment, depressing potential returns. In addition, small black-owned businesses do not usually become large enough to attract acquirers or to take public. To exit an investment, a VC firm must rely on the company's owner and management to buy it out. The amount of capital these parties control thus determines the firm's returns, which, as a result, are probably considerably lower than the multiple of initial valuation expected from a typical deal. The consensus among private-equity and VC firms with knowledge of the black SME sector is that successful deals have a return on investment of 7 to 10 percent. That is comparable to the return on low-yield debt instruments—not very attractive considering that the majority of black SMEs are plagued by deficient capital and collateral and led by inexperienced and unskilled management, resulting in high failure rates.

In South Africa, black entrepreneurs need to depend largely on external financing to fund their businesses. This is clearly necessary given the scarcity of savings and wealth among black South Africans.

The financing vehicle is only part of the equation, however. In a 1995 white paper, the South African government stated that it needed the help of other institutions to address the funding impediments faced by black entrepreneurs and to realize its goal of developing small businesses. Many financial firms believe that the private sector would not participate in BEE initiatives unless the government mandated such action. They also, however, express resentment at government interference in this area. The resulting stalemate has left the needs of black entrepreneurs generally unmet. What is needed is a model that combines the advantages of venture capital with incentives to invest in black enterprises. This requires participation by both the public and the private sector. The difficulty is finding a common ground between the two.

PUBLIC/PRIVATE PARTNERSHIPS

A possible solution is to marry the South African government's agenda for broad-based economic empowerment with the private sector's resource capacity and expertise through a public/private partnership (PPP). Because of the government's support, these partnerships enable VC firms backing black entrepreneurs to earn reasonable returns with limited financial exposure.

The First National Bank (FNB)–Momentum–Umsobomvu Progress Fund is an example of such a partnership. The 100-million-rand Progress Fund is a collaboration among FNB and Momentum—the financial-services and life-assurance divisions of FirstRand Group, one of South Africa's largest conglomerates—and the government-sponsored Umsobomvu Youth Fund. UYF put up 80 percent of the capital, thus shouldering the bulk of the financial exposure, with FNB and Momentum contributing 10 percent each. The fund's aim is to promote entrepreneurship among black youth by backing companies in which black individuals between eighteen and thirty-five years of age either own at least 25 percent of the equity or account for a minimum of one-third of senior managers or half of the employees.

The partnership employs various approaches to overcome the obstacles to VC funding for black SMEs. To counteract the high transaction costs involved in venture capital investing, for example, the Progress Fund subsidizes staff salaries through government grants. It also reduces overhead by using UYF vouchers to hire accounting and IT consultants when a company needs development assistance and by taking advantage of FNB's facilities and tax and legal services.

Since the Progress Fund's mission is social as well as financial, it does not aim to earn typical venture capital returns. Rather, it seeks to minimize the risks of its investments. Although the fund doesn't ask for collateral, it does require that the SMEs it finances have positive projected cash flows and either significant medium- to long-term contracts with the government or private sector or confirmed orders for their products or services that account for a sizable part of their predicted revenues. In addition, the Progress Fund takes a direct role in running the businesses it backs. With one client, for example, the fund's managing director, Duncan Randall, personally co-signed all the checks the company wrote via an online banking service. It also builds competent management teams by targeting college-educated blacks with industry experience and deep roots in the black townships.

Finally, the Progress Fund structures its investments as quasi-equity. This provides it with both a periodic return and a viable exit strategy. The investment starts out as debt, paying a coupon amount calculated not to be burdensome to the company: the prime rate minus three percentage points plus a percentage of sales. It typically converts, at a valuation of two to three times earnings, to an equity stake of approximately 25 percent, which the company buys out over time. In this way, the Progress Fund extracts value over the life of the investment.

WEAKNESSES OF THE PPP MODEL AS REPRESENTED BY THE PROGRESS FUND

The Progress Fund overcomes several of the obstacles to the VC financing of black SMEs. Nevertheless, it has deficiencies. The most immediate is insufficient staff to carry out its mandate of investing 100 million rands in five to seven years. Randall's team consists of eight investment professionals with varying degrees of experience in VC consulting, project management, and operations. Deciding whether or not the fund will make an investment takes from three to six months. Due diligence and negotiations, which are extremely labor intensive, account for most of this processing time. Also time- and labor-consuming is the fund's direct involvement with its clients' operations. Although this detailed oversight is effective in elevating black entrepreneurs' skills and lowering their failure rate, it risks bogging the fund down in minutiae when it should be seeking out new investments.

More, and more-experienced, personnel would help alleviate this problem. Hires are needed in particular to search for and evaluate deals and allocate funds. Attracting and retaining appropriate staff, however, is costly. VC professionals, whose compensation is typically tied to returns, require extra incentives to work for a fund whose returns are significantly below the industry standard of 25 to 30 percent.

Another problem, mentioned earlier, is the scarcity of talented, experienced black entrepreneurs. Progress Fund has targeted young black professionals, but so have many large corporations, which need to fill their quotas of historically disadvantaged people to receive preferential treatment from the government. Since the number of college-educated blacks is limited, a bidding war has ensued. Young, educated black professionals must ask themselves whether it is in their interest to turn down a high-paying job for an uncertain entrepreneurial venture. The overwhelming response has been no.

One particularly difficult challenge faced by the PPP model in general is the tension between its mandate of performing a social good and the necessity of making sufficient profits to remain self-sustaining. The government's mission is to act as a catalyst to attract private capital to black SMEs. To do this, it must demonstrate a long-term dedication to propping up the sector. It has finite funding resources, however, and cannot subsidize capital investments in SMEs if they are unsuccessful. The difficulty of striking the proper balance is illustrated by the Progress Fund's first completed deal, announced at the beginning of March 2003: the buyout of a construction equipment rental company. A black youth shareholder, Bangile Kambile, and an employee trust together hold 67 percent of the equity and are supported in running the company by the old, experienced management team, which will retain 33 percent equity. The deal thus accords with the fund's mandate of empowering and nurturing young black entrepreneurs. On the other hand, because the rental company is well-established and one of the largest in the Eastern Cape, this is a relatively low-risk investment that many private-equity firms would make. In Progress Fund's defense, it is attempting to counteract the history of major losses associated with BEE initiatives by establishing a profitable track record. The danger is that the fund may continue committing to the rental-company type of deal rather than funding true start-ups that have more need of its help but also exhibit more risk. The fund will need to review its portfolio constantly to ensure that it achieves the proper mix of start-ups, expansions, buyouts, and equity buy-ins, with an increased emphasis on enterprises that, because of their riskiness, would not have otherwise had access to financing.

IN CONCLUSION

To solve its economic development issues, South Africa must find ways to make the financing process less of an obstacle for black SMEs and to attract talented black youth to entrepreneurship. The goal requires both an augmentation of the current PPP model and thinking outside the box for novel solutions. Moreover, the problem of developing black entrepreneurial talent has more long-term solutions than short-term ones. However, PPPs present the greatest potential for overcoming the impediments to financing black SMEs.

One problem with the PPP model, noted previously, was the lack of sufficient personnel to evaluate potential VC investments. A PPP could attract seasoned investment professionals and senior executives by offering salaries, funded by the VC firm, commensurate with their experience combined with the lifestyle benefits of a less stressful work environment. Younger professionals might be lured by the promise of greater responsibility than they would have at traditional private-equity firms. BEE VC funds could further market themselves as excellent private-equity training grounds.

One approach to developing entrepreneurial talent would be for PPPs to work with existing South African entrepreneurs to supply smart, hard-working young blacks with vocational training, mentoring, and apprenticeships. In addition, funding should be provided for the teaching of entrepreneurship at the elementary, high school, and college levels.

In terms of the functioning of the PPPs themselves, the partnerships should concern themselves with the quality of their investments rather than the quantity. Setting a target for the number of SMEs to be funded within a certain period puts in question the sustainability of the businesses and their ability to create the black SME sector that South Africa needs.

To encourage PPPs to finance more SMEs rather than larger, less risky enterprises, the government should loosen and simplify certain regulations that create heavy burdens for young businesses. The tax compliance process is especially cumbersome. So is registration, and some of the necessary offices are open only on weekdays, when a new entrepreneur might expect to be busiest. With these structural problems addressed, more black-owned SMEs may be willing to undertake the challenge.

REFERENCES

Adelzadeh, Asghar. 2003. On the path to nowhere. *Mail and Guardian Online* (April 10).

BBC News. 2002. Micro-lenders under pressure (February 28). http://news .bbc.co.uk/2/hi/business/1847036.stm.

Berger, Allen N., and Udell, Gregory F. 1998. The economics of small business finance: The roles of private equity and debt markets in the financial growth cycle. *Journal of Banking and Finance, 22,* 613–673.

Black Economic Empowerment Commission. 2000. Presentation for the Portfolio Committee on Trade and Industry, Cape Town, South Africa (September 13). www.pmg.org.za/docs/2000/appendices/000913BEE .htm.

Brealey, Richard, and Myers, Stewart. 1996. *Principles of corporate finance,* 5th edition. New York: McGraw-Hill.

Canadian International Development Agency. 2003 (accessed). www .acdi-cida.gc.ca/.html.

Central Statistical Services. 1998. The people of South Africa: Population census 1996. Report 1, 03–01–11. www.statsonline.gov.za/census01/ census96/HTML/CIB/CIB1996.pdf.

Chandra, Vandana, and Nganou, John Pascal. 2001. *Obstacles to formal employment creation in South Africa: Evidence from recent surveys.*

Presented at Development Policy Research Unit and Friedrich Ebert Stiftung Conference on Labor Markets and Poverty in South Africa, Johannesburg (November 16). www.commerce.uct.ac.za/DPRU/chandra&nganou.pdf.

Department of Trade and Industry. 1995. White paper: National strategy for the promotion and development of small business in South Africa (March 20). http://www.gov.za/whitepaper/1995/smallbus.htm.

Driver, Amanda, Wood, Eric, Segal, Nick, and Herrington, Mike. 2001. Global Entrepreneurship Monitor, 2001 South African executive report. University of Cape Town Graduate School of Business (December). www.gsb.uct.ac.za/cie/GEM/SouthAfrica2001.pdf.

International Finance Corporation (IFC). 2003. Africa project development facility. IFC Small and Medium Enterprise Department. www.ifc.org/sme/html/apdf.html.

International Monetary Fund. 2002. Republic of Senegal: Poverty reduction strategy paper (May). www.imf.org/External/NP/prsp/2002/sen/01/100502.pdf.

KPMG Corporate Finance. 2001. KPMG and the Southern African Venture Capital and Private Equity Association 2001 Private Equity Survey (published April 2002). www.savca.co.za/downloads/SAVCA %20 KPMG%20Private%20Equity%20Survey%202001.pdf.

Luiz, John. 2000. Small business development, entrepreneurship and expanding the business sector in a developing economy: The case of South Africa. *Journal of Applied Business Research, 2*(18), 1–16.

Phillips, Bruce. 1993. Equalizing opportunity through small business development: A South African perspective. *Review of Black Political Economy, 22* (Fall), 141–150.

Progress Fund. 2002. FAQs. www.progressfund.co.za/data/sb_group/3/.

Randall, Duncan. 2003. Progress Fund managing director. Interview by authors, March 20, Johannesburg, South Africa.

U.S. Central Intelligence Agency. 2003. Central Intelligence Agency world factbook. www.cia.gov/cia/publications/factbook/index.html.

Vietor, Richard H. K. 1997. *South Africa: Getting in GEAR.* Cambridge, Mass.: Harvard Business School.

Chapter 11

CLOSING THE SKILLS GAP IN POST-APARTHEID SOUTH AFRICA

Piotr Pikul, Kathy Wang, and
Craig Wynn

When the African National Congress (ANC) government introduced the idea of black economic empowerment (BEE) in 1994 (see chapter 10), corporations responded by quickly appointing high-profile black executives and directors and ceding partial ownership to BEE companies. In this phase, ownership and control were the two most prominent indexes of progress. By the end of the ANC's first term in 1999, however, it appeared that BEE had succeeded only in creating a powerful black elite without helping the massive underclass. Whites remained in operational and equity control of most companies. In 2000, therefore, the government changed tactics. Equity transfers became only one path to achieving black empowerment. Affirmative action laws set targets for employment at all levels of authority, and human resources development, training, enterprise development, social investment, and procurement policies were also emphasized. In response, industries established voluntary BEE charters, which set targets in all these areas with time frames for achieving them. A BEE scorecard was created to enable industries to measure their progress.

OWNERSHIP AND CONTROL

By 2003, ownership and control were no longer seen as ends in themselves. Still, they are featured in every industry charter and are a favorite topic of discussion in the government and the media. Charters typically specify a target of at least 25 percent black ownership by a certain date, of which 10 percent must represent direct ownership. Old Mutual, a South African London-listed insurance company with an international presence, for example, is seeking to increase the percent of shareholders' equity held by blacks to 10 percent by the end of 2010 from the current 4 to 5 percent, and BP Southern Africa (BPSA), a multinational energy company, has committed to 25 percent ownership by historically disadvantaged groups, such as blacks and disabled persons, by the same date. The charters also call for blacks to make up one-third of membership on boards and executive staffs by a given date, thus preventing the former practice of merely appointing figurehead black CEOs or chairmen while vesting true control in the white executives and directors. Progress in this area has been slower than with other BEE-related mandates. At FirstRand, a financial services group, two out of thirteen board directors are black, while at Old Mutual, one in five top executives are of Indian descent.

In the 1990s, ownership and control transfers were effected through deals implemented by special-purpose BEE vehicles. Today, the white-controlled companies themselves decide to whom they should sell their equity, by what date, and under what conditions. They seek partners with high ethical standards and demonstrated records of delivery. They also look for enterprises that have a broad base of active shareholders, to ensure that benefits accrue to the many and not just to a small elite, and that have the ability to invest their own capital, thus sharing in the risks as well as the rewards of the partnership. A good example is BPSA's empowerment deal, signed in August 2001, with the Mineworkers Investment Corporation (MIC) and Women's Development Bank Investment Holdings, both of which have histories of joint investments and proven records of using funds to support social development at the grassroots level. The deal gives BPSA's two partners equity stakes resulting in three seats on its board, 25 percent shareholder voting rights, and leadership positions on board subcommittees involved with training, employment diversity, and representation (that is, equity) in the company.

EMPLOYMENT EQUITY, TRAINING, AND EDUCATION

Employment equity requires that a company's management reflect the country's demographic makeup. To achieve this, a company must set targets for the representation of blacks and other disadvantaged groups at all levels of management. The financial services charter, for instance, requires that by 2008, blacks in general and black women in particular represent, respectively, 20–25 percent and 4 percent of senior management, 30 percent and 10 percent of middle management, and 40–50 percent and 15 percent of junior management.

Corporations must create plans for meeting such targets without destroying value. As Jacob Modise, chief operating officer of Johnnic Holdings, a leading South African BEE media company, told us, "People have to do the job. It is not enough to just have window dressing; you have to be able to run the business." Recruiting qualified black management candidates is not easy, however. Demand far outstrips supply, a mismatch worsened by the high rate of HIV/AIDS in the workforce and the brain drain in industries such as information technology, whose skilled professionals leave the country for better salaries and opportunities abroad. Increasing education among black workers should ease the hiring competition among South African companies. But as the country becomes integrated into the global economy, other nations will enter the game and begin vying for South African companies' highly skilled employees.

Advertising is often ineffective in attracting candidates from disadvantaged groups. As alternatives, companies have partnered with government and grassroots organizations to promote positions and have resorted to recruitment agencies and career fairs.

Historically white companies have also had to enhance their profiles so that members of these groups perceive them as desirable places to work.

Retaining qualified employees is as challenging as hiring them. The few skilled employees are highly sought after and do not feel compelled to remain in one place. Companies must offer increased responsibilities and competitive compensation to retain the best and the brightest. Long-term career plans, mentorship, incentives, and continuing education all play roles.

Education has been a favored tool in attracting and retaining employees. Centralized training programs and corporate universities are now common in the private sector. The financial services charter mandates that each financial institution establish undergraduate and postgraduate diplomas and degrees in financial services in conjunction with institutions of higher learning. Old Mutual Business School, for example, trains employees using faculty and curricula from institutions with which it has established partnerships, such as London Business School and University of Cape Town (UCT) Graduate School of Business. A company's program may be accredited through its industry's Sector Education and Training Authority (SETA) to participate in South Africa's National Qualifications Framework. This enables employees to earn educational credits for workplace experience and vocational training. First National Bank (FNB) has the FNB Learning program, for instance, offering coursework that is accredited up to NQF Level 6 (equivalent to a degree from a two-year or technical college). FNB is a subsidiary of the FirstRand financial services group and one of the four largest South African banks.

Employees are not the only beneficiaries of accreditation. The companies themselves receive financial rewards. Under BEE, businesses must spend 1 percent of their payroll budget on training, and leading companies consistently spend more. Old Mutual, for instance, puts 7.2 percent of its 2003 payroll into training, including 2.2 percent at Old Mutual Business School. Companies accredited through SETA get tax credits for their education outlays, up to 1 percent of their payrolls. Old Mutual receives this tax credit because its program is accredited through its partnership with UCT.

Another common tool for attracting and developing talent is the bursary. Bursaries are scholarships granted to disadvantaged students wishing to pursue degrees at institutions of higher education. Some cover tuition only; others include living expenses and employment at the sponsoring company over holidays. In return, most companies ask or require that recipients work for them for a certain period after they achieve their educational goals. Old Mutual has an extensive bursary program for training actuaries and accountants, two traditionally all-white professions. The scholarships cover full tuition for an approved accounting degree at South African universities and include allowances for books and other expenses. In addition, other incentives are offered, including employment at Old Mutual during university holidays.

BPSA does not support bursaries. However, BPSA partner MIC runs the JB Marks Education Trust Fund, which, since 1997, has provided 2,499 bursaries worth 17.4 million rands to National Union of Mineworkers members and their dependents.

PROCUREMENT AND DISTRIBUTION POLICIES

Corporations have reached beyond their own facilities to develop the capabilities of disadvantaged populations both upstream and downstream in the production flow. BPSA's BEE procurement policy, for instance, mandates that the company buy 30 percent of the nonhydrocarbon commodities and supplies it uses through accredited contractors and suppliers. To be accredited, an enterprise must be at least 51 percent black-owned or receive a score of at least five in a system that assigns points for black ownership, black management or control, black skills transfer, support for BEE procurement, women in management, and disabled employees. Qualifying suppliers also receive training, help in negotiating institutional financing and material prices, and assistance with productivity enhancement and strategy development. In a similar vein, the financial services charter specifies that financial institutions must provide black-owned small and medium enterprises with support to enable them to benefit from targeted procurement programs, promote early payment for services these enterprises provide, and encourage existing suppliers to become accredited. Financial institutions must also assist other BEE-accredited companies through skills transfer, staff exchanges, and technical and administrative support.

Downstream assistance is illustrated by BPSA's targets for its branded service stations. These are owned by individual dealers. BPSA aims to increase the representation of historically disadvantaged groups among its dealers to 47 percent by 2010. To this end, it has committed to invest 20 million rands each year in five retail sites set aside annually for owners from these groups. In another example, the financial services charter specifies that by 2008, 80 percent of the population should have access to—that is, be within twenty kilometers of—banking transaction and savings products and services, and an as yet undefined percentage should have access to life insurance products and services.

SOCIAL INVESTMENT

Finally, corporations have committed to improving conditions outside their factories and production chain. The financial services charter, for instance, mandates that between 2004 and 2014, financial institutions spend 0.5 percent of their posttax operating profits annually on community education facilities, secondary and higher educational programs, bursaries and scholarships, community training, skills development for the unemployed, adult basic education, financial literacy, youth development programs, and job creation.

PROGRESS REPORT

Education statistics seem to suggest impressive gains between 1994 and 2001 (the last year for which a full set of data is available). For instance, the pass rate for the Senior Certificate examination increased during this period from 58 percent to almost 62 percent, and the proportion of black full-time students rose to 61 percent at universities and 84 percent at the vocational *technikons*. In 2001, almost half a million black students were enrolled full time or long distance in higher education facilities, and the percentage of black students graduating approached 66 percent, narrowing the gap with coloreds (75 percent), Indians (76 percent), and whites (82 percent).

The progress indicated by these numbers, however, may be unsustainable and even largely illusory. Education is widely perceived to have declined in quality, and higher pass rates are attributed to lowered standards. As a result, even as more students are graduating from high school, fewer of these graduates are getting jobs. Much the same pertains to college students. Critics charge that affirmative action has not bridged the knowledge and skills gaps among students of different races but has only shifted the focus from achievement to racial balance. The educational successes that have been recorded, moreover, are not in the areas that could be most useful in reducing the high level of unemployment. Critical shortages of skilled workers still exist, for example, in professions such as information technology.

In Conclusion

Despite the discouraging data, initiatives like black economic empowerment charters and lifelong learning will eventually improve life for the disadvantaged majority in South Africa. The fact that the government seeks not just to redistribute resources to the majority but to create a country that is competitive in a globalized economy should encourage private-sector participation and lead eventually to prosperity for both businesses and citizens.

Corporations should view black economic empowerment less as a means of redressing past injustices than as a way to bring the majority into the formal economy and create a stronger, broader-based consumer class. Black economic empowerment policies create long-term economic value for companies and should therefore be regarded as investments rather than costs.

For instance, transfers of ownership and control to the black population have to be more than simple handovers. New owners, directors, and executives must be given time to learn how to operate a business and create value. A good model for such transfers is BPSA's joint venture with empowerment groups that allows these groups to provide training and development of necessary management skills. With regard to employment equity, companies need to focus on policies that nurture skilled recruits from the majority population. Bursary programs and scholarships are good ways to identify, train, and recruit disadvantaged persons. Here, Old Mutual's accounting and actuary scholarships are good models.

Training should also be regarded as an investment with an expected long-term return. Accreditation, which allows employees to transfer their acquired skills and knowledge to other areas and companies, is best achieved through centralized training departments or corporate universities. Trained employees should be free to pursue opportunities elsewhere. Such knowledge dispersion has long-term benefits for companies since it closes the skills gap in the wider society, contributing both to the availability of skilled labor and the growth of the consumer sector. Finally, policies like that of the BPSA that encourage suppliers to gain BEE accreditation and increase the number of black-owned dealerships are good examples of fostering skills throughout the production chain. The success of such policies depends heavily on choosing genuine partners. In the past, some BEE companies served as fronts for nonempowered businesses and thus precluded learning opportunities. Customer education, like that mandated in the financial services charter, increases the consumer class.

References

Alexander, Paul, and Pillay, Dev. 2004. Old Mutual Business School executives. Personal interview, Cape Town, South Africa (March).

Anderson, Benny. 2004. (head of First National Bank Learning Division). Personal interview, Johannesburg, March.

Cohen, Leon. 2004. (chairman of PG Bison). Personal interview, Johannesburg, March.

Ford, Steven, and Graham-Parker, Grahame. 2004. (Community Employment Initiative founders). Personal interview, Cape Town, March.

Innocenti, Nicol Degli. 2004. Companies simply realize it's the right thing to do. *Financial Times,* April 13.

Leke, Acha, Loch, Mark, and Maltz, Noah. 2004. (McKinsey & Company Johannesburg office consultants). Personal interview, Johannesburg, March.

Mbeki, Thabo. 1999. Opening of Parliament speech. June 26, 1999.

Modise, Jacob. 2004. (chief operating officer of Johnnic). Personal interview, Cape Town, March.

Moyo, Peter. 2003. Transforming our business in South Africa: The financial services charter (December 4). http://www.oldmutual.com/download /2478/04Dec2003.

Oyegun, Bebe. 2004. Transformation manager of BP Southern Africa. Personal interview, March, Cape Town, South Africa.

Project Literacy. 2004. *Education statistics* (April 30). www.projectliteracy .org.za.

Reed, John. 2003. South Africa's cappuccino effect: Will economic empowerment do more than create a sprinkling of black tycoons? *Financial Times,* November 5.

Reed, John. 2004, South Africa's new dividing lines: Ten years after the end of apartheid, the ANC's big challenge is to create jobs. *Financial Times,* April 22.

Republic of South Africa. 1996. *Constitution of the Republic of South Africa.* May. www.info.gov.za/documents/constitution/index.htm.

Republic of South Africa. 2001. *Education in South Africa: Achievements since 1994.* Department of Education, May. www.education.gov.za/dynamic/ imgshow.asp?id=246.

Republic of South Africa. 2003. *Education statistics in South Africa at a glance in 2001.* Department of Education, June. www.education.gov.za/ emis/emisweb/01stats/EducationStats2001.pdf.

Republic of South Africa. 2003. *Financial Sector Charter.* Financial Services Sector. www.treasury.gov.za/press/other/2003101701.pdf.

Republic of South Africa. 2003. *Broad-Based Black Economic Empowerment Act.* www.info.gov.za/gazette/acts/2003/a53-03.pdf.

Republic of South Africa. 1998. *Employment Equity Act.* Legislature. www
.info.gov.za/gazette/acts/1998/a55-98.pdf.

Republic of South Africa. 2004. *Budget 2004 at a glance.* National Treasury.
www.treasury.gov.za/documents/budgets/2004/review/Glance.pdf.

United Nations Development Program. 2004. *Human development reports,*
April 30. www.undp.org/hdr2003/indicator/indic_2_1_1.html.

U.S. Library of Congress. 1996. *South Africa: Library of Congress country
study,* May. http://lcweb2.10c.gov.

PART 4

MEETING THE AIDS CHALLENGE

Chapter 12

SUSTAINABLE FOUNDATIONS FOR HIV/AIDS CARE: TREATMENT AND DELIVERY IN SOUTH AFRICA

Stephanie Chan, Deepa Gupta, Kara Palamountain, and Aparna Saha

For people in developed nations who have HIV/AIDS, education, awareness, and access to critical medications have transformed the disease from a death sentence to a chronic illness. In South Africa, in contrast, the inadequate educational infrastructure and lack of access to affordable drugs have allowed the virus to remain an implacable killer. The United Nations AIDS/World Health Organization (UNAIDS/WHO) estimates that in 2003 alone, 370,000 people died from AIDS, a number that is expected to increase to 10 million by 2015.

Although the global community has begun to address this crisis, it has often been hindered by the actions and, sometimes, inaction of the South African government. Businesses operating in the nation, hit by productivity losses, employee health and training costs, and a shrinking and impoverished consumer base, have attempted to pick up some of the slack in combating the epidemic. Many large companies have done risk assessments, formulated nondiscrimination policies, implemented awareness and prevention programs, instituted voluntary testing and counseling, and assisted their employees with care and treatment. Smaller enterprises, however, lack the capital to provide such programs. And those with the wherewithal worry about being flooded with HIV-positive employees.

One industry—the pharmaceuticals sector—has offered solutions beyond its own workforce, transforming the delivery of AIDS treatment and care in the country as a whole. Here we look at the contributions of a particular drug company, Abbott Laboratories, whose Abbott Access program (Access) might serve as a model for HIV/AIDS care in other African nations.

The success and efficiency of the International Healthcare Distributors (IHD) company provide a compelling example of how private partnerships can benefit both individual companies and the countries they serve. This case study shows how it should be feasible for pharmaceutical companies and their partners to initiate similar warehousing strategies in other African nations.

THE SOUTH AFRICAN GOVERNMENT AND THE AIDS EPIDEMIC

The African National Congress (ANC), South Africa's governing body, has responded to the HIV/AIDS crisis controversially and often illogically. One prominent example was its response to the Global Fund to Fight AIDS, Tuberculosis and Malaria (Global Fund), a public/private partnership established at the Group of Eight summit in July 2000. Its mission is to reduce infections, illness, and deaths caused by the named diseases, as well as to contribute to poverty reduction. The South African government failed to sign an agreement with the fund to release the first US$40 million disbursement of a five-year, US$165 million grant to KwaZulu-Natal, one of the provinces hardest hit by the epidemic. It further tried to block the grant after it was approved in June 2002 by arguing that KwaZulu-Natal originally submitted its application directly to the fund and that South Africa had not yet established a Country Coordinating Mechanism to review such applications.

The obstruction in the case of the Global Fund grant is not the only instance of the ANC's seemingly self-defeating AIDS policy. President Thabo Mbeki has questioned the relationship between HIV and AIDS and refused to provide the AIDS drug AZT to rape victims or pregnant women. ANC Health Minister Manto Tshabalala-Msimang has broadly rejected antiretrovirals (ARVs), stating that they are not a cure for HIV/AIDS and citing concerns about their toxicity, the availability of laboratory services, and limited infrastructure and educational resources, particularly in the rural areas.

Predictably, these stances have been attacked both globally and domestically. The Treatment Action Campaign, a South African AIDS activist organization, for example, publicly charged the minister of health and trade and the minister of industry with failure to provide adequate treatment, including ARV drugs, to AIDS victims.

Although it provides only halfhearted support of treatments for AIDS patients, the government actively promotes prevention efforts. These include the free distribution of condoms (350 million in 2002) and voluntary HIV counseling and testing at approximately one thousand public health sites. The ANC also supports programs such as loveLife, which was launched in 1999 and funded by the Bill and Melinda Gates Foundation and the Henry J. Kaiser Family Foundation. At its launch it had the goal of halving the rate of new HIV infections in the fifteen-to-twenty age group before 2006 through communications and social marketing campaigns.

The National Association for People Living with AIDS and similar organizations regard initiatives like loveLife as wastes of valuable resources that could be better devoted to providing ARV drugs to HIV-positive patients. South African professionals whom we interviewed explained that the ANC position is based on the ideal of equitable allocation of resources: While prevention messages can be affordably provided to the entire South African population, the spending required for ARV therapies would force the government to prioritize treatments to some patients, thereby excluding others. The government's position is understandable, but many medical professionals and leaders of nongovernmental organizations (NGOs) believe prevention can be effective only if a treatment program for HIV-infected individuals exists. As one physician noted, "Why get tested for HIV/AIDS when there is no treatment option for you? You only face public scorn and make life harder for yourself."

South Africa's primary treatment option is to improve patients' immune systems through better food security and nutrition. This approach has had little success. The government now provides ARV therapies to survivors of sexual assault and claims to be seeking to reduce the barriers—high drug prices and inadequate health infrastructure—to implementing a nationwide program. It will be some time, however, before treatment can keep pace with the millions of new infections each year.

ABBOTT'S HIV/AIDS PROGRAM— COLLABORATION AND DISTRIBUTION

Abbott Laboratories is one of several pharmaceutical companies in South Africa that distribute antiretrovirals at or below cost. Its HIV-care program, Abbott Access, is tasked with facilitating the delivery of ARV therapies at no profit in countries that the United Nations defines as least developed. Abbott Laboratories seeks to collaborate with host governments, allied organizations, and local NGOs.

Before Abbott Access can operate in a country, the country's government must grant regulatory approval for each product the company will distribute. Approval is typically based on how the government perceives the need for the therapies, its desire to support in-country treatment, and its concerns about patient safety. South Africa does not have a formalized approval process; companies must be persistent and keep communicating with the relevant officials. For this purpose, Abbott has installed a program manager in Johannesburg.

The ANC does not support a nationwide ARV program, but it does allow private medical offices, insurance providers, and other community health-care programs to distribute the drugs. Abbott, accordingly, has formed partnerships with these entities. To ensure that it chooses partners that can do the job properly, the company relies on its partnership with Axios International, a global management consultancy experienced in private- and public-sector partnerships with organizations like UNAIDS and in public health programs in developing countries. Through its dedicated staff, the organization enables Abbott to make accurate, timely assessments of the hundreds of applications the company receives for its drugs, assuring that approved facilities provide proper voluntary counseling and testing as well as drug administration that focuses on adherence to a regimen and follow-up care. Axios also facilitates cooperation among the many multinational companies and NGOs involved in HIV/AIDS prevention and treatment in South Africa, avoiding duplication of services and programs and making the distribution and administration of medication more efficient and effective. For example, Axios may recommend that a facility receive products through Abbott Access and also adopt educational programs offered by another partner.

DISTRIBUTION: INTERNATIONAL HEALTHCARE DISTRIBUTORS

Abbott gets its treatments to Axios-approved doctors, insurance providers, and NGOs through International Healthcare Distributors, a central drug repository located in Johannesburg. Founded in 1993, IHD also serves ten other major multinational pharmaceutical manufacturers: Aventis, Bayer, Boehringer Ingelheim, Bristol-Myers Squibb, Eli Lilly, MSD, Novartis, Roche, Schering, and Wyeth. Abbott joined the partnership in 1998, a few years before launching Abbott Access, hoping to leverage IHD's local and continental drug distribution network and so streamline its own supply-chain management.

IHD provides Abbott with cost-effective logistical and warehousing support and a range of distribution services. It has a technologically sophisticated system that includes air-conditioned warehouses, stringent cold-chain maintenance (that is, maintaining proper vaccine temperatures during storage and handling to preserve potency), batch tracking from manufacturer to end dispenser, and an Internet-based online ordering system called Futurewave. The security of the system and its tracking capabilities are crucial, given the value of ARV treatments and the preferential pricing Abbott offers to its clients. By keeping detailed records of where a batch was sold, at what price, and to whom, IHD can quickly track down recovered or stolen stock.

Perhaps the most important feature of Abbott's partnership with IHD, though, is that the company retains control of its drugs, unlike in traditional wholesale arrangements, in which ownership of the product is transferred to the wholesaler. This arrangement enables Abbott to negotiate prices and trading policies with countries and end dispensers and ensure that strict quality standards applied in manufacturing are maintained throughout the distribution chain.

PROGRAM RESULTS

Abbott's goals for Access have focused on increasing and broadening the distribution of its treatment and diagnostic products. In these terms, the program has been successful. In December 2002, for instance, the number of countries where the company's ARV drugs and diagnostic tests were available had increased to 24 and 48, respectively, up from 9 and 27 the year earlier. Currently, the number of countries has risen to 130. For 2003, the company's distribution goal for diagnostic tests was seven million; the distribution goal for its antiretrovirals was 680,000 grams, double the goal for 2002. Good progress toward these goals was indicated by first quarter 2003 sales of Abbott's ARV therapies and tests, which surpassed the total for 2002. The company also set a target of treating at least 70,000 South Africans by the end of 2003. Since then, the company has continued to contribute money to the development of new treatments as well as to make its products affordable in order to increase the number of individuals using these preventive measures. Abbott distributes HIV/AIDS treatment at a rate of $500 per patient per year to help facilitate its accessibility for all people.

Abbott attributes much of Access's success to its lean structure, which allows Abbott to communicate directly with Axios about applicants and minimizes the bureaucratic layers between it and drug dispensers. Communication with end dispensers is further facilitated by the partnership with IHD, which also enables Abbott to ensure product integrity and prevent illegal trading of its products. Another factor contributing to the program's success is Axios's central role in coordinating the activities of multinationals and NGOs that are engaged in improving health in the region. Finally, there are various marketing initiatives, including promotional groundwork done by the Abbott staff in Johannesburg, direct mail campaigns, and participation by the program's representatives in international conferences, where they spread the word about the success of Abbott Access in preventing and treating HIV/AIDS.

EXPANDING THE PROGRAM

Despite its success, Abbott Access can become more effective in fighting HIV/AIDS in South Africa and throughout the entire continent. To do so, it must move beyond its focus on product distribution. Following are some areas into which the program could consider expanding.

INCREASING MEDICAL EDUCATION

Abbott and Axios staff members already conduct informal education sessions for providers. By explaining how HIV/AIDS is transmitted and how Abbott's drugs fight it, the sessions not only

enhance the clinical knowledge of providers—whose medical training, in many cases, included little or no discussion of the disease—
but also ease their acceptance of ARV treatments. Furthermore,
they help Abbott Access expand its network of end dispensers by
illustrating the positive results of ARV treatment and encouraging
hospitals to incorporate the Abbott therapies as first-line agents in
treatment protocols. Given these benefits, the company may want
to formalize and expand its medical education program through
partnerships with NGOs and academic institutions.

MEASURING END-DISPENSER EFFICACY

No matter how widespread their distribution, drugs do no good
unless they are properly administered. In fact, ARV can cause considerable harm if not taken correctly and consistently, since inconsistent use may allow the virus to evolve into super strains. Ensuring
proper drug administration would be a natural extension of the
Access program. This would require developing a measurement of
treatment efficacy. One way to do this would be to distribute a form
to end dispensers to be filled out and submitted biannually. It
would ask for the number of people served; their age, race, gender,
and income level; and their health progress since beginning treatment in terms of counts of CD4 lymphocytes and white cells, nutri-
tional status, and other indicators, depending on the technology
available to the respondent.

Collecting these data would serve several ends. First, it would
provide evidence of the effect of ARV therapies on the quality of
patients' lives. Second, it would give Abbott Access a better understanding of the populations it currently serves and point to those it
may be missing. And third, it would motivate end dispensers to
maintain high standards for regimen adherence and drug administration. Programs with inadequate performance might receive assistance from Abbott's other programs, NGOs, private medical
providers, or insurers that are successfully meeting the criteria. This
would ensure continuous program improvement and help to prevent the development of drug-resistant strains.

INFLUENCING PUBLIC POLICY

Public policy is perhaps the area in which it is most difficult for private companies to effect positive change. It is, however, probably the most important for ensuring the continuation of access to antiretroviral drugs. The data collection described in the previous section may provide enough evidence to convince government officials that supporting small-scale national treatment programs is both beneficial and cost-effective.

IN CONCLUSION

The ANC cites several obstacles to implementing an ARV program: high drug prices, inadequate health infrastructure, and difficulties with ensuring treatment compliance. Several countries have demonstrated that these obstacles can be overcome. Brazil, for instance, largely produces its own, relatively cheap, generic equivalents to ARV drugs and has addressed the infrastructure problem by creating a network of HIV/AIDS clinics (see chapter 13). As for compliance, 69 percent of Brazilian patients have achieved 80 percent adherence to the treatments. As a result, the country's national ARV program, initiated in 1997, has kept the infection rate relatively low, stabilizing the epidemic and paying for itself in decreased costs realized through lower hospitalization rates and improved overall public health.

In South Africa, although pharmaceutical companies provide therapies at prices that are considerably lower than the market price, the drugs are still beyond the reach of most of the population, with the exception of well-off urban citizens. Although it is easier to monitor and ensure adherence to the drug regimen in a smaller sample of users, as the drugs become more widely accessible, this issue will need to be addressed. Despite these problems, though, Brazil's example suggests that South Africa should be able to develop a reasonably successful treatment program and realize the concomitant financial and health benefits.

References

A continent in peril. 2001. *Time.* www.time.com/time/2001/aidsinafrica/
map_flash.html.

Arndt, Channing, and Lewis, Jeffrey. 2000. The macro implications of
HIV/AIDS in South Africa: A preliminary assessment (August).
www.worldbank.org/afr/wps/wp9.pdf.

Axios International. 2003 (accessed). About Axios. www.axios-group
.com/en/about.asp.

Axios International. 2003 (accessed). Access to HIV Care. www.accesstohiv
care.org/en/welcome/.

Daly, Kieran, and Parr, Julian. 2003 (accessed). The business response to
HIV/AIDS: Impact and lessons learned. www.iblf.org/csr/csrwebassist
.nsf/content/f1d2a3b4c5h6.html#report.

Global Business Coalition on HIV/AIDS. 2003 (accessed). Why is
HIV/AIDS a business issue? www.businessfightsaids.org/about_why
.asp.

Global Fund to Fight AIDS, Tuberculosis and Malaria. 2003 (accessed).
Frequently asked questions. www.globalfundatm.org/faq_gfund.html.

Henry J. Kaiser Family Foundation. 2003. South Africa's failure to sign
Global Fund agreement shows government has 'no intention' of providing AIDS treatment, opinion piece says (April 22). http://kaisernet
work.org/daily_reports/rep_index.cfm?DR_ID=17291.

International Healthcare Distributors. 2003 (accessed). Profile. www.ihd.com.

Johnson, Cindy. 2003. Customer service representative with International
Healthcare Distributors. Interview with the authors, March 17,
Johannesburg, South Africa.

Joint Monitoring Committee on Improvement of Quality of Life and Status
of Women. 2001. How best can South Africa address the horrific
impact of HIV/AIDS on women and girls? (November). http://196
.25.195.137/committees/report/jmciqlsw.htm.

Mahlangu, Theo. 2003. Access initiative project manager in Johannesburg.
Interview with the authors, March 17, Johannesburg, South Africa.

Pakendorf, Andreas. 2003. Pharmacist and researcher with a perinatal HIV
research unit. Interview with the authors, March 17, Johannesburg,
South Africa.

Pressly, Donwald. 2001, June 5. No to anti-retroviral AIDS drugs. *Business
Day (South Africa).* www.virusmyth.net/aids/news/bdavrs.htm.

Reuters. 1999. South African President Thabo Mbeki questions AZT
(October 28). www.virusmyth.net/aids/news/southafrica.htm.

South African Press Association. 2000. Expert panel will look at AIDS with fresh eyes (February 28). www.virusmyth.net/aids/news/sapapanel .htm.

Smetherham, Jo-Anne, and Khumalo, Buhle. 2003. AIDS activists turn up heat on ministers. *The Star (South Africa),* March 21. www.accessm ed-msf.org/prod/publications.asp?scntid=2432003143179&contentty pe=PARA&.

Chapter 13

MEETING THE HIV/AIDS CHALLENGE IN BRAZIL

Joshua Bennett, Nageswara Pobbathi,
Andy Zhilei Qiu, and Ryan Takeuchi

HIV/AIDS imposes a severe burden on the developing world. Not only does it usually affect people in the most productive years of their lives, crippling the economy, but also treating the disease puts a terrific strain on scarce resources, of both families and governments.

Ten years ago, there were many reasons to doubt that Brazil's AIDS program could succeed. Not least among these were the difficulties of treating the disease and the cost of the therapies relative to the country's per capita gross domestic product. In addition, pharmaceutical companies might well have seen the Brazilian market as too risky. In general, neither the governments nor the vast majority of patients in the developing world can afford the prices routinely charged for AIDS medications in North America and Europe. Discounting treatments can be costly to the companies if the drugs are reexported to the developed world or if many other countries begin demanding similar deals.

Despite these potential obstacles, Brazil has been able to provide state-of-the-art therapies for its rapidly increasing pool of AIDS patients while keeping its budget constant. The country's AIDS program demonstrates that a developing market can be viable for pharmaceutical companies. We look here at the factors that have made Brazil's program so successful, the risks pharmaceutical companies face in the country's market, and how they can address these risks and compete there more successfully.

AIDS today is generally treated with a "cocktail" of three or more antiretroviral (ARV) drugs. The annual cost can average US$10,000 or even, for new therapies such as Fuzeon, $20,000. The expense of buying these drugs is only part of the problem developing countries face in combating the disease. Many of them also lack the necessary infrastructure to ensure that medications are delivered to patients and that these patients are educated about the complex regimens for taking them. Monitoring compliance with the drug regimens is also required, to prevent the virus from mutating into resistant strains.

To help developing countries cope with AIDS, many public-interest organizations contend that it is necessary to lower their drug costs. One way to accomplish this would be to give poor countries access to cheaper generic versions. Article 31 of the Agreement on Trade-Related Intellectual Property Rights (TRIPs) can help provide that access.

Article 31 is an attempt to balance drug companies' right to make a profit, thus preserving their ability and motivation to develop future products, against the health and welfare of developing countries. The article permits World Trade Organization (WTO) member states to limit patent rights in a national health emergency either by using the patent itself or by issuing a compulsory license to a third party. Exactly when and in what circumstance the article should be invoked, and how much harm this does to pharmaceuticals and their ability to innovate, continues to be a subject of debate. Such protections are very important to the high-tech industries in general and to the pharmaceutical sector in particular. Drug companies spend ten to fifteen years and $800 million, on average, to bring a new product to market in the United States; if they wish to expand sales overseas, they may incur additional costs. To recoup their expenditures and earn a profit, they need legal protection for a certain period during which the creation of copycat drugs is barred to allow them to recover their research investments.

BRAZIL'S AIDS TREATMENT MODEL

The Brazilian AIDS/HIV program has been cited as a model for combating a health epidemic. Access to AIDS treatment, as well as to health care and basic medications in general, is a constitutional right in Brazil. The country developed an AIDS program in São Paulo as early as 1983. By 1985, it had instituted a national program based on prevention, treatment, and respect for the basic rights of people living with the disease. The program has had consistent support from both the public and the highest tiers of government, even as enrollment has risen and administering the program has become more difficult. Political resolve has been bolstered in part by the early and effective advocacy of well-funded groups representing homosexuals, who, as in the United States, were the earliest AIDS sufferers.

Government support for AIDS treatment has translated into regulatory policies and the permanent allocation of financial resources at national, state, and local levels. Brazil currently provides more than 140,000 of its citizens with free ARV therapies. As a result of its program, AIDS mortality rates in the country have fallen from a peak of 18,000 in 1996 to 15,000 in 2003.

A high debt burden, together with constraints imposed by the International Monetary Fund in return for support it provided during Brazil's economic crises in the 1990s, has put pressure on the government's AIDS budget. The country has, however, partly contained the costs of providing free treatment by purchasing domestically produced generic drugs.

Before Brazil became party to the TRIPs Agreement in 1996, the country's pharmaceutical companies could legally infringe on patents, including those on seven antiretroviral drugs. Buying these ARVs from domestic manufacturers has kept the government's spending on the AIDS program within bounds. In 2000, for instance, the Health Ministry disbursed $301 million on treatments, the same figure as for 1999 even though the number of patients in the program had risen by 33 percent. If it had had to import the same amount of medicine, the government's cost would have been about $1 billion.

It is questionable whether such savings can continue. AIDS drugs are constantly evolving and improving to counter viral resistance, but only the older antiretroviral drugs are produced in Brazil. As a result, the country now imports 81 percent of the ARVs it uses in its program.

PRICING DRUGS IN BRAZIL

After the Brazilian government passed legislation to comply with international TRIPs Agreement standards in 1997, international drug companies, attracted by the market's growth potential, started to make serious investments in the country. Between 1997 and 2000, the research-based pharmaceutical industry committed approximately $2 billion to Brazil. Much of the foreign investment has gone into facilities, such as the $200 million manufacturing plant GlaxoSmithKline opened in Rio de Janeiro in 1998. Today, Brazil's pharmaceutical industry is the largest in Latin America in terms of value and the sixth largest in the world, estimated to comprise about $5 billion in prescription drug sales.

PRICING PRESSURES

The Brazilian government has historically controlled the prices of pharmaceutical products. Recently, it has added Article 31 to its arsenal. In late 2000, caught between a relatively fixed budget for its AIDS program and escalating costs stemming from increased enrollment and from court orders to provide new (and expensive) drugs to all HIV-positive patients, the government threatened drug companies with compulsory licensing if they did not reduce the cost of their AIDS cocktails. Two factors lent credibility to this threat. First, the country's domestic generic drug industry already had experience producing AIDS drugs. Second, its physicians have relatively little political clout. In developed markets, physicians would mount strong opposition to any attempt to limit access to drugs they were currently prescribing. In Brazil, however, many of the doctors treating AIDS patients are doing so in rural clinics and lack specific training in AIDS treatments, so they depend on the government for guidance.

Brazil's tactic worked. In April 2001, for example, Merck cut the prices of two of its antiretrovirals, one of which at the time accounted for 10 percent of the country's AIDS program budget, by nearly two-thirds from list price. Although Abbott refused to negotiate under threat, most drug companies followed Merck's example. Bristol-Myers Squibb's new protease inhibitor is sold at a 76 percent discount off its U.S. price, and other medications have been marked down 40 percent or more.

Risk of Global Customized Pricing

Even taking into account sales and marketing costs, drug companies achieve average operating margins in excess of 30 percent. Such margins are needed to justify research and development investments, but they also give the pharmaceuticals some leeway in customizing the prices of their products to individual markets' ability to pay. Some customization is necessitated by government regulations. For example, more than 88 percent of global drug sales take place in North America, Europe, and Japan. Because of price controls in the last two regions and Canada, pharmaceutical companies charge higher prices in the United States, which thus accounts for the bulk of their profits.

Just as pharmaceutical companies benefit by charging more (thus fattening margins) in the United States, where the government imposes no controls, they can profit by charging less (thus increasing volume) in developing countries like Brazil, where manufacturing and sales costs are relatively low. Cutting prices would seem to be a profitable tactic for marketing AIDS drugs in the developing world, where many patients currently lack access to antiretrovirals and cannot afford to pay a lot for them. Doing so in Brazil, however, could pose risks both to industry profits and, in the longer term, to AIDS sufferers.

Risks of Reimportation

Although prices for the same drug vary from country to country, this opens the way for a secondary market in which customers in high-paying nations reimport pharmaceuticals from nations where costs are lower. The greater the difference in prices between markets, the greater the incentive for such reimportation. If the secondary market were to operate unfettered, price customization would break down, and all wholesalers would purchase drugs at the lowest price available globally. Although drug flow among countries is never completely uninhibited, limited reimportation does occur.

In recent years, reimportation has become a topic of heated debate in the United States, where consumers have been taking advantage of Canada's government-controlled prescription drug prices. The result has been a three-way battle among local U.S. governments with overstretched budgets, major pharmaceutical companies trying to protect their profits, and Canadian distributors worried about meeting domestic demand while satisfying the foreign market. In a similar development, at least $15 million of HIV drugs priced at a discount and destined for use in Africa were found in the European market in 2002.

In the United States–Canada case, it has been argued that reimportation, by decreasing the supply of low-cost drugs relative to demand, will increase prices for Canadians and land U.S. consumers back where they started. A similar situation could occur in Brazil with AIDS drugs—and with harsher consequences. In the short term, reimportation could generate shortages in Brazil. In the long term, it could increase overall drug costs, which would be passed on to the Brazilian government, making the program harder to sustain.

Although reimportation is technically possible in Brazil, several factors militate against it actually occurring. First, the Health Ministry is the sole purchaser of AIDS drugs, the majority of which are distributed through government-funded clinics, and this purchase and distribution process is subject to close public scrutiny. The government can thus easily be held accountable for drugs that are illegally redirected out of the country. Second, drug purchases are precisely matched to the number of patients in the healthcare system, resulting in few excess drugs.

Risks of Forced Price Discounts

Brazil's success in treating AIDS and in winning substantial price discounts for branded AIDS drugs from pharmaceutical companies could inspire imitation both internally and externally. HIV/AIDS is not the leading cause of death from disease in Brazil. Malaria, hepatitis, and diabetes are all prevalent in the country and are often deadly. Since what constitutes a national health crisis under TRIPs is subject to interpretation, it is conceivable that the Brazilian government could negotiate reductions in the prices for treatments of these diseases as it did for AIDS drugs. A politician might, for example, promise increased access to malaria drugs through price negotiations as an election platform. Carried far enough, such actions could effectively negate the benefits achieved in 1996, when the government enacted patent protection for drugs, and lead to a decrease in pharmaceutical investment in Brazil.

Similarly, other countries could be inspired by Brazil's example to demand discounts from pharmaceutical companies. This possibility is all the more real because many experts from the Brazilian program hold key positions in the World Health Organization (WHO) and act as advisers to the programs of other developing nations. If other states do follow Brazil's lead, it is difficult to predict whether pharmaceutical profits would rise or decline. As stated previously, price customization—even if forced on companies through negotiations—could lead to higher overall profits. However, if increased access to the drugs led to reimportation, the impact could be negative.

Although still a risk, neither internal nor external imitation of Brazil's AIDS-drugs negotiations is likely to occur. For one thing, for the Brazilian government to employ the same tactic for other disease treatments would be difficult. AIDS is the only disease for which the government is the sole purchaser of drugs. Assuming this role for other illnesses would entail taking the economically and politically costly step of disrupting existing channels and contracts.

Moreover, other diseases lack the public awareness and level of advocacy by nongovernmental organizations (NGOs) that AIDS has garnered. It is notable that pharmaceutical companies express little concern about internal expansion of negotiating tactics.

As for external expansion, other countries would have serious problems attempting to copy Brazil's tactics. The ability to sustain a program like Brazil's depends on a combination of a strong health-care infrastructure, a government with a social agenda that gives priority to AIDS treatment, dexterity in negotiating with pharmaceutical companies, and commitment by NGOs. Brazil's health-care infrastructure, by ensuring proper delivery and administration of drugs together with patient education and monitoring, also ensures that the government's price negotiations with AIDS drugs manufacturers result in improvements both in access to treatments and in outcomes. Many of the nations that most need lower pharmaceutical prices, such as those in sub-Saharan Africa, lack the necessary infrastructure. Treatment for river blindness, a disease common in Africa, is much simpler than that for AIDS, requiring only one pill per year, yet it took Merck and the WHO five years to set up a system to distribute the medication in the continent. Creating infrastructure for AIDS treatment would almost surely take longer. In addition, countries that do not, like Brazil, concentrate all AIDS-drug purchasing in the government's hands would have difficulty winning the same volume-based discounts. Finally, Brazil's domestic generic drug industry gives it a stronger negotiating hand than most other developing countries would have.

Risk of Reduced Investment in AIDS Research and Development

Reincorporation of forced drug discounts puts pressure on drug company profits. This in turn could reduce the investment for research, raising the risk to AIDS programs and patients. As stated earlier, a major challenge in fighting this disease is that the virus develops resistance to therapies. This virtually ensures that patients taking current therapies will eventually require new drugs. Research and development are expensive, and pharmaceutical companies must continuously question whether these are the best uses of their investment dollars, especially when they could be putting the time and money into cures for diseases that are more concentrated in the developed world, such as cancer. If reimportation and aggressive negotiating tactics were to significantly reduce the profitability of AIDS drugs, companies might decide the answer was no, stanching the flow of new AIDS drugs. This would be disastrous for AIDS programs.

Such a worst-case scenario is a legitimate concern. Brazil, however, represents only a small percentage of AIDS sales and, as was pointed out, presents little risk of drug reimportation. Cuts in AIDS research and development are thus unlikely to result from Brazil's policies. In addition, pharmaceutical companies would probably want to avoid the public relations meltdown that reducing their investments in AIDS research would cause.

MAKING THE BRAZILIAN AIDS MARKET WORK FOR PHARMACEUTICAL COMPANIES

The market for AIDS treatments in Brazil has three characteristics that must enter into any calculus of the opportunities to be found there. First, because of constraints on the government's budget, the market cannot be expected to grow significantly. Second, because of the country's excellent infrastructure and centralized purchasing, pharmaceutical companies face fewer risks in Brazil than in other developing nations. Third, the number of drugs is increasing, intensifying competition among their makers.

The viability of Brazil's market depends crucially on its AIDS patients' continued access to therapies. Although the pharmaceutical industry has collaborated with the government to improve delivery infrastructure, efforts have been hampered by the government's desire not to appear too close to the companies with which it negotiates. The industry might be able to avoid the perception of conflict of interest by partnering with the government through separate entities created for the purpose, through arrangements with NGOs, or by some other means. However they are handled, continuing to undertake projects in cooperation with the government would not only ensure that the Brazilian AIDS market remains viable but could also free up more of the government's limited budget for drug purchases. In general, assisting efforts to improve infrastructure and access to drugs will benefit the pharmaceutical industry.

Beyond working to grow the Brazilian market for AIDS drugs as a whole, pharmaceutical companies must strive to increase their market share. To succeed, they need to differentiate their products. As we said earlier, many Brazilian physicians lack extensive training in AIDS treatment and so tend to prescribe the therapies that are recommended by the independent scientific committee the government relies on in determining its own drug purchases and treatment specifications. This committee has historically looked only at efficacy in making it decisions. Drugs that provide novel benefits will thus be much more likely to win market share. That said, price is increasingly entering into the committee's determinations, and so affordability improves a drug's chances of inclusion in government-recommended treatment regimens.

Finally, a company has more control over the pricing of its drug if the process for manufacturing it is complex, like that for Abbott's Kaletra. The harder it is for generic producers to duplicate a drug, the less weight government threats to issue compulsory patents carry in negotiations. A proper balance, however, must be struck between complexity and cost. Fuzeon, a HIV fusion inhibitor, is very complicated to manufacture, which should put Roche, its producer, in a strong negotiating position. But the Brazilian government chose to limit access to the drug, primarily because of its high annual cost of $20,000 per person. Companies that can combine complexity and novel benefits with low costs will be most likely to gain traction in the Brazilian market for AIDS drugs.

In Conclusion

Together with the existence of a thriving domestic generic drug industry, the structure of Brazil's AIDS program and its infrastructure have enabled the country to win necessary price concessions from pharmaceutical companies. They have also made it easier for these companies to make concessions. The combination of centralized purchasing and a strong delivery infrastructure eliminates the need to use third parties to get drugs to patients, reducing the risk of reimportation. The difficulty of reproducing the program reduces the risk that Brazil's negotiating tactics will spread to other countries. Pharmaceutical companies can thus safely lower the prices of their AIDS drugs in the country.

Pharmaceutical companies can contribute to keeping Brazil's AIDS program viable, thus ensuring a continuing market for their products, by helping to increase patients' access to it. To succeed in the market, they should try to design AIDS drugs that address medical needs that are currently unmet and whose manufacture is too complicated to be easily copied but is accomplished at a relatively low cost. Achieving all these goals may seem difficult, if not impossible. It should be remembered, though, that just a short time ago, similar doubts could have been voiced about the future of the Brazilian market for AIDS drugs.

REFERENCES

AIDS.org. 2004 (accessed). Living with HIV: How do I start? www.aids.org/factsheets/201-How-Do-I-Start.html.

AIDS.org. 2004 (accessed). What is AIDS? www.aids.org/factsheets/101-What-is-AIDS.html.

Almeida, Jaime, Director of New Business, Abbott Laboratories; Marcos Lobo de Freitas Levy, Boehringer Inelheim; Luiz Henrique de C. Lopes, Pfizer; Irapuan Oliveira, Head of Institutional Relations, Abbott Laboratories; and Antonio Carlos Salles, Manager of Corporate Subjects, Bristol-Myers Squibb. 2004. Personal interviews at Interfarma headquarters, March 16, São Paulo, Brazil.

Armstead, Terry, Martha Penna, and Irapuan Oliveira (president, general manager, and head of institutional relations, respectively), Abbott Laboratories. 2004. Personal interviews, March 18, São Paulo, Brazil.

Associated Press Newswires. 2003. Brazil closes second deal this month for AIDS drug discount, two more under negotiation (November 19). www.aegis.com/news/ads/2003/AD032415.html.

BBC News World Edition. 2002. Industry tackles AIDS drug scandal (October 3). http://news.bbc.co.uk/2/hi/europe/2296157.stm.

Castelo, Adauto. 2004. Professor, Division of Infectious Diseases, São Paulo Federal University. Personal interview, March 17, São Paulo, Brazil.

Center for Drug Evaluation and Research. 2001. *Guidance for the industry—M4: Organization of the CTD.* Washington, D.C.: U.S. Department of Health and Human Services, Food and Drug Administration (August).

Cohen, Jillian. 2000. *Public policies in the pharmaceutical sector: A case study of Brazil.* LSCHD Paper Series 54 (January). Washington, D.C.: World Bank.

Cohen, Jillian, and Lybecker, Kristina. Forthcoming. AIDS Policy and Pharmaceutical Patents: Brazil's Strategy to Safeguard Public Health.

Constitution of Brazil. 1988. www.senado.gov.br/bdtextual/const88/const88i.htm.

Davis, Jennifer, and Nelson, Todd. 2002. *HIV and AIDS therapeutics.* RBC Capital Markets, May 3.

Dintruff, Robert. 2004. Director of Global Care Initiatives, Abbott Laboratories. Personal interview, March 8, in Chicago, Ill.

Embassy of Brazil in the United Kingdom. 2004 (accessed). Brazil's population. www.brazil.org.uk/page.php?pid=99.

Finkelstein, Joel. 2004. Drug reimportation looms as U.S. safety task force is named (March 15). *amednews.com,* www.ama-assn.org/amednews/2004/03/15/gvsb0315.htm.

Ganesan, Senthil. 2003. *Brazil: The perennial underachiever.* Hyderabad, India: ICFAI Knowledge Center.

Harrington, Mark. 2000. *Brazil: What went right? The global challenge of access to treatment and the issue of compulsory licensing.* Speech at Tenth National Meeting of People Living with HIV and AIDS, Rio de Janeiro, Brazil (November 3). www.aidsinfonyc.org/tag/activism/brazil.html (accessed April 3, 2004).

Hay, Andrew. 2003, November 18. Brazil plays hardball on AIDS drug discounts. *Reuters.*

Joint United Nations Programme on HIV/AIDS. 2004. A joint response to HIV/AIDS (April 2). www.unaids.org.

Kaiser Foundation. 2001. The history of HIV treatment. Daily HIV/AIDS Report (June 8). www.kaisernetwork.org/daily_reports/print_report.cfm?DR_ID=5073&dr_cat=1.

Kaiser Foundation. 2003. Drug access: Brazil authorizes importation of generic AIDS drugs; move could reignite WTO debate. Daily

HIV/AIDS Report (September 5). www.kaisernetwork.org/daily_
reports/rep_index.cfm?hint=1&DR_ID=19712.

Magee, Mike. 2004 (accessed). Importing drugs from Canada and beyond.
Health Politics with Dr. Mike Magee. www.healthpolitics.com/
media/prog_32/slides_prog_32.pdf.

Malloy, Megan, Ho, May-Kin, Noensi, Erick, Tsai, Kuhn-Shen, Schwimmer,
Aaron, and Georgetis, Emily. 2003. Trimeris Inc. Goldman Sachs
Equity Research (April 8).

Médecins sans Frontières Campaign for Access to Essential Medicines. 2003.
*Drug patents under the spotlight: Sharing practical knowledge about phar-
maceutical patents.* Geneva, Switzerland. May.

Medici, André. 2004 (accessed). Causes of mortality. Embassy of Brazil in
the United Kingdom. www.brazil.org.uk/page.php?cid=235.

Mercer Human Resources Consulting. 2003. A look into the Brazilian
healthcare market (April 3). www.mercerhr.com/summary.jhtml/
dynamic/idContent/1087840.

O'Keeffe, Geraldine, Farmer, George, and van Hulten, Bartjan. 2002. HIV
treatment: Current and future trends. Sector Note, Fortis Bank
(December 18).

Oxfam International. 2003. Robbing the poor to pay the rich? How the
United States keeps medicines from the world's poorest. Oxfam
Briefing Paper 56 (December). www.oxfam.org.uk/what_we_do/
issues/health/bp56_medicines.htm.

Peloia, Geraldo. 2004. Manager of Roche Pharmaceuticals. Personal interview, March 16, São Paulo, Brazil.

Pharmaceutical Research and Manufacturers of America (PhRMA). 2002.
Delivering on the promise of pharmaceutical innovation: The need to
maintain strong and predictable intellectual property rights. White
Paper on the Intersection of Intellectual Property and Antitrust Law in
the Pharmaceutical Industry (April 22). Washington, D.C.: PhRMA.

Rosen, Sydney, Simon, Jonathan, Vincent, Jeffrey, MacLeod, William, Fox,
Matthew, and Thea, Donald. 2003. AIDS is your business. *Harvard
Business Review* (February 2003).

Small, Gretchen. 2001. Brazil battles for right of all nations to affordable
medicines. *Executive Intelligence Review* (March 23). www.larouchepub
.com/other/2001/2812BrazilAIDS.html.

Standard & Poor's. 2003. Healthcare: Pharmaceuticals. Industry Survey
(December 3). www.netadvantage.standardpoor.com.

Teixeira, Paulo. 2002. The Brazilian response to the HIV/AIDS epidemic:

Prevention, treatment and human rights. Global Health Council (May). www.globalhealth.org/conference_2002/onsite/downloads/teixeira.ppt.

Tren, Richard. 2004. On AIDS, Brazil's new way forward. TCS Daily (February 11). www.techcentralstation.com/021104D.html.

UK Cabinet Office's Performance and Innovation Unit. 2001. Health in developing countries: A proposed package for support by the international community (March 30). www.iphn.org/20010330%20%20Consultation%20Paper.doc.

U.S. Centers for Disease Control and Prevention. 2004 (accessed). What causes AIDS? www.cdc.gov/hiv/pubs/faq/faq36.htm.

Wadia, Roy. 2001. Brazil's AIDS policy earns global plaudits. CNN.com (August 16). www.cnn.com/2001/WORLD/americas/08/14/brazil.AIDS/index.html.

Whitaker, Daniel. 2001. The pharmaceutical marketplace in Latin America. *Pharmaceutical Industry Dynamics* (June).

World Trade Organization. 1994. Standards concerning the availability, scope and use of intellectual property rights. TRIPS: Agreement on Trade-Related Aspects of Intellectual Property Rights. www.wto.org/english/docs_e/legal_e/27-trips_04_e.htm.

World Trade Organization. 2003. Implementation of paragraph 6 of the Doha Declaration on the TRIPS Agreement and public health. General Council (September 1). www.wto.org/english/docs_e/legal_e/27-trips_04_e.htm.

World Trade Organization. 2004 (accessed). The multilateral trading system—past, present and future. The WTO in Brief: Part 1. www.wto.org/english/thewto_e/whatis_e/inbrief_e/inbr01_e.htm.

PART 5

CORPORATIONS AND THE ENVIRONMENT

Chapter 14

GREEN MANAGEMENT IN THE EUROPEAN UNION

*Lamtiurida Hutabarat, Marc Major,
and Doug Stein*

In the era since the adoption by most industrialized nations of the Kyoto Protocol, an international treaty designed to limit global greenhouse gas emissions, the European Union (EU) has been among the greenest of the world's major political blocs. Its Environmental Action Programme, which is currently in its sixth incarnation, commits the EU to an ambitious ecological program: combating climate change, preserving biodiversity, reducing chemical use, conserving natural resources, and reducing waste. The member states have in the past pursued these goals mainly through strict regulation and monitoring. More recently, however, they have focused on cooperative approaches in which businesses are encouraged by incentives, rather than forced by regulations, to make their operations greener.

Here we examine the factors driving increased environmental awareness by studying three EU-based companies known for their environmentally conscious policies and actions: textile and furniture producer Otto Versand, consumer-goods titan Unilever, and petrochemical giant BP Amoco. In particular, we seek to determine what motivates these companies to reduce their environmental impact and what short- and long-term costs and benefits they can realistically expect from their actions.

ENVIRONMENTALISM IN THE
EUROPEAN UNION

The 1970s marked the start of a growing consensus in Europe that something needed to be done about environmental damage. This resulted in legislation aimed at managing specific sources of pollution. The 1980s brought more comprehensive end-of-pipe solutions, particularly in Germany, where threats to the Black Forest by acid rain catalyzed new laws regulating waste disposal and water and air pollution. The 1982 Seveso Directive governing risk and accident management in the EU was similarly inspired by an environmental threat: in this case, the 1976 release of a cloud of dioxin from a chemical plant in Seveso, Italy.

By the 1990s, however, lawmakers on both sides of the Atlantic had begun to realize that attempts to legislate away every environmental problem created massive bureaucracies and threatened to make operating businesses, particularly small and medium-sized ones, almost impossible. It was determined that traditional command-and-control regulation, in which the government dictates companies' goals and how the companies should reach them, often merely encourages the regulated entities to cheat and is thus less effective in many situations than more cooperative approaches.

With this in mind, the EU, like the United States, has incorporated more market approaches into its environmental programs. In 2005, for instance, the EU inaugurated the Greenhouse Gas Emission Trading Scheme, in which all twenty-five member states participate. In emissions trading, a regulatory body sets an acceptable level for each pollutant and divides the total into units called credits or permits. Companies whose emissions are beneath the limit may sell credits to others that breach the cap. The community has also introduced ecolabeling (for example, the German Blue Angel and Green Dot) that enables consumers to choose products based on how environmentally friendly they are. On the production side, EU companies are forced to consider the costs of polluting and of exploiting diminishing resources by a system of green taxes and subsidies. Carbon taxes proposed in Germany and the UK exemplify this approach, as do various planned and existing subsidies for projects such as environmental-technology research and development, conservation, and nature preservation. Perhaps the most ambitious of these projects is a program, announced in 2002, to research and develop vehicles powered by hydrogen fuel cells.

Of course, command and control is still alive and well. In this regard, the EU has introduced some groundbreaking measures. The Directive on End-of-Life Vehicles, for example, which was adopted in 2000, requires that automobiles sold in the EU be 85 percent recyclable by weight and that automakers take back their vehicles at the end of their useful lives. If this program proves successful, it will be extended to other products.

THREE GREEN COMPANIES

Although no company has zero impact on the environment, a few have endeavored to make their operations ecologically responsible. Unilever, Otto Versand, and BP Amoco are clearly among them. These companies' environmental initiatives do not appear to be driven by government regulations. Rather, all three try to stay ahead of the regulatory curve, to gain as much lead time as possible in engineering needed solutions and differentiating themselves from their competitors.

UNILEVER

The Anglo-Dutch company Unilever is the leading supplier of food, household, and personal-care products, employing 265,000 people and selling in nearly every country in the world. Despite its size, the company has worked hard to reduce its impact on the environment. It has instituted recycling programs, reusing material from toothpaste tubes in Brazil, for example, and has been steadily increasing the amount of renewable energy it employs—up to 90 percent at its tea estates in India. The company also promotes biodiversity. To cite one instance, the farmers who grow peas in Britain for Unilever's Birds Eye brand are required to protect and encourage the many bird species, some of them endangered, that nest and feed in their fields.

The company compounds the impact of its environmentalism by extending it through its supply chain. A particular focus is the sustainable use of water. Unilever is attempting to reduce both the amount of water its factories consume and the volume of their discharges. It also ensures that what is discharged has as few pollutants as possible, to the extent that, in certain cases, the effluent can be used in fertilizer. At the other end of the chain, the company has several projects to educate consumers in better, more efficient water usage.

OTTO VERSAND

Founded in 1950 by Werner Otto as a shoe-catalog business, Germany's Otto Versand today is the world's largest mail-order group, encompassing eighty-three retail companies in twenty-three countries and employing more than 70,000 people. Its main catalogue comprises 1,400 pages and has a monthly circulation of about 10 million. Environmental protection has been on the company's agenda since 1986, given equal emphasis with its economic goals. To guarantee continual improvement, management identifies eco-performance targets, as well as measures to reach them. It evaluates its progress, publishing the results in a sustainability report.

The ecological ethos permeates all Otto Versand's functional areas. The company's sites division, for example, is always looking for ways to save energy and water and reduce waste, while the packaging division tries to avoid bulky materials that are environmentally unfriendly. The textile division strives to use only organic cotton and is hoping to increase to 79 percent the percentage of materials tested for substances harmful to humans. The transportation division, meanwhile, has succeeded in reducing the CO_2 emissions from its massive fleet of delivery trucks by about 40 percent from 1994 levels. Extending its commitment beyond the group itself, Otto Versand will work only with suppliers that comply with its environmental and social standards, avoiding pollutants in their production processes and regulating child labor.

BP AMOCO

Alternately hailed as a forward-thinking business and derided as just another large oil company with a nifty flower logo and shiny green veneer, BP Amoco is indisputably one of the major players in the global petrochemical industry. It has enormous influence over not only the production of vital commodities but also the public's understanding of the proper role of a modern industrial corporation.

As supplier of just 1.5 percent of the world's energy and 3 percent of its oil and gas, BP Amoco has limited control over the production and use of these commodities, which themselves account for only a portion of the total human impact on the environment. The company leverages its influence, however, by serving as a model among both its peers and the public for how a multinational company can and should behave with regard to the environment. In a key strategic move aimed at creating shareholder value, BP Amoco has positioned itself as being outside the mainstream of global energy companies, drawing attention to its relatively high ecological consciousness through its new sunflower logo and green coloring.

BP Amoco's outlier stance is perhaps most evident with regard to climate change, one of the most contentious issues facing the energy sector. In 1996, the company officially separated from the Global Climate Coalition (GCC), based in Washington, D.C., which counts among its members most big oil companies and many utilities, coal companies, and auto companies. The innocuously named lobbying and public relations organization has been on the front lines in challenging the science underlying regulations limiting greenhouse-gas emissions in order to prevent their enactment. BP Amoco found the GCC's position intellectually unjustified. It also wanted to avoid the fate of Royal Dutch Shell, which was savaged in the press in 1995 over its disposal plans for an offshore oil storage platform named the Brent Spar.

In 1997, BP Amoco's colorful and controversial chief executive, Lord Browne of Madingley, grabbed headlines with a speech at Stanford University calling for companies and governments to address the rising concentration of carbon dioxide in the atmosphere and the rising temperature of the earth's surface. Later that year, the company matched his words with action, beginning its own internal emissions-trading scheme to reduce carbon from its processes (though not from use of its products). In 1998, it announced its intention to reduce emissions 10 percent from 1990 levels by the year 2010. The company met this ambitious target in 2001—nine years ahead of schedule and at no net cost. In fact, from 1998 through 2002, the project actually improved BP Amoco's financial performance by a total of $600 million. Since 2002, the company has aggressively pursued a program of growth without increased emissions, achieved largely by applying state-of-the-art engineering to less-efficient plants it has acquired.

For the long term, BP Amoco is investing vast sums in solar-, wind-, and hydrogen-energy technologies. As of 2002, BP Solar enjoyed a 20 percent global market share and was growing at 30 percent a year; the company's target for the division is 40 percent annual growth. It recently added an experimental wind park to one refinery, although in market studies, BP Wind has learned that communities resist large windmills, perceiving them as ugly and oversized. More immediately, the company is promoting natural gas (to vast stores of which, not coincidentally, it has easy access) as a "bridge fuel" between what management perceives as humanity's petroleum-based past and its hydrogen-based future. In collaboration with DaimlerChrysler, it is testing hydrogen-fuel-cell buses in Stuttgart and Hamburg. Currently, however, development of hydrogen vehicles is limited by the high costs of prototypes and lack of a fuel distribution network. Producing hydrogen on a large scale in an environmentally friendly way is also a problem.

In discussions with us, company officials identified as a business imperative the importance of looking beyond fossil fuels.

WHY GO GREEN?

As noted earlier, these three companies' environmental programs are largely the products of internal pressures rather than external regulations. The chief motivations seem to be morality, risk avoidance, competitive pressure, and investor influence.

MORALITY

Unilever, Otto Versand, and BP Amoco are unusual in the degree to which morality—in the sense of obligation to employees, society, and the world at large, both now and in the future—pervades their organizations and informs their policies. Otto Versand chief executive officer Michael Otto, for example, ties a company's "right to exist" to the degree to which it has a higher purpose than pure profit. For his company, this higher purpose is "to introduce acceptable environmental and social standards throughout the world, at the same time seeing to it that these are more readily enforceable." Similarly, for Unilever, the right to exist derives from government, customers, and communities, which may revoke it if the company does not hold up its end of the bargain with environmentally and socially sound policies.

RISK AVOIDANCE

Companies that do not act in environmentally responsible manners face the risks of lawsuits, tighter regulations, and damage to their brand. These points were made by Claros Consulting of London in a report it compiled for concerned ExxonMobil shareholders. The Claros report stated that because Exxon had let itself "become the obvious chief climate change villain," it could lose up to $3 billion in brand value as well as considerable power to recruit and retain employees and to influence policy-makers around the world. The company had also exposed itself to the nontrivial risk of being sued for damage related to climate change. Given the cost of recent tobacco industry settlements in the United States, Claros estimated the potential costs of maintaining a defense in such litigation at up to $1 billion annually, with damage awards possibly costing one hundred times that.

COMPETITIVE PRESSURE

The Claros report notes that if ExxonMobil supported mandatory greenhouse-gas reductions, it "could boost the value of its huge gas reserves, . . . generate revenues from emissions trading, . . . [and become] a total energy business, increasing global market share, through diversification into clean energy." By limiting environmental investments and mitigation expenditures, the company is improving its current bottom line. But it is also setting itself up to be strategically outmaneuvered in the long term by more progressive competitors, such as BP Amoco, which are positioning themselves now to thrive in a world where the Kyoto Protocol has the force of law. For small companies, a long-term vision is often easier, since profits may not exist at all in the short term. Those with innovative environmental technologies can use the network provided by the European Business Council for a Sustainable Energy Future (e5), which lobbies on behalf of environmental companies, to find larger partners with distribution capability for speeding their innovations to market.

INVESTOR PRESSURE

As noted previously, being behind the curve in complying with coming environmental regulations can hurt a company's bottom line in the long term, damaging shareholder value. Not surprisingly, then, investors are taking the issue seriously. Banks are also beginning to recognize environmental irresponsibility as a risk factor and are lowering their interest rates on loans to companies that have mitigated a portion of this risk.

Evaluating the trade-offs between financial returns and sustainable practices, however, is not easy. Many companies are developing sustainability and corporate social responsibility reports to supplement their annual reports, but they generally do not understand how to explain or quantify the pluses and minuses of their policies properly. Social indexes can help investors cull undesirables (arms manufacturers, cigarette and alcohol sellers, gambling establishments, certain lumber and oil companies) out of their portfolios. The FTSE4Good index series and the Dow Jones Sustainability Index, for example, rank companies by performance criteria outlined online at www.ftse4good.com and at www.sustainability-index.com, respectively.

Institutional investors, who control large blocks of stock, are particularly well placed to pressure companies to behave responsibly. Recognizing that the financial risks and consequences of climate change will continue to increase, a group of thirty-five institutional investors representing assets in excess of $4.5 trillion commissioned Innovest Strategic Value Advisers to launch the Carbon Disclosure Project (CDP) in spring 2002. The project is charged with getting the 500 largest companies in the world by market capitalization to disclose "investment-relevant information concerning their greenhouse gas emissions." Since the launch, the number of participating institutions has nearly tripled—to 95 from 35—and represented assets have more than doubled, to more than US$10 trillion. The number of leading institutions backing CDP demonstrates that the mainstream investment community is now seriously engaging with the strategic and financial implications of responding to climate change.

In Conclusion

Forward-thinking companies have the opportunity to move toward green management and sustainability. As Unilever, Otto Versand, and BP Amoco demonstrate, such a strategy, if implemented and managed correctly, can yield tremendous benefits and competitive advantage. Changes in production and technology that reduce usage of natural resources such as energy, minerals, water, and timber can yield substantial profits, not only paying for themselves over time but, in many cases, reducing initial capital outlays. Companies thus do well by making choices that sustain both business and the environment.

References

Ball, Kevin. 2003. Vice president for energy enhancement, BP Amoco. Interview with the authors, March, Europe.

Boulding, Kenneth. 1966. The economics of the coming Spaceship Earth. www.geocities.com/combusem/BOULDING.HTM.

Browne, John. 1997. Addressing global climate change. Speech presented at Stanford University, Stanford, Calif. (May 19).

Browne, John. 2002. Beyond petroleum: Business and the environment in the twenty-first century. Speech presented at Stanford University, Stanford, Calif. (May 11). www.bp.com/centres/press/stanford/highlights/index.asp.

Browne, John. 2002. The environmental challenge: A European business perspective. Speech presented at Humboldt University, Berlin, Germany (March 29).

Carbon Disclosure Project. 2003 (accessed). Home page. www.cdproject.net.

Claeys, Patrick. 2003. Representative, BP Amoco. Interview with the authors, Europe, March.

Dow Jones Sustainability Indexes. 2003 (accessed). Corporate sustainability. www.sustainability-index.com/htmle/sustainability/corpsustainability.html.

Haumann, Ursula. 2003. (representative, German Green Party). Interview with the authors, March, Europe.

Hawken, Paul. 1993. *The ecology of commerce.* New York: HarperBusiness.

Le Menestrel, Marc, De Bettignies, Henri-Claude, and Van den Hove, Sybille. 2001. Should business influence the science and politics of global environmental change? The oil industry and climate change, part A. INSEAD Case Studies. www.caseplace.org/cases/cases_show.htm?doc_id=160912.

Le Menestrel, Marc, De Bettignies, Henri-Claude, and Van den Hove, Sybille. 2001. Should business influence the science and politics of global environmental change? The oil industry and climate change, part B. INSEAD Case Studies. www.caseplace.org/cases/cases_show.htm?doc_id=160912.

Lovins, Amory B., Lovins, L. Hunter, and Hawken, Paul. 1999. A road map for natural capitalism. *Harvard Business Review* (May/June).

Mansley, Mark. 2002. Risking shareholder value? ExxonMobil and climate change: An investigation of unnecessary risks and missed opportunities. Claros Discussion Paper. www.campaignexxonmobil.org/pdf/RiskingValue.pdf.

Miller, Scott, Bahree, Bhushan, and Ball, Jeffrey. 2002. A Global Journal Report: Europe launches hydrogen initiative. *Wall Street Journal,* October 16.

Otto, Michael. 2003. Annual press conference, Hamburg, Germany, September 4. www.otto.com/en/ueber_uns/ueber_uns_bericht_drotto .html.

Porter, Michael, and van der Linde, Claas. 1995. Green and competitive. *Harvard Business Review* (September/October), 120–134, 196.

Reinhardt, Forest. 1999. Bringing the environment down to earth. *Harvard Business Review* (July/August).

Reinhardt, Forest, and Richman, Emily. 2001. Global climate change and BP Amoco. Harvard Business School Case 700106, February 28.

Rivers, Richard. 2003. Senior vice president, Unilever. Interview with the authors, March, London.

Speight, Paul. 2003. EU Director General in Brussels. Interview with the authors, March, Brussels.

Unilever. 2003 (accessed). Corporate responsibility. www.unilever.com/ investorcentre/corporatesocialresponsibility/.

Unilever. 2003 (accessed). Global challenges: Local actions. www.unilever.nl/ Images/Global%20Challenges%20Local%20Actions_tcm20-5100 .pdf.

Willard, Bob. 2002. *The sustainability advantage.* Gabriola Island, B.C.: New Society Publishers.

Chapter 15

ECOEFFICIENCY IN CHILE AND PERU

Stacy Gibbons, Maren Lau, Stacy McAuliffe, and Jessica Watson

> Environmental protection and economic development
> are complementary rather than antagonistic processes.
> —*William D. Ruckelshaus,*
> *Toward a Sustainable World*

Ecoefficiency is a management philosophy that seeks to create financial value by lessening ecological impact. It has been discussed and implemented globally in a range of policy and business contexts since 1992. Today, socially responsible corporations operating in the international market deploy ecoefficient strategies to increase profits, gain competitive advantage, and lessen industry's impact on the environment.

The particular form an ecoefficient strategy takes depends partly on the context in which it is implemented. To date, most such efforts have occurred in industrialized nations, for two reasons: Such countries have the financial and technological capabilities to create ecoefficient innovations, and their governments and civic organizations have historically had the resources and inclination to give priority to and enforce corporate environmental responsibility. Lesser-developed countries differ from industrialized ones with respect to resources and the will to carry out environmental programs. They also differ in these respects among themselves. One would expect, therefore, that their particular manifestations of eco-efficiency would vary greatly as well. This chapter explores the effect of social, political, and economic context on the form and implementation of ecoefficient strategies by comparing the operations of Tetra Pak, an environmentally conscious multinational packaging manufacturer and retailer, in Chile and Peru. The neighboring countries share regional similarities but have many cultural, political, and economic differences. It also attempts to determine what benefits, if any, Tetra Pak has reaped from its ecoefficiency efforts in these two countries.

PUSHING THE BOUNDARIES OF BUSINESS

Ecoefficiency is a direct descendant of the broader and more established management philosophy of sustainable development. The latter seeks to link high and stable levels of economic growth and employment with social progress, protection of the environment, and prudent use of natural resources. Ecoefficiency approaches this project from a business perspective, integrating environmental responsibility with profitability and not just image enhancement. The idea is that leading companies can lower costs and add value to goods and services by increasing efficiency in resource utilization, simultaneously reducing waste and pollution and decreasing environmental harm. For example, two companies, A and B, in different industries might enter into a symbiotic relationship in which A uses the by-products of B as the input for its own production. In this way, A lowers its resource costs, B gains an additional revenue stream, and environmental waste is reduced.

More generally, companies achieve ecoefficiency through some combination of the following practices: reducing the amount of material and energy resources consumed in the production of their goods or services, decreasing the dispersion of toxic by-products, recycling, and maximizing the sustainable use of renewable resources. Although these practices do not require partnerships among companies or industries like that between A and B in the illustration, they are easier to implement within a supply and distribution network of ecologically conscious players. Paper mills sourcing from renewable forestry companies, technological innovators selling energy-efficient equipment to manufacturing clients, and mining companies hiring consultants to implement emission reductions are all examples of supply chain partnerships created by companies committed to ecoefficiency.

ENVIRONMENTAL MANAGEMENT SYSTEMS

The business maxim "only what gets measured gets done" holds true for ecoefficiency programs. To continue their ecoefficient policies, companies must be able to see the policies' social and economic benefits. For this, they need to set goals for sustainable development and measure their progress toward attaining them. Program implementation, goal setting, and progress measurement are all functions of an environmental management system (EMS). An EMS consists of the following elements:

- A policy for integrating environmental concerns into all aspects of operations, including research and development, manufacturing, finance, marketing, and distribution;
- An action plan translating the policy into objectives and identifying how human and financial resources will be deployed in reaching them;
- Organizational structures establishing assignments, delegating authority, and assigning responsibility for actions;
- Procedures for monitoring progress;
- Actions to eliminate potential nonconformance;
- Internal training programs and information dissemination; and
- Communication of environmental goals and performance to the outside world.

In addition to measuring progress toward internally set goals, it is useful for a company to assess its environmental performance relative to industry competitors. This requires a set of clearly defined standards that are universally accepted and adaptable to different businesses and environments. The Geneva-based International Organization for Standardization (ISO) created the ISO 14000 to fill this role. It provides standards for environmental auditing and performance evaluation in such areas as environmental labeling, product life cycles, use of natural resources, and pollution.

Tetra Pak Global

Like all management strategies, ecoefficiency must be tailored to the company implementing it and the country where it is being applied. The following sections examine how Tetra Pak has incorporated sustainable practices into its business in general and how it has adapted the practices to the particular economic, social, and political environments of Chile and Peru.

Company Overview

Tetra Pak manufactures aseptic packaging—cartons that keep the food and beverages they contain safe, clean, and unspoiled without refrigeration—as well as plastic bottles, cups, and bags; plastic and foil pouches, glass bottles and jars, and metal cans. The company also offers complete processing, packaging, and distribution systems for clients' food products, plus software, training, follow-up service, and marketing assistance. Founded in Sweden in 1951, the company employs 21,150 people and produces or sells its products and services in more than 165 countries. Customers include Coca-Cola, Nestlé S.A., Parmalat, Unilever BestFoods, and Arla Foods.

Tetra Pak is organized along business and geographical lines. Its marketing activities are divided into two regions: Europe/Africa and Asia/Americas. In both Chile and Peru, it has marketing companies that sell packaging through new-market development and by growing existing client relationships. Neither country has a manufacturing plant. Instead, the marketing companies import packaging from Tetra Pak factories in Argentina and Brazil.

ENVIRONMENTAL POLICIES AND PRACTICES

One of Tetra Pak's founders, Ruben Rausing, proclaimed that each of the company's packages should "save more than it costs." This applies both to the customer—whose savings are in the form of reduced waste space and spoilage as well as the elimination of expensive refrigeration—and to the manufacturer, which economizes through efficient resource exploitation. The savings also extend to the environment. Less refrigeration means lower energy use, and minimized material input reduces forest destruction.

With such benefits in mind, Tetra Pak began during the mid-1980s to extend its founder's goal to include an ecoefficiency mandate that it believes differentiates the company from other packaging producers. Initially, it considered the environmental impact only of its plants, measuring effects such as contaminant emissions. In the late 1980s, however, Tetra Pak came under fire from some environmental groups in the United States because its packaging was not recyclable. When, to encourage recycling, Maine passed a law requiring a deposit on bottles and cans, Tetra Pak was temporarily banned from the state. External pressure to recycle on the back end of its process combined with the company's own legacy of product-design efficiency on the front end to create an ambitious ecoefficiency policy.

Because of its highly integrated business model, Tetra Pak must minimize environmental impact at many stages of the manufacturing and distribution process. Since production creates the most negative effects, the company has concentrated its efforts there—using paper made from sustainably harvested forests, for instance, and reducing energy and water consumption in processing its raw materials. Today Tetra Pak considers and, when possible, measures its environmental impact at five levels: design; raw-material use and supply chain; operations; customers, consumers, and community; and waste management.

ONE STEP AHEAD

Tetra Pak issued its first corporate environmental report in 1999 and has updated it several times since. In 2002, through its global program titled "One Step Ahead," the company articulated a program for achieving environmental leadership in the diverse socioeconomic and political contexts in which it operates. Being at the ecological forefront means different things in different countries. To be one step ahead in Germany, for example, where the sophisticated Green Dot recycling system places significant waste-management responsibility on corporations, Tetra Pak must set different goals than it might in Venezuela, which has neither the infrastructure nor the political will for recycling.

To accomplish its environmental leadership goals, Tetra Pak required each of its marketing companies to analyze the situation in the country where it operated. They assessed Tetra Pak's environmental performance against local consumer demands and concerns, competitors' activities, existing and expected legal requirements, and issues raised by environmental organizations. Based on these analyses, management created goals and policies that would put Tetra Pak one step ahead in each market.

TETRA PAK IN CHILE AND PERU

As noted earlier, Chile and Peru differ significantly in terms of economic strength and political stability. In both countries, however, Tetra Pak faces similar challenges: a lack of consumer awareness regarding the environment, the relatively recent introduction of environmental impact legislation, and the high cost of waste management.

CHILE

Chile received international acclaim as a model for rapid economic growth throughout the 1990s, becoming known as the "tiger of Latin America." Driven by the neoliberal economic policies fostered during the seventeen-year regime of General Augusto Pinochet, the country's economy grew at an average annual rate of 7.3 percent between 1990 and 1998. By and large, this growth was propelled by industries whose core activities involved the extraction or consumption of natural resources—namely, mining, forestry, fishing, and manufacturing. These activities had a significant downside: negative environmental repercussions. For example, approximately 60 percent of the total industrial solid waste in Chile is not yet controlled, and the amount of waste is increasing. Reacting to the ecological damage done by unchecked growth in both production and consumption, environmental groups have lobbied for a reduction in industrial contaminants, and government authorities have begun imposing strict restrictions on vehicle circulation in heavily polluted urban areas. Businesses have also begun questioning the long-term sustainability of their extraction and production processes.

Government's Role in Environmental Management
In the wake of the 1992 Earth Summit in Rio de Janeiro, the Chilean government created several entities to help reverse the environmental destruction already done and to steer the country's businesses toward ecoefficiency. Leading these efforts is the National Commission of the Environment (Conama), a cross-ministerial body established in 1994 that has branch offices in each of Chile's twelve regions. Conama's ambitious environmental agenda focuses on water treatment, waste management, and control of air quality in urban areas. The government has also committed to a national plan to conserve Chile's rich biodiversity and to increase the number of publicly and privately protected forests.

Chile subjects new industrial projects to an environmental impact review before approving them for implementation. Although the effectiveness of the government's System to Evaluate Environmental Impact (Seia) has not been studied, it represents a vital step toward building corporate compliance with environmental norms and laws. Another such step is the Clean Production Accords (APL), established in 1998. These voluntary agreements are meant to encourage the use of ecoefficient technologies in every industry, from mining and manufacturing to construction and agriculture. To date, seven sector-specific accords have been signed as well as three broader ones, in agroindustry and foods, mining, and bottling and packaging.

Corporate Environmental Responsibility

Acción Empresarial ("Business Action") is a nonprofit organization dedicated to promoting corporate social responsibility, including environmental sustainability, among companies operating in Chile. To date, its members include forty companies, half of which are multinational and the other half Chilean owned and operated. Through its seminars and workshops, newsletter, and case studies as well as practical guides to the environment, ethics, responsible marketing, and community involvement, Acción Empresarial educates businesses about social responsibility and encourages them to incorporate it in their operations. The organization's influence is limited, however, because many small and medium businesses cannot afford its membership dues.

Another nonprofit organization, Sustentable ("Sustainable"), helps companies in Chile navigate the process for environmental permitting. Its team of experienced civil engineers consults with clients on waste management and emissions control, providing them with a catalog of clean technologies that will help them improve their environmental records and achieve ISO 14000 certification. Like Acción Empresarial, Sustentable does not reach many smaller companies.

Tetra Pak Chile

Tetra Pak's environmental management program in Chile has focused largely on helping to solve the very evident waste management problems of Santiago, the capital city, where approximately 60 percent of the population lives. Only 1 percent of Chile's waste is recycled. This is largely because the costs are prohibitive for sorting and delivering recyclables not presorted by consumers. In 2000, Tetra Pak Chile introduced a campaign to increase community awareness of recycling—and, specifically, of recycling the company's containers. Because recycling was not a high priority for Chilean consumers, the company's strategy was to associate it with a social cause relevant to many: homelessness. Tetra Pak joined forces with the nongovernmental organization (NGO) Un Techo para Chile ("A Roof for Chile") to manufacture shelters for the homeless using panels of Tectan, a cellulose-based wood substitute made from recycled Tetra Pak containers. The campaign *No botes la casa, recicla la caja* ("Don't throw away a house, recycle the carton") established collection points for used containers throughout Santiago's metropolitan region, which accounts for 60 percent of the country's food consumption and 60 percent of its Tetra Pak container use. The receptacles themselves were made of Tectan, so that consumers could better visualize the end product, and were tagged with instructions on how to recycle the packages. Nearly all the area's supermarkets participated, representing 80 percent of the city's food sales. This level of participation was important, since it enabled the campaign to collect large volumes of containers at a few centers rather than small numbers from many individual households, which would have been prohibitively expensive.

Chile's glass and plastic recyclers did not want to make the capital investment needed to modify their plants to handle Tetra Pak containers, so the containers were sent to Argentina. There they were made into Tectan panels that were then returned to Chile and used to construct sixty basic shelters in Santiago. The campaign was such a success that after two weeks the television ads were suspended due to oversupply of postconsumption packaging.

In August 2002, Tetra Pak Chile signed an agreement with Pizarreño S.A, Chile's largest producer of construction and roofing panels. Tetra Pak now supplies the containers collected by the *No botes la casa, recicla la caja* campaign free of charge to Pizarreño, which processes them into fiber panels, donating a number of them to Un Techo para Chile.

The *No botes la casa, recicla la caja* campaign spurred other companies to begin their own recycling programs. Like Tetra Pak's, these programs are affiliated with social causes. This suggests that Chilean businesses and consumers still do not accept recycling as a valuable activity in and of itself.

A postcampaign study done in 2002 determined that Tetra Pak had the best environmental image of any packaging company in Chile. This has not yet translated into a noticeable increase in supplier or client preference, however. In Chile, as in Latin America as a whole, economic problems have made price the prime consideration for consumers, and because of its additional input costs, Tetra Pak containers are often more expensive than glass or plastic bottles. The situation could be reversed in the future if the government requires suppliers to minimize the negative environmental impact of their operations.

PERU

Peru's economic growth, though much slower than Chile's, is also fueled by extractive industries. In 1999, for example, extraction and primary processing accounted for 87 percent of the country's exports. Again as in Chile, the country's dependence on these industries has led to environmental degradation, which Peruvians have largely ignored. In a 1998 survey asking about the country's most important problems, only 5 percent of respondents named the environment as a concern. Over the past decade, however, Peruvians, like other South Americans, have become more aware of environmental issues and sustainable practices. This has translated into government action.

In 1994, Peru's government established the National Commission on the Environment (Conam), charging it with promoting the sustainable use of natural resources, introducing measures of environmental quality such as ISO 14000, and supporting environmental education in the schools. One of Conam's long-term objectives is to assess environmental management's contribution to reducing poverty and increasing competitiveness.

Business has also recognized the importance of sustainable practices to Peru's success in an increasingly globalized world. In 1992—a time of crisis caused by the dissolution of Congress, escalating attacks by the terrorist organization Shining Path, and economic reforms that were driving businesses out of the country—a group of corporate leaders got together to form Peru 2021. Their goal was to reverse the country's downward spiral and help it attain sustainability by 2021, the bicentennial of its independence from Spain. Currently, the association's projects fall into three categories:

corporate social responsibility, education, and sustainable development. The implementation of the projects takes into account the differing needs and conditions of the multitude of regions within Peru. An example is the five-year Cadena Productiva Sostenible Proyecto (Sustainable Productive Chain Project), for which the goal is to develop and train a pool of consultants to help small and medium enterprises implement environmental management systems so they can obtain ISO 14001 certification.

TETRA PAK PERU

Peru's dominant consumer market, like Chile's, is its capital city. Lima represents 39 percent of the country's population and 54 percent of its consumption. The market in the city for Tetra Pak, however, is quite small. This is partly due to local customs and tastes: Tetra Pak is the leader in fresh-milk packaging, but Peruvians prefer evaporated milk, produced principally by Gloria and Nestlé, which supply their own cans. This has left Tetra Pak with a fragmented client base that comprises manufacturers of other foodstuffs, such as tomato paste, juices, and soups.

Peru, as noted earlier, mirrors Chile in terms of low consumer and business awareness about environmental issues. According to Tetra Pak surveys, a mere 2 percent of Peruvian consumers understand what actions might prevent environmental degradation. Only one Tetra Pak client is ISO 14000 certified, and most adopt conservation measures only when required by law.

Because waste management incentives do not exist for businesses and because consumers do not recycle in their homes, the company decided to turn to education. It developed the program *Recicla y gana una sonrisa* ("Recycle and win a smile") and introduced it in primary schools, where environmental educational had recently been introduced. The program demonstrates the benefits of recycling and offers prizes to schools that bring the most used Tetra Pak containers to partner supermarkets.

As in Chile, Tetra Pak Peru also attempted to popularize recycling by associating it with the social cause of housing. The company entered into a joint venture with a small recycling plant on the outskirts of Lima, providing it with $12,000 to modify its equipment to handle Tetra Pak containers. As of May 2003, the plant was to begin turning used packaging that Tetra Pak Peru provided, free of charge, into cables and Tectan panels to make into houses for Lima's homeless. Unlike in Chile, the company hasn't found an NGO through which to administer the housing, so it will distribute the homes to the public and publicize the program at its own cost.

IN CONCLUSION

We anticipated as we began this study that Chile's more advanced economy and stringent regulatory enforcement would lead to more widespread, sustainable business practices in Chile than in Peru. To a large extent, we saw that this was true. We also found that the major impetus for Chilean companies' adoption of these practices, and for the government's regulation in this area, was the desire to become more competitive in international markets. We observed that Peru, although lagging behind Chile in awareness of ecoefficiency, demonstrates growing support for the strategy. Peru has several committed public and nongovernmental agencies, in some cases modeled on Chilean agencies, whose focus is ecoefficiency. Peruvian companies are currently less exposed than Chilean companies to international markets, but as the mining and textile industries become involved in global trade, the business community will feel growing pressure to become more ecoefficient.

Both countries could benefit from more stringent and transparent environmental legislation, which would not only improve domestic environmental standards but would also increase the two countries' competitiveness in environmentally sensitive markets such as those of Europe and North America. The same goal would be served by the formation of more civic associations like Acción Empresarial and Peru 2021, which promote the diffusion of technological information and implementation of environmental management systems. This would be particularly significant for the small and medium enterprises that are largely excluded from ISO certification because of the high costs involved.

In Chile and Peru, where sustainable business practices are relatively new, Tetra Pak's promotion of consumer recycling puts it "one step ahead." Although it is unclear what the financial implications for the company are, its campaigns to promote recycling have spurred environmental awareness. Moreover, the company has not realized ecoefficient gains in the entire product life cycle in Peru and Chile, since most manufacturing activities take place in nearby countries. Nevertheless, Tetra Pak's investments in Peru and Chile have to be seen in the context of its overall strategy of becoming a market leader through its association with environmental sustainability. By supporting social campaigns such as Chile's *No bote la casa, recicle la caja* and by driving market demand through educational programs like Peru's *Recicla y gana una sonrisa,* the company is building a loyal customer base for tomorrow in both countries.

Sustainable business practices are still new to Chile and Peru. Yet at the government, civil society, and business levels, they are slowly working toward a degree of ecoefficiency that will put them on a par with more developed countries. Tetra Pak's work in these markets demonstrates that the long-term perspective of a multinational corporation can influence consumer awareness in ways often not achievable through legislation. Governments now need to structure legislation to give domestic enterprises the resources to convert this impetus into a new understanding of competitiveness and market positioning.

REFERENCES

Abogabir, Ximena. 2003. Casa de la Paz. Interview with the authors, March 18, Santiago, Chile.

Acción Empresarial. 2003 (accessed).www.accionempresarial.cl.

Calderón, Beatriz. 2003. Acción Empresarial. Interview with the authors, March 19, Santiago, Chile.

Chimeli, Ariaster. 2003 (accessed). *An economic measure of national environmental stringency.* Faculty working paper, Department of Agricultural and Consumer Economics, University of Illinois at Urbana-Champaign. www.ace.uiuc.edu/faculty/Braden/manuscripts/string .PDF.

Cornejo, David Solano. 2002. Educación ambiental en el Peru: Estudio de caso. Entorno Peru. http://entornoperu.tripod.com/expertos001.htm. Accessed February 2003.

Day, Robert. 1998. Beyond ecoefficiency: Sustainability as a driver for innovation. Perspectives Beyond Ecoefficiency. www.perspectivesbeyondeco efficiency.htm. Accessed April 2003.

Del Valle, Jorge Mario. 1998. Comisión Nacional del Medio Ambiente Información. Acerca de Conam. www.conam.gob.pe.

De Simone, Livio, and Popoff, Frank. 2001. Ecoefficiency: The business link to sustainable development. World Business Council for Sustainable Development. www.wbcsd.org.

EcoNews Peru. 2003 (accessed). www.econewsperu.com/inicio.htm.

Ecosustainable Developments. 1999. Ecosustainable Hub. www.ecosust ainable.com.au/links.htm.

Environment and Urban Development Division, Country Department I, Latin America and the Caribbean Region. 1994. *Chile: Managing environmental problems: Economic analysis of selected issues.* Report 13061-CH. Washington, D.C.: World Bank.

Favre, Julio. 2002. *Eco-rentability and competitiveness: Challenge for Peru.* Paper presented at Conam's Eco-Dialogue Conference, Iquitos, Peru. www.conam.gob.pe/Ecod2002/EcoRentab_archivos/frame.htm. Accessed April 2003.

Galarza. Elsa. 2003. Centro de Investigación de la Universidad del Pacífico. Interview with the authors, March 27, Lima, Peru.

Global Giving Matters. Q & A with Stephan Schmidheiny. 2002. May. www .synergos.org/globalgivingmatters/features/0204schmidheiny.htm.

Gobierno de Chile Comisión Nacional del Medio Ambiente. 2003 (accessed). Agenda ambiental país: Por un desarollo limpio y sustentable 2002–2006. www.conama.cl/portal/1255/channel.html.

Gobierno de Chile Comisión Nacional del Medio Ambiente. 2003 (accessed). Chile: Examples of sustainable development. www.conama .cl/portal/1255/channel.html.

Government of Chile. 2000. Todo Chile: Oportunidades de inversión regional. www.todochileinversiones.cl/reciclaje.htm.

Huggard-Caine, Patrick. 2003. Peru 2021. Interview with the authors, March 27, Lima, Peru.

Klein, Edward. 2003. Vice president of environmental affairs, Tetra Pak. Telephone interview with the authors, March 13, Illinois.

Muratoglu, Suleyman. 2003. Tetra Pak Chicago. Interview with authors, March 4, Vernon Hills, Ill.

National Roundtable on the Environment and the Economy (NRTEE). 2002. Measuring ecoefficiency in business: Feasibility of a core set of indicators. www.nrtee-trnee.ca/eng/programs/Current_Programs/htm.

Panayotou, T. 2003 (accessed). Environmental regulation and sustainable development. Corporación Adina de Fomento. www.caf.com/attach/4/default/EnvironmentalRegulationandSustainableDevelop.

Parliament of Canada House of Commons Standing Committee on Industry. 2003 (accessed). Ecoefficiency and the knowledge economy. Productivity and innovation: A competitive and prosperous Canada. www.parl.gc.ca/InfoComDoc/36/2/INDU/Studies/Reports/indy20/18-ch10-e.html.

Pérez, Clemente, and Santa María, Martín. 2003. Sustentable. Interview with the authors, March 19, Santiago, Chile.

Peru 2021. 2002. Promoting ecoefficiency in the business community. Internal company presentation, Environmental and Sustainable Development Committee: Peru 2021.

Producción Limpia. 2001. Prevención y eficiencia. Consejo Nacional de Producción Limpia. www.produccionlimpia.cl.

ProInversión. 2002. Analysts' view on the Peruvian economy. Peru. www.proinversion.gob.pe/english/boletines/documentos/AV0212.pdf.

Ruckelshaus, William D. 1989. Toward a sustainable world. *Scientific American, 261*(3).

Schaper, Marianne, and Onffroy de Vérez, Valérie. 2001. Evolución del comercio y de las inversiones extranjeras en industrias ambientalmente sensibles: Comunidad Andina, Mercosur y Chile (1990–1999). Comisión Económica para América Latina y el Caribe (Economic Commission for Latin America and the Caribbean) Serie Medio Ambiente y Desarrollo.

Smart Communities Network. 2003 (accessed). Definitions and principles. www.smartcommunities.ncat.org/.

Sustainable Development. 2001. What is sustainable development? Sustainable Development: UK government approach. www.sustainable-development.gov.uk/what/index.htm.

Teillery, Solange. 2003. Tetra Pak Chile. Interview with the authors, March 18, Santiago, Chile.

Tetra Pak. 2002. Facts and figures. Tetra Pak worldwide. www.tetrapak.com.

Tetra Pak. 2002. One step ahead: Corporate environmental report. www.tetrapak.com.

Ugat, Lucero. 2003. Tetra Pak Peru. Interview with the authors, March 28, Lima, Peru.

U.S. Environmental Protection Agency. 2002. Voluntary environmental management systems/ISO 14000. www.epa.gov/OW-OWM.html/is014001/index.htm.

Vildósola, Julio. 2003. Environmental lawyer. Interview with the authors, March 18, Santiago, Chile.

Wilson, J. 2001. Dirty exports and environmental regulation: Do standards matter? World Bank Development Research Group. www1.worldbank.org/wbiep/trade/Standards/files/EnvironmentStds.pdf.

World Business Council for Sustainable Development. 1997. Ecoefficiency and cleaner production: Charting the course to sustainability. United Nations Development Program. www.undp.am.

World Business Council for Sustainable Development. 1997. Frequently asked questions. United Nations Development Program. www.undp.am.

Chapter 16

FLEX-FUEL TECHNOLOGY
IN BRAZIL

*Henry Lai, Matt Lippert, Guilherme
Silva, Avi Steinberg, Pratish Sthankiya,
and Justin Twitchell*

Given the geopolitical, economic, and environmental issues surrounding oil-based technologies, many organizations are
exploring alternative fuels. One example is in Brazil, where flexible-
fuel vehicles were recently introduced to the Brazilian automobile
market.

Flexible-fuel vehicles are automobiles that can run on any
combination of ethanol and gasoline. By using ethanol, these vehicles not only reduce environmental impact but also perform better
than their gasoline-fueled counterparts. As a result, flexible-fuel
technology provides a unique means of enabling all parties (market
and nonmarket) to achieve their respective goals (for example, making profits or protecting the environment).

In this chapter, we examine the key factors responsible for the
rapid growth of the market for flexible-fuel vehicles in Brazil. We
will discuss this growth in the context of (1) consumer demand, (2)
availability of technology, and (3) ethanol infrastructure. We assert
that the convergence of these three factors is necessary for the adoption of flexible-fuel technology, and we note that Brazil is uniquely
positioned to take advantage of this technology because of its
unique ethanol infrastructure, which was developed out of past initiatives to reduce petroleum use.

FLEXIBLE FUEL IN BRAZIL: BACKGROUND

A flexible-fuel (flex-fuel) vehicle is one that can run on a combination of fuels, usually gasoline and ethanol. Unlike other alternative-fuel vehicles, a flex-fuel vehicle has one fuel tank and one drive system (that is, one engine and fuel system). Flex-fuel vehicles in Brazil can run on pure ethanol, pure gasoline, or any mixture of the two.[1] The flexible-fuel vehicles in Brazil have a special sensor in the fuel system that analyzes the ethanol/gasoline mixture and adjusts the fuel injection and timing to the mixture. From a driver's perspective, the only decision required is whether to purchase ethanol or gasoline; the vehicle takes care of the rest.

Current Brazilian flex-fuel vehicles are different from the ethanol-only vehicles that dominated Brazil in the 1980s. These vehicles, which represented over 90 percent of new-car sales in the mid-1980s, were dedicated entirely to ethanol. The strong market for them was created by the oil crisis and skyrocketing gasoline prices—Brazil was heavily dependent on foreign oil—and the government's role in developing an ethanol infrastructure. When gasoline prices and ethanol supplies dropped, the market for ethanol-only vehicles declined to less than 1 percent of new market sales.

In March of 2003, Volkswagen introduced flex-fuel cars to the Brazilian market; since then, it has grown rapidly. In 2004, flex-fuel vehicles represented 20 percent of all new car sales, and this figure was expected to grow significantly. In 2006, 86 percent of cars and light commercial vehicles sold were flex-fuel. There are even predictions that 100 percent of new-car sales in Brazil will be flex-fuel cars. This prediction has been supported by spokesmen at Volkswagen, Ford, and GM who, during our interviews, confirmed that these automakers intend to have 100 percent of their Brazilian production consist of flex-fuel vehicles within the next three to five years.

In the following section, we examine the three key drivers of this rapid growth in Brazilian demand for flex-fuel vehicles: consumer demand, availability of economical technology, and the existence of an ethanol infrastructure.

CONSUMER DEMAND FOR FLEXIBLE FUEL
IN BRAZIL

Since April of 2003, sales of flexible-fuel cars have grown in real numbers and as a percentage of total car sales in Brazil. We have identified four factors driving consumer purchases of flexible-fuel vehicles in Brazil: (1) lower total cost of ownership, (2) increased vehicle performance, (3) environmental benefits, and (4) support of the Brazilian economy.

LOWER TOTAL COST OF OWNERSHIP

A leading driver of consumer demand for flexible-fuel vehicles is the lower total cost of ownership relative to owning a gasoline-powered vehicle. Total cost of ownership includes the purchase price, fuel costs, maintenance, and resale value.

Purchase Price

Although manufacturing costs for flexible-fuel vehicles are currently higher than those for gasoline-only vehicles, manufacturers have not passed on that additional cost to the consumer. As manufacturers increase production of flexible-fuel vehicles to meet rising demand and as more manufacturers enter the market to compete, the unit cost of production should decrease in the long run, and the cost to the consumer will be determined by the market. Retail price will be determined in part by the market's view on total cost of ownership, which will be influenced by the amount the consumer is willing to pay. Because flexible-fuel vehicles are at a relatively early stage in the product's life cycle, production costs are slightly higher than their likely long-run average as manufacturers progress up the learning curve and fail to yet fully realize economies of scale. Our discussions with executives from Volkswagen, Ford, and General Motors (GM) in Brazil suggested that on average, production costs are approximately US$200 higher per unit for flexible-fuel vehicles. This additional cost is not considered material, and favorable federal tax incentives offset it. Thus, as part of a strategy to stimulate and maintain demand, manufacturers are not passing the additional production cost on to consumers.

Fuel Costs

Fuel is the most important area for cost savings and is usually the largest ongoing cost of owning a vehicle. The option of using either gasoline or ethanol (or any combination thereof) affords owners the opportunity to lower fuel costs by purchasing the cheaper[2] of the two fuels. With oil prices (which directly affect gasoline prices) relatively high, ethanol is an attractive alternative, and owners of flexible-fuel vehicles face no switching costs. For example, in a 2004 Associated Press article, a São Paulo owner of a flexible-fuel vehicle stated that she used to spend $17 per week on gasoline and now she spends $10 per week on ethanol. A weekly saving of $7 annualizes into a significant savings of approximately $350, or 5 percent of the average family's annual income in Brazil.[3] Thus the ability to switch between gasoline and ethanol without penalty ensures that consumers will be able to minimize their fuel costs.

Ethanol is currently cheaper than gasoline, but that has not always been the case. Ethanol shortages in the early 1990s and falling oil prices made ethanol-based vehicles extremely unattractive. The advantage of flexible-fuel vehicles over dedicated gasoline- or ethanol-powered vehicles is that the owner can switch easily between the two fuels to take advantage of relative price differences. The recent greater rate of increase in gasoline prices relative to ethanol prices further justifies the benefits of using flex-fuel vehicles.

Maintenance Costs

Despite the new technology behind flex-fuel vehicles, their maintenance costs are no different than those of gasoline-powered vehicles. The automotive executives with whom we spoke unanimously agreed on that point. Because of the relatively recent emergence of these cars, data on their long-term maintenance needs (for example, frequency of repairs, long-term costs) are not sufficiently available to allow conclusions.

Resale Value

Because flex-fuel vehicles have been on the market only for a short time, there are no reliable data on their relative resale values. However, we believe that the resale value of a flexible-fuel vehicle will be at least as high as that of the gasoline-powered vehicle, as the former offers much higher value to the consumer (that is, lower total cost of ownership, increased performance, and environmental benefits). The industry executives with whom we spoke agreed unanimously with this hypothesis.

INCREASED PERFORMANCE

Ethanol offers superior performance to gasoline in terms of increased power. Specifically, ethanol has both a higher octane rating than gasoline and a higher specific energy per kilogram. The higher octane rating allows engines to run at higher compression ratios, which translate directly into greater horsepower and torque. Simultaneously, the higher specific energy of ethanol means that more energy is released for every kilogram of ethanol burned. This specific energy translates into higher horsepower and better performance. As an example, the flexible-fuel version of the Ford Fiesta, when operating on ethanol, has 13 percent more power than the gasoline-only version.

However, ethanol does not provide the same fuel efficiency as gasoline. At a mixture of 10 percent ethanol and 90 percent gasoline (E-10) very little fuel efficiency is lost by using ethanol,[4] but increasing the relative ethanol content of the fuel decreases fuel efficiency. Based on competitive fuel-efficiency data provided by Ford, vehicles fueled by 100 percent ethanol are 36 percent less fuel-efficient than comparable vehicles fueled by gasoline. Thus, consumers will have to refuel more often if they use 100 percent ethanol. Consumers should recognize this difference in fuel efficiency when determining which fuel will be more cost-effective.

ENVIRONMENTAL BENEFITS

One reason that Brazilians purchase flexible-fuel vehicles is that they prefer "clean" cars. The clean aspect of flexible fuel comes from its use of ethanol, which is widely regarded as a greener fuel than gasoline on the basis of its lower rate of harmful emissions and its net positive energy balance.

Reduction of harmful emissions includes both reductions in carbon dioxide (CO_2) and the elimination of toxic compounds. Due to the closed-loop nature of ethanol production and use, the fuel has significantly reduced CO_2 emissions. For example, the widespread use of ethanol as a fuel during the 1980s in Brazil is estimated to have reduced CO_2 emissions in Brazil by 50 million tons. In 1990–1991, ethanol usage provided a net reduction of 9.45 million tons of CO_2. In addition to the CO_2-related benefits, ethanol fuel does not contain environmentally toxic and carcinogenic compounds such as tetra-ethyl lead, benzene, or the additive MTBE, which are found in gasoline.

Ethanol also has a net positive energy balance—that is, it is a renewable fuel that provides 8.3 times more energy output than it takes to produce it. In contrast, gasoline and diesel fuel—both non-renewable—have a negative energy balance.

SUPPORTING THE BRAZILIAN ECONOMY

A final incentive for some buyers of flexible-fuel vehicles is the benefit for the Brazilian economy. Specifically, they believe that buying these vehicles is good for Brazil's employment picture. This is consistent with the opinion held by a majority of Brazilians that the purpose of corporations is to generate employment and develop the country.[5] Because flexible fuel is a Brazilian product, all manufacturing of flex-fuel vehicles takes place domestically. When consumers purchase a flexible-fuel vehicle, they know that the vehicle was built in Brazil and that they are keeping their money in the Brazilian economy. Additionally, to the extent that the increased use of flexible-fuel vehicles raises the demand for ethanol, purchasers of flex-fuel vehicles will be helping Brazil to reduce its consumption of foreign oil and supporting the development of domestic fuel and agriculture (for example, sugar cane production).

TECHNOLOGY AVAILABILITY

Despite Brazilian consumer demand for more cost-effective and environmentally friendly vehicles, flexible-fuel vehicles could not have been introduced as successfully if the technology had not already been developed and proven. Although it was not fully commercialized until recently, modern flexible-fuel technology was developed in the mid-1980s and was soon proven to be reliable. Because the technology was more mature than substitutes such as fuel cells and electric-car technology, the risks associated with investment in the manufacturing of flexible-fuel vehicles were minimal.

Not surprisingly, the flexible-fuel technology used by Volkswagen, Ford, and GM is similar. All three major auto manufacturers use an electronic control module (ECM) from Magneti Marelli. The ECM is similar to a computer's motherboard, coordinating multiple processes such as sensing of oxygen content in the exhaust, fuel injection, and engine spark. Also, each manufacturer currently installs a cold-start system, which assists in the initial cranking of the engine in cold weather[6] if a consumer is using ethanol in the main fuel tank. However, Volkswagen is planning to phase out its cold-start system, as the company believes its fuel-injection system eliminates issues of low ethanol combustibility. Finally, because ethanol is more corrosive than gasoline, each manufacturer has upgraded the components (that is, hoses, linings, and valves) in the fuel system.

Flexible-fuel technology has evolved both from Brazil's experience in manufacturing and operating ethanol-only vehicles and the experience of the United States in creating variations of flexible-fuel systems (such as E-85, a mixture of 85 percent ethanol and 15 percent gasoline).

When ethanol technology was first developed as an ethanol-only system, it faced several challenges. Plastic components required protection against water absorption. Ethanol is a corrosive substance, and so upgrades of the traditional fuel tank and fuel lines were required; metallic components, including the exhaust system, needed to be made of stainless steel. Similarly, electric insulation was used to prevent galvanic corrosion in the fuel pump. Because ethanol has lower volatility than gasoline, ethanol-only vehicles had difficulty with cold-weather starts. Consequently, cold-start systems, which used gasoline to start the car in cold weather, were created.

Mixtures of ethanol and gasoline have been used in many markets since World War I, but these mixtures tended to be gasoline with ethanol as an additive. Ford was the first manufacturer to commercially produce a vehicle that could run on a mixture that was predominantly ethanol. In 1985, Ford produced a Taurus in the United States that ran on E-85 (85 percent ethanol), and subsequently E-85 technology was commercialized in several other vehicles. Currently, more than 3.5 million vehicles in the United States run on E-85 fuel. However, E-85 can be purchased at only approximately 200 refueling sites in North America, significantly limiting its usage.

Ford introduced the first concept flexible-fuel car in 2000 in Brazil, and Volkswagen introduced the first commercial flexible-fuel vehicle there in 2003. General Motors and Ford introduced their first commercial flexible-fuel vehicles within 12 months of Volkswagen's launch. Ford, the third manufacturer to enter the market for flexible-fuel vehicles, improved the technology it had first demonstrated in 2000, developing an engine capable of operating at a higher compression ratio, more alcohol-resistant components, and unique engine-control software algorithms. The increased compression ratio of 12.3:1 on the Ford Fiesta allows the engine to take full advantage of alcohol's higher octane rating (108, versus 93 for gasoline). As a result, the Ford Fiesta has the highest compression ratio and best fuel efficiency of all flex-fuel vehicles in its category.

Flexible-fuel options were initially available only for vehicles with 1.6-liter engines, but the executives we interviewed from Ford, GM, and Volkswagen unanimously stated that they expected flexible-fuel engines to be available for all of their vehicles in the future. In fact, manufacturers will have to consider whether to eliminate gasoline-only engines as an option. Manufacturing vehicles with multiple options for fuel systems can increase the complexity of manufacturing operations and related costs. However, vehicles manufactured in Brazil are exported to other countries that do not have a strong ethanol infrastructure and would not currently benefit from flexible-fuel technology. If manufacturers eliminate the gasoline-only versions and export only flexible-fuel vehicles, they would face decreased revenues and would have to absorb the incremental cost of approximately $200 per vehicle or pass it on to the consumers. In tightly competitive markets, it may not be possible to pass on this cost.

Next-generation flexible-fuel vehicles will likely incorporate natural gas as a third option. For example, GM is introducing a tri-fuel vehicle, and Volkswagen intends to do so. Ford's strategy is to wait and see how the technology develops. But given the ethanol infrastructure and the success of flex-fuel vehicles in Brazil, it is unlikely that solar-powered or fuel-cell vehicles will emerge as competitive substitutes in the foreseeable future.

ETHANOL INFRASTRUCTURE

A final and critical factor enabling the introduction and rapid growth of flexible-fuel technology in Brazil is the existence of a robust infrastructure for producing and distributing ethanol throughout the country.

HISTORY OF ETHANOL IN BRAZIL

In addition to its contribution to the ever-popular *caipirinhas* and *cachaça,* sugar cane has always been a potential fuel source in Brazil, used as both an additive and a pure fuel. Brazil's history of ethanol and flexible-fuel technology has had five stages:

1. Ethanol as a gasoline additive (pre-1970s)
2. Ethanol as a response to oil dependency (1970s)
3. Ethanol as a dominant fuel source (1980s)
4. Gasohol and the collapse of ethanol (1990s)
5. Rise of flex-fuel (present)

Since World War I, Brazil, like many other countries, has been distilling ethanol as a gasoline additive. In the 1920s and 1930s, ethanol was routinely blended with gasoline by every industrialized nation except the United States. In fact, Henry Ford called ethanol the "fuel of the future." Sugar has always been a key agricultural product for Brazil, and ethanol blending was used primarily to hedge international sugar prices by providing an outlet for excess sugar. In 1966 and 1967, driven by low sugar prices, the use of ethanol as an additive to gasoline peaked at 14 percent in São Paulo and 6 percent overall in Brazil.

However, as Brazil experienced the two oil crises of the 1970s, the role of ethanol changed significantly. ProAlcool, a federal program promoting the use of ethanol, was created in 1975 in response to the oil embargo of 1973. Its mandate, according to Arnaldo Vieira de Carvalho, was "to reduce crude oil imports by increasing production of sugar-cane-derived ethanol to displace gasoline." By 1979, when the second oil crisis occurred, ethanol had replaced 14 percent of all gasoline usage. At this time, ethanol was blended with gasoline. However, after the 1979 crisis and the sudden spike in oil prices, auto manufacturers began to produce ethanol-dedicated vehicles—cars that ran only on ethanol.

During the 1980s, ethanol emerged as the dominant fuel source. Brazil had invested in ethanol infrastructure—both production and distribution—and consumers throughout the country found ethanol at the pumps. To promote ethanol, the Brazilian government provided three incentives: (1) guaranteed purchases by Petrobras (the state-owned energy company), (2) low-interest loans for ethanol firms, and (3) fixed gasoline and ethanol prices, where ethanol was sold for 59 percent of the price of gasoline. In the 1980s, sales of ethanol cars reached 99 percent of new-car sales, with nearly 5 million cars in operation. Ethanol had displaced 60 percent of gasoline use, and the fuel was set to be blended at 20 percent for ethanol/gasoline mixes. The increased consumption and production of ethanol had other positive effects on the Brazilian economy, creating 700,000 additional jobs throughout the supply chain, and pollution in urban areas was reduced. While the average annual salaries of the jobs created were up to four times less than the national average salary, the additional jobs were in rural areas, which traditionally had high levels of unemployment.

However, in the early 1990s, the market for ethanol vehicles collapsed due to a decrease in oil prices and a shortage of ethanol. Global oil prices were decreasing, and Petrobras had discovered oil-fields and cultivated oil production in Brazil. At the same time, the market price for sugar increased, creating ethanol shortages throughout the country. Additionally, ProAlcool suffered from internal issues, such as government control of fuel production, which inhibited the organization's ability to react effectively to these changes. By 1993, sales of ethanol vehicles dropped to less than 1 percent of new-car sales, and consumers were skeptical of ethanol as a pure fuel source.

Today, ethanol continues to be available as a pure fuel source and in a blend with gasoline, a mixture referred to as gasohol. The proportion of ethanol blended with gasoline is set by the government on an annual basis (24 percent as of March 2005) and it is used as a way to hedge against fluctuations in the international sugar and oil prices.

CURRENT ETHANOL SUPPLY CHAIN

Brazil's unique history with ethanol has helped it to have the most sophisticated production and distribution infrastructure in the world. This infrastructure is one of the key reasons that flexible-fuel technology has had such great success in Brazil.

The current ethanol supply chain consists of sugar cane plantations, ethanol distilleries, and ethanol distributors. As of March

2005, there are approximately 70,000 sugar cane plantations, 320 distilleries, and six distributors in the Brazilian supply chain. Ethanol is produced from sugar cane in the distilleries and distributed through six large companies: Agip, Esso, Shell, Texaco, Petrobras, and Ipiranga. These six distributors provide ethanol to more than 25,000 gas stations throughout Brazil.

The total worldwide production of ethanol in 2004 was 38.27 million kiloliters, of which Brazil is the largest contributor, producing more than 15 million kiloliters, or 42 percent of total production. Moreover, Brazil was the lowest-cost producer of ethanol— $0.20 per liter versus $0.32 per liter (United States) and $0.58 per liter (European Union). Investment in ethanol production continues, with 34 new distilleries under construction, a 10 percent increase in sugar cane growing area, and $5 billion of investments in other infrastructure projects.

A key player in this supply chain is Petrobras, the formerly state-owned energy company. Petrobras comprises the holding company that drills and processes crude oil and Petrobras BR, which manages the distribution of gasoline, diesel, and ethanol to the consumer. Based on our interview with Petrobras executives, Petrobras BR not only has a major share of the market (over 35 percent) but also has taken responsibility for promoting the stability of the country's ethanol supply. It has entered into long-term contracts with ethanol producers, upgraded its storage capabilities, and created large reserves of ethanol.

The government also plays a critical role in the supply of ethanol by providing significant tax incentives for ethanol sales relative to gasoline sales. In addition to the tax incentives provided to auto manufacturers for building ethanol-based engines,[7] the government provides tax subsidies for sales of ethanol, such that the effective price of ethanol is less than 70 percent that of gasoline.

The government's interest in ethanol is driven by a desire to continue reduction of dependence on foreign fuel and to improve environmental conditions. As discussed in the environmental section, use of ethanol as a fuel has several environmental benefits, including reduction in the amount of CO_2 released. Effectively minimizing carbon emissions provides an opportunity for Brazil to benefit from carbon credit programs that allow countries that reduce their carbon emissions below a specified level to sell their excess allowances (credits) to other countries. As consumers purchase more ethanol and less gasoline, the federal taxes received from fuel sales should decrease. However, financial opportunities based on reduced carbon emissions could allow the Brazilian federal government to offset these tax declines.

One of the key consumer issues in the supply chain is the supply of ethanol. When international sugar prices rise, sugar cane producers prefer to sell more volume to sugar refiners and less to ethanol distillers, leading to a potential shortage of ethanol. While this risk can be regulated through nonmarket policies toward ethanol reserves and prices, the flexible-fuel technology allows consumers to individually mitigate this risk by switching fuels as supply changes.

Overall, ethanol production and distribution in Brazil are strong, and Brazil is a significant exporter of ethanol. However, when Brazil is compared with the second-largest producer of ethanol, the United States, the uniqueness of its infrastructure is very clear. Both countries export ethanol, but only Brazil has a strong internal distribution network. Brazil can distribute this ethanol to each of the more than 25,000 gas stations in Brazil as either pure ethanol or a gasohol blend. In comparison, ethanol in the United States is only blended into gasoline, and there is no infrastructure to deliver pure or even high ethanol (E-85) mixtures to gas stations. In summary, Brazil's position as the leader in both ethanol production and ethanol distribution is a critical enabling factor for the adoption of flexible-fuel vehicles in Brazil.

In Conclusion

The combination of consumer demand, economical availability of technology, and robust ethanol infrastructure is required for the successful adoption of flexible-fuel technology. In the Brazilian market, all of these factors converged, with the uniqueness of Brazil's ethanol infrastructure a critical component.

Given differing infrastructures and consumer preferences, alternative technologies may be more appropriate for some markets.

However, with the increasing need to address environmental concerns and meet emission goals such as those defined in the Kyoto Protocol, flexible-fuel technology represents a promising opportunity for many countries to leverage market forces to achieve nonmarket environmental objectives. Next we present a high-level set of criteria for the likelihood of success of flexible-fuel vehicles (as derived from our analysis of Brazil):

IS THERE CONSUMER DEMAND FOR FLEXIBLE-FUEL VEHICLES?

Although demand for flexible-fuel vehicles could be based on cost savings, performance, or environmental or patriotic preferences, it is unlikely to be based on cost savings in markets other than Brazil. The current cost savings in Brazil are driven by the ubiquity of both ethanol and gasoline, of which ethanol is currently significantly less expensive. However, no other country currently has the same distribution network for ethanol, and as Brazil is the lowest-cost producer of ethanol it is unlikely that ethanol would be as inexpensive elsewhere. If a government wished to promote the adoption of flexible-fuel vehicles, it would likely have to subsidize the price of ethanol (or tax the sale of gasoline) and ensure that ethanol was readily and consistently available to consumers. However, performance, environmental concerns, and patriotic preferences could be key drivers in many countries. For example, in the United States, certain segments of consumers are interested in greener vehicles that would reduce levels of environmental damage as well as U.S. dependence on foreign oil and high performance. If flexible-fuel vehicles can be presented as a compelling solution to these problems, it would be reasonable to expect that consumer demand would materialize.

IS ECONOMICALLY FEASIBLE TECHNOLOGY AVAILABLE?

Availability of ethanol-related technology does not seem to be a limiting factor. Based on our conversations with auto manufacturers and Petrobras, we learned that the technology currently being used in Brazil could easily be exported to other markets, without modifications. Although other markets may use ethanol derived from a different source (corn, wheat, sugar beets), they could still make use of the current technology in its current form. Moreover, given each auto manufacturer's plan to extend flexible-fuel options to all of their vehicles, it is possible that Brazil could export the vehicles to these markets.

IS THERE ADEQUATE INFRASTRUCTURE FOR DELIVERING ETHANOL TO CONSUMERS?

Infrastructure is the key constraint, as no other country has an ethanol distribution infrastructure as effective as Brazil's. Most other countries would need to import ethanol from either Brazil or the United States. Specifically, countries such as China and India, in which demand for ethanol is rapidly growing, are unable to meet their ethanol requirements domestically. However, once imported ethanol arrives in these countries, there is no mechanism to deliver 100 percent pure ethanol to consumers. Many countries offer mixtures of ethanol and gasoline. The most common mix is E-10—10 percent ethanol and 90 percent gasoline. However, to fully take advantage of flexible-fuel technology, significant investment in distribution infrastructure would be required.[8] A government considering this type of investment would need to consider the costs of building the infrastructure versus the benefits of improving the environment, reducing dependence on foreign oil, and, in some cases, indirectly subsidizing agriculture that would be used to produce ethanol. For many countries, this may not currently be a cost-effective investment.

While flexible-fuel vehicles in Brazil represent an excellent market solution to non-market issues such as improving the environment and reducing oil dependence, this solution may not be as viable in other countries or markets that do not have the consumer demand or, more critically, the infrastructure to support flexible-fuel technology.

NOTES

1. Some U.S. consumers will be familiar with flex-fuel in the context of flexible-fuel vehicles and E-85 gasoline. Although these are related to Brazilian flex-fuel technology, a key difference is that U.S. flexible-fuel vehicles run on any combination of E-85 (an ethanol/gasoline mixture) and unleaded gasoline.

2. "Cheaper" should be defined as the lowest cost of fuel per mile (or kilometer) driven. Given potential differences in fuel efficiency between ethanol and gasoline, a savvy consumer will not take into account only the difference per liter at the gas station. However, for consumers with significant cash constraints, the absolute price difference may also be relevant.

3. According to IBGE, the Brazilian statistical agency, the average Brazilian family income in 2003 was $7,019.25.

4. Tests and studies suggest that fuel economy may decrease by approximately 2 percent in fuel-injected cars, such that a car averaging 30 miles per gallon on the highway would average 29.4 miles per gallon using an ethanol-blended fuel (10 percent ethanol)—not enough to be detected by the average driver.

5. According to a recent survey, 93 percent of Brazilians believe that the mission of companies is to generate jobs and 60 percent believe that the mission also includes helping to develop the country. In contrast, only 10 percent believe that the mission should include generating profits for investors.

6. Cold weather can be considered roughly any temperature less than 11 degrees Celsius, as pure ethanol does not easily form a rich enough mixture of fuel vapor to air to support combustion at temperatures below that.

7. Depending on the engine size, the government gives a tax reduction of between 2 and 7 percent per vehicle for ethanol-based engines.

8. The Renewable Fuels Association estimates that it would cost $50,000 to convert a single gas station to ethanol in the United States. To convert all 170,700 U.S. gas stations, it would cost approximately $8.5 billion, according to a 2005 Euromonitor estimate.

REFERENCES

Anfavea. 2004. Vendas internas no atacado de nacionais por combustível—1957/2003. Anuário estatístico da indústria automobilistica brasileira. Accessed February 25, 2005. www.anfavea.com.br.

Associated Press. 2004. Brazil buys into flex-fuel cars (August 30).

Benson, Todd. 2004. More Brazilian drivers turn to ethanol. *New York Times,* October 20.

CETC (CanMet Energy Technology Centre). 2005. Ethanol the "green gasoline. Accessed February 25, 2005 www.nrcan.gc.ca/es/etb/cetc/cetc01/htmldocs/factsheet_ethanol_the_green_gasoline_e.html.

Chin, Roberto (General Motors). 2005. Interview with author. São Paulo, Brazil, March 15.

Coelho, Antonio Carlos Lopes (Petrobras). 2005. Interview with author. Rio de Janeiro, Brazil, March 24.

Consulado Geral da India, 2005. Brazil fuel-alcohol program. Accessed February 25, 2005, www.indiaconsulate.org.br/comercial/p_exporta-dores_indianos/ethanol.htm.

Davis, Gregory W. 2001. *Project: development of technologies to improve cold start performance of ethanol vehicles.* Flint, Mich.: Kettering University Automotive Engine Research Laboratory.

Ethanol—Driving Towards a Greener Future. 2005. Benefiting the environment. Accessed February 26, 2005, www.ethanol-crfa.ca/vehicle.htm.

Ethanol.Org. 2005. What is fuel ethanol? Accessed April 23, 2005, www.ethanol.org/whatisethanol.html.

Euromonitor. 2005. Gasoline station retailing in the United States. Accessed April 23, 2005, www.euromonitor.com/Gasoline_Station_Retailing_in_United_States.

Exame. 2005. O stigma do lucro. *Exame,* March 23.

Geller, Howard. 1985. *Ethanol fuel from sugar cane in Brazil.* American Council for an Energy-Efficient Economy.

IBGE. 2005 (accessed). www.sidra.ibge.gov.br.

Kovarik, Bill. 1998. Henry Ford, Charles F. Kettering and the fuel of the future. *Automotive History Review, 32,* 7–27.

La Rovere, Emilio. 2004. *The Brazilian Ethanol Program,* Federal University of Rio de Janeiro, Presentation for International Conference for Renewable Energies, June 1, 2004.

Lindau, Luis Antonio. 2002. *An overview of the CNG vehicular market in Brazil.* Lastran—Laboratório de Sistemas de Transportes—EE/UFRGS—Escola de Engenharia da Universidade Federal do Rio Grande do Sul. Porto Alegre, RS, Brasil.

Oliveira, Diogenes de (Ford Motor Company). 2005. Interview with authors, Salvador, Brazil, March 21.

Ramos, Raimundo (Volkswagen Brazil). 2005. Interview with author, São Paulo, Brazil, March 17.

Renewable Fuels Association. 2005. Home page. Accessed February 25, 2005, www.ethanolrfa.org.

Ribeiro, S. K., Costa, C. V, David, E. G., Real, M. V., and D'Agosto, M. A. 2000. *Transporte e mudanças climáticas.* Mauad, Rio de Janeiro, Brasil.

Steinbruch, B. 2002. O motor afogou. *Folha de São Paulo,* caderno B, p. 2 (June 4).

Vieira de Carvalho, Arnaldo. 2003. *The Brazilian ethanol experience as fuel for transportation.* Report for the World Bank's Biomass Energy Workshop.

Chapter 17

Environmentally Friendly Technologies in China's Auto Industry

*John Eisel, Jonathan Glick, Adrienne
Kardosh, Coleman Long, David Mayer,
and Doug Roth*

The world has never before faced the rapid emergence of an economy the size of China's. Driven both by the country's own burgeoning industrialization and by its increasingly open relations with the rest of the world, China's gross domestic product (GDP) is growing at a rate of 8 percent a year. Along with economic expansion has come expanded automobile use. Published figures on the number of cars currently on the road in China vary widely, ranging anywhere from 20 million to 68 million vehicles as of 2003. Estimates of growth within the industry also vary, with some experts claiming that the number of vehicles will double every six years and others saying every two years. The automobile explosion has created a major environmental problem: Traffic emissions now represent the major threat to clean air in China. Planners in Shanghai have estimated that 90 percent of the city's air pollution is attributable to automobile exhaust. This pollution exacts an economic cost: The World Bank estimates that related health-care and lost-productivity costs amount to 5 percent of the country's GDP.

A potential solution to the air pollution problem may be found in environmentally friendly automotive technologies, such as hybrid and fuel-cell-powered cars. The adoption of such technologies, moreover, may be far easier in China, with its tradition of centralized planning, than it has proved to be in Western countries like the United States. In this chapter, we examine the opportunities this situation presents both for China and for the automobile manufacturers operating there.

CHINA'S AUTOMOTIVE MARKET

The Chinese market probably provides the greatest growth opportunity, globally, for car manufacturers. Rapid wealth creation has brought car ownership within reach of an ever-increasing percentage of the population, and a growing number of drivers are purchasing multipurpose vehicles (MPVs).

In 2002, average GDP per capita in major urban areas such as Beijing was 19,000 renminbi (US$2,289) and rising at 22 percent per year. At the same time, the cost of a new small car was approximately 45,000 renminbi ($5,421) and falling. For the expanding middle classes, new cars are now affordable. And a growing second-hand market has broadened the pool of potential consumers.

China's economic expansion, in addition to making vehicle ownership more accessible, has also made it more necessary. As cities outgrow their boundaries and middle class families move from urban centers to new, more luxurious suburbs, cars are needed for commuting and for traveling within communities. To handle the increased vehicle volume, Beijing has completed its fifth and sixth ring roads and at this writing was building a seventh.

In addition to becoming necessities, cars are also increasingly becoming status symbols. Chinese consumers look for outwardly rugged vehicles with plush, pampering interiors. Currently, the market is dominated by sedans. The MPV segment, however, is growing explosively, although from a very low base. The key environmental implication is that the average engine capacity is increas-

ing. This will compound the environmental impact from the underlying growth in private automotive ownership.

Manufacturers

Feeding the Chinese population's appetite for more and larger automobiles is a booming automotive industry, which by 2008 is
expected to be turning out nearly 5 million vehicles a year, or even,
according to some more aggressive estimates, 7.4 million.

The largest industry players are partnerships between domestic
and international manufacturers. The top three manufacturers,
which together generate 70 percent of total sector revenues and take
in 89 percent of sector profits, are Shanghai Volkswagen (VW), a
joint venture among Volkswagen (50 percent), Shanghai
Automotive Industry Corporation (25 percent), and several other
Chinese companies; FAW Volkswagen, a joint venture among VW
(30 percent), First Automotive Works (FAW) (60 percent), and
Audi (10 percent); and Guangzhou Honda, a joint venture between
Guangzhou Automobile group and Honda. Along with VW,
Honda, and Audi, most other international automotive companies
have also established relationships in China. These include General
Motors, which is the fourth largest manufacturer in China;
DaimlerChrysler; Ford, whose presence is relatively limited; and
major Japanese players Nissan and Toyota.

The Environmental Problem

Vehicles whose engines are powered by gasoline or diesel fuel emit
a wide variety of pollutants—principally carbon monoxide (CO),
oxides of nitrogen (NO_x), volatile organic compounds (VOCs), and
particulates—that have an increasing impact on urban air quality.
In addition, the action of sunlight on NO_x and VOCs leads to the
formation of ozone, a secondary pollutant that affects rural areas far
from the original emission site. Acid rain is another long-range pollutant caused, in part, by vehicle NO_x emissions.

The growth in car ownership has increased the presence of all of these substances in China's atmosphere. The situation is made worse by the poor emissions standards of many domestic brands of cars. In response, China's State Bureau of Machinery Industry has required that all cars produced since July 1998 meet emissions-control standards equivalent to those set by the European Union. Cars weighing less than 3.5 tons must reduce CO, hydrocarbon, and NO_x emissions by between 43 percent and 66 percent. To encourage consumers to move to more environmentally friendly cars, fuel taxes have also been raised.

Because of China's size and the density of its population, however, merely meeting current world emissions standards will not solve the country's pollution problems. Consider that for China to have the same number of vehicles per capita as Germany, manufacturers would have to produce 650 million cars. This would not only deplete the world's supply of steel and oil but would create a tremendous volume of greenhouse-gas and other noxious emissions. Airborne pollution would impose costs on the economy in the form of illnesses, decreased soil fertility, and increased building and equipment maintenance. Moreover, autos create waste products that are hard to dispose of, including old tires, motor oil, and the vehicles themselves. Unlike many Western countries, China does not have the infrastructure for recycling these materials.

THE TECHNOLOGY SOLUTION

Environmentally friendly automobiles represent both a possible solution to China's pollution problems and an economic opportunity. Moreover, the country's political structure and relative lack of infrastructure could make the transition to these new technologies easier than it has been in more open societies with an older industrial base.

To see the potential impact of green technologies, consider the following scenarios. Assume that the average Chinese motorist drives 7,500 miles a year in a car whose fuel efficiency is 30 miles per gallon (mpg), and assume that these figures remain constant through 2033. Using the prediction for automobile ownership given earlier, this would mean that by 2033 the country would be burning 163 billion gallons, or eight billion barrels, of oil annually. If, however, hybrid technology were introduced that increased fuel efficiency to 60 mpg, oil use would decrease by half, to approximately 81 billion gallons or four billion barrels—a dramatic decrease in pollution.

The Role of Government

It is very difficult for the U.S. government to support any pro-environment policies that are seen as endangering the future of the oil and gas or automotive industries, even if many people believe these policies constitute the best long-term strategy for lessening pollution. In the United States, representatives are elected and must therefore listen to the demands of their constituents—including individuals, nongovernmental organizations (NGOs), industry forces, and other third-party groups—if they wish to stay in office. Of course, many U.S. NGOs are concerned about environmental issues such as global warming; they argue that the government should increase the fuel efficiency of the 125 million cars and 65 million light trucks and vans on the roads. But these groups are outspent by the large lobbyists for the automotive and oil industries. In the 1998 election cycle, for example, individuals and organizations representing the oil and gas, mining, electric, and auto industries gave $48.2 million to candidates campaigning for national office, compared with just $814,712 from the environmental groups, a ratio of nearly 60 to 1. The influence of campaign contributions can be seen in the fact that senators voting to block improved corporate average fuel economy (CAFE) standards received more than twice the campaign contributions from the auto lobby as those who did not. In addition to lobbying the government directly, automobile manufacturers have created public pressure on politicians by using their vast financial resources to launch marketing campaigns to convince the general public that increasing fuel-efficiency standards would reduce their vehicle choice.

The situation is far different in China. Although the country's industrial policy has become significantly more accommodating to market forces, the government's ability to frame industrial strategy is almost absolute. The country has been a centrally planned state led by the Chinese Communist Party (CCP) since 1949, when the People's Republic of China was established under Mao Zedong. Centralization ensures that implementation of governmental policies encounters little, if any, opposition. Automotive manufacturers in the country are particularly unlikely to object, given that many have some type of government ownership. As one executive at GM Shanghai put it, "When the government publishes new long-term policy, we simply accept it as fact."

POLICY GOALS, TECHNOLOGY, AND THE ENVIRONMENT

Although neither the president nor the prime minister is subject to the direct political pressure of pure elections, both are keenly aware that popular discontent with the economy can escalate into large-scale protests. As a result, the main goals of China's centrally planned policies are sustainable economic growth and job creation. In the short term, environmentally friendly policy will lose whenever it appears to conflict with these goals.

Investment in technology is much less likely to present such a conflict. In fact, it is generally viewed as a driver of economic progress and a source of national pride. The Chinese government also sees technological development as a way to mitigate growing unrest among the millions of rural poor and laid-off white-collar workers suffering hardships associated with the country's rapidly developing, more market-oriented economy. Improvements to their daily lives in the form of mobile phones, Internet access, and customer convenience show that the country is headed in the right direction, despite current discomfort. Thus, political considerations also motivate the government to support technological research and development.

Much of China's technology efforts are in its domestic automotive industry. During the country's ninth five-year plan, the

Ministry of Science and Technology named as a key goal the development of environmentally friendly vehicles, and the government invested approximately 100 million renminbi ($12 million) toward reaching it. The tenth five-year plan pushed for even more technological development. As a result, the commercialization of environmentally friendly cars is now explicitly part of China's science plan for the next decade. The country plans to commercialize electric buses in Beijing and Shanghai by 2007, expanding to ten additional cities by 2015. Furthermore, electric cars are to be part of a model motorcade for the Beijing Olympic Games in 2008. As of January 2004, the combined capital investment in green automotive technology by the central and local governments, as well as by state-owned enterprises, totaled 3 billion renminbi ($361 million).

The government's support for environmental technology in the auto industry is also evident in a policy document noting that the "state shall promote hybrid and [cleaner] diesel technologies." Because of the CCP's ability to implement policy declarations, such a document is effectively law. This creates a not-so-subtle pressure on car companies to work with the government on research-intensive technologies. By aligning their product strategies with governmental policy, automakers not only get financial support but also position themselves as key players in an industry that the government ultimately plans to consolidate. To this end, GM is helping develop China's electric bus fleet, Volkswagen is establishing itself as a leader in diesel technology in China, and Toyota is refining its hybrid technology.

The automakers, in addition, are participating in a broad-based group of more than 100 institutions, also including universities and research institutes, that is committed to researching and developing auto-related environmental technology. So far, thanks in large part to the government's aggressive promotion of the necessary research and development, the group had completed prototypes of hybrid and fuel-cell vehicles, developed key parts and engines for fuel cells, and significantly improved high-power nickel-hydrogen and lithium batteries.

Infrastructure

Like its political system, the United States' entrenched automotive infrastructure, based on gasoline-powered vehicles, has been an impediment to the adoption of environmentally friendly car technologies: Too many businesses are wed to using the "old" ways to make money. China, in contrast, is still developing its infrastructure. Highways are being built at a remarkable pace, and gas stations are only now becoming common along the nation's roads. The country is thus in a better position to promote leapfrog technologies that can transform its auto industry.

This is similar to the situation that obtained with regard to communications technology. Many developing countries, including China, never bothered investing in landline infrastructure, going directly from having no telephone service at all to establishing complete mobile-phone networks, which are cheaper in the long term and easier to provide, especially in the more rapidly developing rural areas. In the United States and other Western markets, adoption of advanced communications technologies was slowed down by large companies such as the "Baby Bells," whose businesses were threatened by them.

China is a relative newcomer to car manufacture and ownership, as it was to communications systems, and so it can capitalize on global intellectual capital to position itself in the forefront of environmentally friendly technologies. In the short term, the related infrastructure may be costlier, but in the longer term, it will be cheaper to maintain. And this strategic positioning should ultimately prove more profitable, given the government's strong interest in research and development.

Consumers

The most fuel-efficient, least-polluting vehicles will do nothing for China's environment if Chinese drivers will not buy them. Marketing to these customers poses some unique challenges. If done incorrectly, it can be disastrous for a company or a brand. When Volkswagen, for example, introduced its hatchback Golf into the Chinese market, consumers balked. The reason: The Chinese believe that there is an equal and opposite force for everything, and they viewed the hatchback as off balance, with a front (hood) but no back (protruding trunk). Automakers have not been able to revisit the design since.

The rapid expansion of the car market in China has created a situation that has important implications for marketing campaigns. Consumers are being inundated both with new products and with advertising for them. Unlike car buyers in more established markets, whose knowledge about the products has developed along with the relatively slowly evolving industry, the Chinese must learn the categories, brands, and models all at once. Most Chinese have fewer than five years of driving experience. Technical specifications are therefore less relevant to their purchase decisions; they do not yet feel the importance or impact of a car's mileage per gallon or maintenance costs.

Faced with a confusing array of choices, potential buyers look for proxies for information. For example, they see that Chinese officials travel in Audis and so associate the brand with status, making it a market leader in one of the country's premium segments. For the same reason, Chinese consumers are very susceptible to marketing messages. This gives multinational corporations the opportunity to influence consumer perceptions in a way they cannot in markets where they have a longer history. The Howard Johnson in Shanghai, for instance, is a five-star luxury hotel, instead of the economy lodging the chain provides in the United States. Similarly, Buick has positioned itself as a mid- to high-tier luxury brand. On the down side, Chinese consumers, plied on every side with advertisements and choices, have little brand loyalty and are apt to rely on first impressions. They are more than willing to try new things but will walk away from a brand if they are unhappy with their first experiences with it.

Given these characteristics, Chinese car buyers might be attracted to environmentally friendly vehicles by establishing a link between environmental science and economic or social status. Merely emphasizing the technology's benefits, such as improved fuel efficiency and lower fuel costs, will not convert Chinese drivers. Positioning hybrid engines as the latest and "coolest" technology available, however, will resonate with their desire to have the very best.

The government can also help drive demand by converting the official fleet, as well as buses and taxis, to new, environmentally friendly models. Consumers will see the technology in use, associate it with a high level of prestige, and seek out hybrid models for themselves.

In Conclusion

The tremendous growth of the Chinese automotive industry is dazzling the world, but it is also creating an enormous environmental hazard. Through the development of green technologies, China can address environmental issues that affect the nation. The country is uniquely placed to accomplish this because of its government's structure. Central planning may raise social concerns, but it also removes significant barriers to change that exist in countries like the United States. This is a lesson that organizations wishing to push for social or environmental change in the country need to learn. The Chinese system is different from that of its Western counterparts, and so these organizations, to achieve their goals, must use different, possibly entirely new, strategies.

References

Access Asia Ltd. 2000. Automobiles in China: A market analysis. October. www.accessasia.co.uk/r/CCCars.pdf.

Audi World Site. 2004 (accessed). Production locations: China. www.audi .com/com/en/company/production_locations/china/china.jsp.

Baiping, Shen (national planning director, Leo Burnett). 2004 (accessed). Interview with the authors, Shanghai.

Bureau of East Asian and Pacific Affairs. 2004 (accessed). Background note: China. www.state.gov/r/pa/ei/bgn/18902.htm.

Callander, Steven. 2004. Strategic management in non-market environments (class). Evanston, Ill.: Kellogg School of Management.

CBnet-Industry Updates. 2004. Electric cars on their way to markets. March 22. http://english.people.com.cn/200403/22/eng20040322_138159.shtml.

China Auto. 2004. The current situation of environmentally friendly vehicles in China. January.

China Automobile News. November 10, 2003.

China View. 2004. Electric cars: China's hope to catch up with advanced auto maker. February 20. http://news.xinhuanet.com/english/2004–02/20/content_1323681.htm.

Chou, Frank. 2004. Business development and planning director, GM Shanghai Group. Interview with the authors, Shanghai.

Leung, Frank. 2004. Senior associate, Mercer Management Consulting. Interview with the authors, Hong Kong.

Miller, Ellen S., and Sifry, Micah L. 2000. Campaign finance emissions. *American Prospect Online.* May 22. www.prospect.org/print/V11/13/devi13.html.

National High Technology Research and Development Program of China. *2001 Annual Report.*

Oxford Analytica Daily Brief. 2003. Confident China will see more growth. December 5. www.oxan.com.

Oxford Analytica Daily Brief. 2003. National identity drives technology policy. October 8. www.oxan.com.

Pang, Phillip. 2004. Vice president for sales, Valentic, Inc. Interview with the authors, Shanghai.

Public Campaign. 2000. Paying and polluting more at the gas pump: Campaign contributions prevent tougher fuel efficiency standards. www.publiccampaign.org.

UK Air Quality Information Archive. 2003. The chemistry of atmospheric pollutants. www.aeat.com/netcen/airqual/kinetics.

Watts, Jonathan, and Morris, Steven. 2003. On the Chinese menu: 260 billion eggs and the world's entire catch of fish. *Guardian* (London), July 18.

Wonacott, Peter. 2003. China's traffic grows deadlier: Car-sales boom, new drivers cause chaotic roads, pollution; Ford and GM focus on safety. *Wall Street Journal Europe,* November 20.

Acronyms

ACWF	All-China Women's Federation
AIDC	Automotive Industry Development Center
AIP	Apparel Industry Partnership
AMIC	Automobile Manufacturing Industry Certificate
ANC	African National Congress
ARV	antiretroviral
ASEAN	Association of South East Asian Nations
ATC	Agreement on Textiles and Clothing (of the WTO)
BEE	black economic empowerment
BP	British Petroleum
CCP	Chinese Communist Party
CDP	Carbon Disclosure Project
CEO	chief executive officer
CESAIS	Center for Economic and Social Applications
CO	carbon monoxide
Conam	National Commission on the Environment–Peru
Conama	National Commission of the Environment–Chile
CSR	corporate social responsibility
DLA	Department of Land Affairs
ECM	electronic control module
Elfun	[Electrical Funds] GE Volunteer arm
EMS	environmental management system
EU	European Union

FAMS	Ford Academy of Manufacturing Science
FDI	foreign direct investment
FLA	Fair Labor Association
FLSA	Fair Labor Standards Act
FNB	First National Bank
GCC	Global Climate Coalition
GDP	gross domestic product
GE	General Electric
GEM	Global Entrepreneurship Monitor
GIM	Global Initiatives in Management
GM	General Motors
GRI	Global Reporting Initiative
ICFTU	International Confederation of Free Trade Unions
IHD	International Healthcare Distributors
IIT	Indian Institute of Technology
ILO	International Labor Organization
ISO	International Organization for Standardization
KWV	Co-operative Wine Growers' Association
LDC	less developed country
Merseta	Manufacturing and Engineering Related Sector's Education and Training Authority
MIC	Mineworkers Investment Corporation
MNC	multinational corporation
mpg	miles per gallon
MPV	multipurpose vehicle
NEF	National Empowerment Fund
NGO	nongovernmental organization
OEM	original equipment manufacturer
OSH	occupational safety and health

PPP	public/private partnership
Safcol	South Africa Forestry Company
SAI	Social Accountability International
SAWB	South African Wine and Brandy Company
Sawit	South African Wine Industry Trust
Seia	System to Evaluate Environmental Impact
SETA	Sector Education and Training Authority
SME	small and medium enterprise
SRI	socially responsible investment (investing)
TKV	Tae Kwang Vina Industrial Company
TRIPs	Agreement on Trade-Related Intellectual Property Rights
UCT	University of Cape Town
UN	United Nations
UNAIDS/ WHO	United Nations AIDS/World Health Organization
UYF	Umsobomvu Youth Fund
VC	venture capital
VOC	volatile organic compound
VUFO	Vietnam Union of Friendship Organisations
WCOC	Workplace Code of Conduct
WHO	World Health Organization
WIETA	Wine Industry Ethical Trade Association
WTO	World Trade Organization

INDEX

Abbott Access, 178, 180, 182–85; IHD and, 181, 182
Abbott Laboratories: ARVs and, 182; HIV/AIDS and, xvi, 178, 180–81, 183, 198; preferential pricing by, 182
Acción Empresarial, 224, 228
accreditation, 168, 172
acid rain, 15, 206
Adidas-Salomon: Global Standards and, 43; labor standards and, 1, 31; sweatshop scandal and, 43
advertising, 10, 18, 89, 167
advertorials, 93, 94
affirmative action, 99, 165, 171
AFL-CIO, 31, 36
African National Congress (ANC), 151; ARVs and, 181, 185; BEE and, 165; HIV/AIDS and, 178, 179; land reform and, 134; microlending by, 156
African Terroir, social welfare and, 140
Agip, ethanol and, 244
Agreement on Textiles and Clothing (ATC), 35, 38
Agreement on Trade-Related Intellectual Property Rights (TRIPs): Article 31 of, 190, 192; Brazil and, 191, 192; national health crisis under, 195
agriculture, 239, 247
AIDC. See Automotive Industry Development Center
AIDS. See HIV/AIDS
AIP. See Apparel Industry Partnership
All-China Women's Federation (ACWF), 79
All India Science Talent examination, 108

American Express, 104
AMIC. See Automobile Manufacturing Industry Certificate
Amnesty International, human-rights education and, 31
ANC. See African National Congress
animal welfare, 1, 16
antiretrovirals (ARVs), 182, 191, 193; ANC and, 181, 185; cocktail of, 190, 192; treatment with, 179, 180, 184
apartheid, 134, 146, 155; education and, 151, 152; legacy of, 121, 152; sanctions and, 133; SMEs and, 151, 153, 154
Apparel Industry Partnership (AIP), 43
Arla Foods, Tetra Pak and, 220
ARVs. See antiretrovirals
ASEAN. See Assiciation of South East Asian Nations
Asian financial crisis (1997), 28, 152
Associated Press, on flexible-fuel vehicles, 236
Association of South East Asian Nations (ASEAN), 60
ATC. See Agreement on Textiles and Clothing
Audi, in China, 253, 259
audits. See labor-standards audits
Automobile Manufacturing Industry Certificate (AMIC), 123, 126, 131; implementation of, 124; literacy and, 130
automobiles: environmental impact of, 251, 253, 254; in China, 251, 252–53, 256–57, 259, 260; infrastructure with, 258; recycling, 207

Automotive Industry Development
Center (AIDC), 122–24, 128,
131
Automotive Research Association of
India, 103
Aventis, IHD and, 181
Avon: challenges for, 92–93, 93–95;
customer base of, 89, 91–92,
94, 95; Latin American culture
and, xv; marketing by, 89; sales
staff of, 91–92, 95; social
outreach by, 94; strategies by, x
Axios International Health
Distributors, xvi, 181, 183
AZT (drug), 179

Back, Charles: Fairview and, 139
Balsudha, 108
Baron, David: on
shareholders/financial
performance, 20
Bastiat, Frédéric: on economists, 41
Baxter International, shareholder
pressure and, 12
Bayer, IHD and, 181
Bayman, Scott R.: on local market,
105
BEE. See black economic
empowerment
Beijing Olympic Games, 257
Ben & Jerry's: CSR and, 7, 9; social
agenda of, 19
BestFoods, Tetra Pak and, 220
Beyerskloof, 137, 138
Beyond Petroleum initiative (BP), 2, 7
Bill and Melinda Gates Foundation,
HIV crisis and, 179
biodiversity, 205, 223
Birlasoft, 104
black economic empowerment (BEE),
xvi, 134, 142, 148, 151, 162,
166, 167, 170; advancing, 141;
black elite and, 165; charters,
171; control of, 152;
corporations and, 171; funding
for, 144, 146; importance of,
143; introduction of, 165;

MNCs and, xv; private sector
and, 158; problems for,
145–46; WIETA and, 141;
wine industry and, 135–40,
144–46, 147, 149
Black Economic Empowerment
Commission, 147, 148, 151
Black Economic Empowerment
Consultation Conference, 141
black entrepreneurs: benefits for, 152;
funding for, 156, 158;
nurturing, 161, 162; obstacles
for, 154, 156; racism and, 155;
scarcity of, 161; VC financing
and, 157, 159
Black Forest, threats to, 206
black market, 37, 66
black ownership/control, 166–67,
169, 171–72
BMW, 122; AMIC at, 124–30;
education/training and, xv,
124–25, 127, 128
Body Shop: CSR and, 7; social agenda
of, 19
Boehringer Ingelheim, IHD and, 181
Boje, David: on Global Standards, 43
Booney, Norman: on women in
industry, 78
Bouwland Wines, 137–38
boycotts, 17, 61, 109
BP. See British Petroleum; Beyond
Petroleum initiative
BP Amoco, 212; environmental
awareness by, xvii, 205, 207,
209–10, 211, 213; financial
performance of, 210; solar-/
wind-/hydrogen-energy
technologies of, 210
BPSA. See BP Southern Africa
BP Southern Africa (BPSA), 170;
BEE procurement policy of,
169; black ownership at, 166;
bursaries and, 169;
empowerment groups and, 172
BP Wind, 210
brand building, 68, 69, 92–95
brand equity, 94, 97

brand loyalty, 57, 95, 259; eroding, 64; increased, xiii; risks to, 62
brands, socially responsible, 8, 9
Braustein, Elissa, 80, 82; on FDI/social status, 84; on FDI/wages, 83
Brazilian Association of Personal Hygiene and Cosmetics Industry, 90
Brazilian Health Ministry: AIDS program and, 191; reimportation and, 194
Brent Spar oil buoy, 17, 209
Bristol-Myers Squibb, 181, 193
British Petroleum (BP), 1; climate change and, 6; cost efficiencies of, 5; initiative by, 2, 7
Broad-Based Black Economic Empowerment Act, 134
Browne of Madingley, Lord: emissions trading scheme by, 209–10
Brown v. Board of Education (1954), 149
Buick, in China, 259
bursaries, 169, 170, 172
business: human/social growth and, ix; pushing boundaries of, 218–20; role/behavior of, 2–3; social welfare and, 3; socially responsible, 4, 113, 115; sustainable, 8

Cadena Productiva Sostenible Proyecto, 227
CAFE. *See* corporate average fuel economy
California Public Retirement System (Calpers), 12
Cape Institute for Agricultural Training, 143
capital, x, 19; labor conditions and, 37; rules for, 10
carbon dioxide emissions: increase in, 209, 251; reducing, 208, 210, 238, 244, 245, 254
Carbon Disclosure Project (CDP), 213

carbon taxes, 206–7
Carvalho, Arnaldo Vieira de, 242
CCP. *See* Chinese Communist Party
CDP. *See* Carbon Disclosure Project
Center for Economic and Social Applications (CESAIS), 42
Central planning, xvii, 252, 260
Centre for Science and Environment, Ford India and, 102
change, 16; companies as catalysts for, 19–21; social, 20, 21, 141, 260
charity, 2, 11, 114
Chennai, India, 100; Elfun in, 107
child labor, 16, 32, 46, 61; banning, 59, 60, 62; MNCs and, 27; regulating, 208; South Africa and, 136
Chinese Communist Party (CCP), 256, 257
Cicarelli, Daniela: Avon and, 93
citizenship, marketing, 69. *See also* corporate citizenship
Claros Consulting, 211
Clean Production Accords (APL), 223
climate change, 209; combating, 205, 213; financial risks/consequences of, 213
Clüver, Paul, 138, 139
Coca-Cola: in India, 109; international standards and, 110; Tetra Pak and, 220
code of employment principles, 141
codes of conduct, 32, 34, 66, 68, 71
Comfort School, 107, 108
command-and-control regulation, 206, 207
communications, 93, 179, 258; obstacles to, 72, 98; strategic, 131
community investment, 103–4, 107–8
community involvement, 9, 101, 113, 224
competition, 6, 153, 229
competitive advantages, 8, 9, 15

competitive pressure, 210;
    environmental/social standards
    and, 211–12
competitive strategies, 9, 14, 19;
    benefit-focused, 7; rules of, 10
compliance, 62, 113; monitoring, 64,
    190; problems with, 36; tactics,
    61; teams, 33
Conama. *See* National Commission
    on the Environment
Conservation and Environment Grant
    Programme, 103
Conservation International, Wal-Mart
    and, 2
consumer awareness, 68, 94;
    environment and, 222; MNCs
    and, 229
consumer demand, xvii, 57, 233, 234,
    235–39, 245; CSR and, 99
consumers, 172, 258–60
consumption, 8, 9; production and,
    223
contract labor, women and, 78
Control Data, charitable causes and, 2
Conventions and Recommendations
    (ILO), 58, 59
Cooperative Wine Growers'
    Association (KWV), 140, 143,
    145
corporate average fuel economy
    (CAFE), 255
corporate behavior, 18
corporate citizenship, 69, 105, 106,
    109, 112, 113, 114; conceptual
    issues in, xiii; reports, 1
Corporate Citizenship Council, GE,
    106, 112, 114
corporate culture, establishing, 113
corporate ownership, transfer of, 152,
    171–72
corporate social investments (CSI),
    113; education and, 128–29
corporate social responsibility (CSR),
    ix, 2; benefits-based, 10;
    building, xi, 108, 109–10, 115;
    business case for, 5, 13, 18–19,
    101–3, 106–7, 109; capital

markets and, 18; consumer
    demand and, 99; corporate
    strategy and, 110; defining,
    xi–xii; environmental, 5, 6;
    financial performance and, 4, 5,
    19; governance, 111–13;
    guidelines, 15; HIV/AIDS and,
    xvi; implementing, xiii, 97,
    115; interest in, 1, 15, 19;
    justifications for, 2, 5; lessons
    of, 108; MNCs and, 99, 110,
    111, 113, 114, 115;
    monitoring, xiii, 101; NGOs
    and, xv, 19, 98, 111–12, 115;
    philosophy of, 101, 105–6;
    policies for, xii–xiii, 11; profits
    and, 21; programs, 114;
    promoting, 224; public support
    for, 112; SRI and, 12, 14;
    strategies for, 3–7, 8, 9, 10, 17,
    19, 22n3, 110, 115
corruption, ix, 35; in India, 98, 100,
    102
cosmetics sales, 89, 90, 91
Country Coordinating Mechanism,
    179
CSI. *See* corporate social investments
CSR. *See* corporate social
    responsibility
Cummins Engines, charitable causes
    and, 2

Daimler Chrysler, 253; hydrogen-fuel-
    cell buses and, 210
Davin, Delia: report by, 82
Davis, Ian: on social acceptance, 2
de Klerk, F. W.: election of, 151
Delhi, India, Elfun in, 107, 108
Department of Land Affairs (DLA),
    134, 146; New Beginnings and,
    136
Devco, 140, 143
diesel fuel, 238, 253
Directive on End-of-Life Vehicles, 207
direct selling, 91–92, 94
discrimination, x, 62, 141; workforce,
    45

distribution, xi, 93; policies, 169–70; services, 182; systems, 220

DLA. *See* Department of Land Affairs

domestic labor, women and, 78

Domini 400 Social Index, 12

Double Learning and Double Competing initiative, 79

Dow Chemical, cost efficiencies of, 5

Dow Jones Sustainability Index, 212

Dreyer, 9

E-10, 247

E-85, 239, 240, 245, 247n1

Earth Summit (1992), 223

ecoefficiency, 218, 219, 223; awareness of, 228; described, 217; manifestations of, 218; NGOs and, 228; working toward, 229

Ecoimagination initiative, GE, 2, 6

economic development, 44, 99, 141, 162; environmental impact and, 217, 223; in Brazil, 191; in Chile, 222–23; in China, 251, 252; in India, 98; labor standards and, 42; in Peru, 226–28; SMEs and, 52–53; in South Africa, 151, 153, 155; in South America, 131; sustainable, 218, 256; in Thailand, 28; in Vietnam, 41, 53

economic empowerment, 152; resources/expertise for, 159; women and, 79, 89

Eddie Bauer: Global Standards and, 43; labor standards and, 31

education, xii, xv, xvi, 131, 139, 143, 149, 177; adult, 167–69, 170; apartheid and, 151, 152; community and, 128–29; CSI and, 128; customer, 172; impact of, x, 128–29; improvements in, 103, 111; inferior, 121, 171; medical, 183–84; in South Africa, 121, 122–23, 125, 126, 144;

statistics on, 170; subsidizing, 2; women and, 85; worker, 32, 122, 138, 167

Electrical Funds (Elfun), 105–6, 107; Comfort School and, 108

electronic control module (ECM), 239

Elfun. *See* Electrical Funds

Eli Lilly, IHD and, 181

Elsenburg Agricultural College, 139

emission reductions, 219, 246, 254

emission-trading schemes, 206, 209–10

employment equity, 167–69

empowerment projects, 142–43, 146, 147, 148

EMS. *See* environmental management systems

energy: efficiency, 219; reducing use of, 2; renewable/nonrenewable, 238

entrepreneurship, 162; social, 20. *See also* black entrepreneurs

entry planning, 109–10

Environmental Action Programme, 205

environmental awareness, 219; corporate, 207–10; growth of, 205, 229

environmental impact, 225–26, 246; automobiles and, 253; economic growth and, 223; legislation, 222; MNCs and, 209; reducing, 205, 206, 218, 221, 223, 227, 233

environmentalism, 206–7, 208

environmental issues, ix, x, xviii, 98, 103, 224, 226, 233, 259, 260; addressing, xvii, 71; in China, 253–54, 256–57; flexible-fuel vehicles and, 235; integrating, 219; legislating, 206; NGOs and, 255

environmental laws, 32, 223

environmentally friendly vehicles, 254, 257, 258

environmental management systems
(EMS), 219–20, 223–24;
elements of, 219;
implementation of, 227,
228–29
environmental programs, 206;
internal pressures for, 210;
lesser-developed countries and,
217
environmental protection, 208, 218;
economic development and,
217
environmental responsibility, xii, 6,
212; corporate, 217; profits
and, 218
Ernst & Young, 42
Esso, ethanol and, 244
ethanol, xvii; demand for, 238;
distilling, 242, 243; distribution
of, 243, 245, 247; economic
feasibility of, 246–47;
emergence of, 242; export of,
245; gasoline and, 233, 237,
240, 242, 243, 246, 247,
247n2; government interest in,
244–45; infrastructure for, 233,
234, 241–45, 247; performance
with, 237; production of, 243,
244, 245, 246; shortage of,
236, 243, 245; tax incentives
for, 244; technology, 240
ethanol cars, 247n7;
manufacturing/operating, 239;
sales of, 243
ethics, 10, 101, 113, 115, 224; motives
and, 3; outcomes and, 19
European Business Council for a
Sustainable Energy Future, 212
European Union (EU): ecological
program of, 205; emissions-
control standards and, 254;
environmentalism in, 206–7;
ethanol and, 244; labor
standards and, 30
ExxonMobil: climate change and, 6;
greenhouse-gas reductions and,
211–12

factory owners, labor unions and, 29,
31
Fair Labor Association (FLA), 43, 44,
46
Fair Labor Standards Act (FLSA)
(1938), 59
fairness, standards of, 15, 16
Fair Valley, xvi, 139
Fairview winery, 139
FAMS. *See* Ford Academy of
Manufacturing Science
FAW. *See* First Automotive Works
FAW Volkswagen, 253
FDI. *See* foreign direct investment
financial goals, 13; social goals and,
12, 14
financial literacy, 111, 170
financial performance, 4, 10, 13, 21,
210, 212; CSR and, 19;
measuring, 14; shareholders
and, 20
financial services charter, 167, 168
Financial Times, on social acceptance,
2
First Automotive Works (FAW), 253
First National Bank (FNB), 159, 168
First National Bank (FNB) Learning
Program, 168
First National Bank (FNB)-
Momentum-Umsobomvu
Progress Fund, 159
FirstRand Group, 159, 168; black
directors at, 166
5 Percent Club, members of, 2
FLA. *See* Fair Labor Association
flexible fuel, 234, 239, 242
flexible-fuel vehicles, 233, 247n1;
consumer demand for, 234,
235–39, 245, 246; economic
support from, 238–39;
environmental benefits of, 235,
237, 238; export of, 247; fuel
costs for, 236; maintenance costs
for, 236; next-generation, 241;
performance of, 237; purchases
of, 235, 238; resale value of,
237; success of, xvii, 246

FLSA. *See* Fair Labor Standards Act
FNB. *See* First National Bank
Ford, Henry, 2, 101, 242
Ford Academy of Manufacturing
    Science (FAMS), 103, 126, 130
Ford Asia Pacific, 100
Ford Escort, 100
Ford Fiesta, flexible-fuel version of,
    237, 240
Ford India, 109; accident rate at, 102;
    auto-industry growth and, 100;
    corruption and, 102; environ-
    mental issues and, 103; social
    responsibility and, 104; standards
    for, 101, 102; women at, 102
Ford Motor Company, 97, 122;
    AIDC and, 127, 128; AMIC
    and, 124–30; certification
    program of, 113; in China, 253;
    community-development
    project in, 103; CSI and, 129;
    CSR and, xv; education/
    training and, xv, 124, 126, 127,
    128, 131; ethanol and, 240;
    flexible-fuel vehicles and, 234,
    235, 237, 239, 240, 241; global
    reputation of, 109; health care
    and, 111; in India, 99–104;
    lessons for, 108–14; Mamelodi
    and, 128; performance of, 100;
    standards for, 101, 102, 110;
    women's issues and, 114
Ford Motor Company Center for
    Global Citizenship (Kellogg
    School of Management), ix, xii
Ford Taurus, E-85 and, 240
foreign direct investment (FDI), ix,
    28, 48, 64; aggregate levels of,
    49; attracting, 114; in China,
    77, 81; financial status and,
    85–86; in India, 98–99; labor
    costs and, 52; labor standards
    and, 65; social status and,
    84–85, 85–86; in Vietnam, 49,
    50–52; wages and, 82–83;
    women and, xiv–xv, 79–80,
    80–83, 84–85, 85–86

freedom of association, 33, 62
free trade, 2; labor standards and, 60
FTSE4Good fund, 12
FTSE4Good index series, 212
fuel cells, 239
fuel-cell vehicles, 241, 252, 257
fuel taxes, 254
fusion inhibitors, 198
Futureware, 182
Fuzeon, 190, 198

Gap, 33; human rights and, 68
gasohol, 242, 243, 245
gasoline, 238, 253; ethanol and, 233,
    237, 240, 242, 243, 246, 247
gasoline-only vehicles, 235, 241
GCC. *See* Global Climate Coalition
GE. *See* General Electric
GE Capital, 104
GE Fund, 106, 107, 112
GE India, 105
GE Lighting, 104
GEM. *See* Global Entrepreneurship
    Monitor
GE Motors, 105
GE Plastics, 104, 105, 106, 107
"Gender, FDI, and Women's
    Autonomy" (Braustein), 80
Gender and the South China Miracle
    (Lee), 85
General Electric (GE), 97;
    certification program of, 113;
    Corporate Citizenship Council
    of, 112; CSR and, xv, 114–15;
    Ecoimagination initiative and,
    2, 6; education and, 111; Elfun
    and, 107; environmental
    practices and, 106; guidelines
    by, 106; in India, 104–8;
    international standards and,
    110; lessons for, 108–14;
    revenues of, 105; volunteerism
    and, 108; women at, 107
General Motors (GM): in China, 253,
    257; flexible-fuel vehicles and,
    234, 235, 239, 240, 241; trifuel
    vehicles and, 241

Gifford, Kathie Lee, 61
GIM. *See* Global Initiatives Management
GlaxoSmithKline, 192
Global Climate Coalition (GCC), 209
Global Entrepreneurship Monitor (GEM), 153, 155, 156, 157
Global Fund to Fight AIDS, Tuberculosis and Malaria, 178
Global Initiatives Management (GIM), ix, xii
globalization, ix, 57–58, 59–60
Global Reporting Initiative (GRI), 101, 111
Global Standards, 43, 44
global warming, 1, 15, 57–58, 209, 255
Gloria, 227
GM. *See* General Motors, 257
GM Shanghai, 256
goals, 219; conflicting, 64–67; emission, 246; financial, 12, 13, 14; policy, 256–57; setting, 219; social, 12, 14
Graduate School of Business (University of Capetown), 144
Graham, George: on Ford accident rate, 102
Green & Black's, CSR and, 7
Green Dot, 206, 222
greenhouse gas emissions, 5, 12, 213; limiting, 205, 209, 211–12, 254
Greenhouse Gas Emission Trading Scheme, 206
Green Management in the European Union, ix
Greenpeace, Royal Dutch/Shell and, 16–17
green taxes/subsidies, 206–7
GRI. *See* Global Reporting Initiative
Grobbelaar, Jan, 124
Group of Eight summit, Global Fund and, 178
Guangshou Automobile group, 253
Guangshou Honda, 253

Gujarat, aid for, 103
Guy Laroche, 91

Häagen-Dazs, social responsibility and, 9
"hard skills" program, 126
Hass, Robert: on brand loyalty, 57
health benefits, 11, 94, 95, 102
health care, 102, 181, 185, 196; focusing on, 111; improvements in, 6, 103, 104; NGOs and, 67; pollution and, 251
health insurance, 67, 70
health issues, x, xii, 45, 123, 139, 141; NGOs and, 183
Healthy Futures program, 107
Heinz, education/community benefits and, 2
Helena Rubenstein, 91
Henry Ford Health Systems, 101
Henry Ford Research Chair, 103
Henry J. Ford Foundation, 112
Henry J. Kaiser Family Foundation, 179
Hershatter, Gail: survey by, 84, 85
Hershey's, education/community benefits and, 2
HIV/AIDS, x, xii, 104, 138, 167, 198–99; ANC and, 178–80; in Brazil, 189–90, 191–92, 195; burden of, 189, 190; counseling/testing for, 179, 180; deaths from, 177, 191; homosexuals and, 191; NGOs and, 184, 196, 197; treating, xvi–xvii, 177–78, 179, 183–85, 191–92, 193, 195, 196
HIV/AIDS drugs: cocktail, 190, 192; cost of, 189, 190; marketing, 193; pricing, 192–97; reimportation of, 194–95; shortages of, 194
Home Depot: shareholder pressure and, 12; supply chains and, 1
homeless shelters, 225, 228
homosexuals, HIV/AIDS and, 191
Honda, 253

Honig, Emily: survey by, 84, 85
Howard Johnson, 259
human resources development, 122, 129
human rights, 1, 17, 59; brand building and, 68; education, 31; improving, 30; labor standards and, 67; violation of, 58
Human Rights Watch, 31
hybrid vehicles, 252, 255, 259, 260
hydrogen-based fuels, 210
hydrogen fuel cells, 207
hydrogen vehicles, 210
hygiene, 106, 108

IBM, education/community benefits and, 2
ICC, 86
IHDs. *See* International Healthcare Distributors
IIT. *See* Indian Institutes of Technology
Ikea, labor standards and, 1
Ikon, 100, 103
ILO. *See* International Labor Organization
Impact of Labor Audits in Vietnam, The, ix
income inequality, 52, 53
Indaba Wines, 143
Indian Institutes of Technology (IIT), 103, 107
Industrial Development Corporation, 156
industry learnerships, described, 123–24
information technology (IT), 104, 157, 159, 167
Infosys, 114
Inheritance Law (1985), 79
Innovest Strategic Value Advisers, 213
Instituto Avon, 94
Intel, 86
intellectual property rights, 2, 35, 37
International Confederation of Free Trade Unions (ICFTU), 31

International Healthcare Distributors (IHD), 178, 181–83
International Labor Organization (ILO), 57, 63; child labor and, 59; human rights and, 30, 59; labor standards and, 28, 32, 58, 60; Thai Labor Organization and, 29; UN and, 59; Versailles Treaty and, 58
International Monetary Fund, 191
International Organization for Standardization (ISO), 102, 220
investor pressure, 210; environmental/social standards and, 212–13
Ipiranga, ethanol and, 244
ISO 14000, 220, 224, 227
ISO 14001, 102, 227
IT. *See* information technology

Jackson, Austin, 138
Jacobs, Arthur, 136
J. B. Marks Education Trust Fund, MIC and, 169
job creation, 45, 47, 153, 170; sustainable, 256
John F. Welch Technology Center, 104, 108
Johnnic Holdings, 167
Jung, Andrea, 93

Kaletra, 198
Kambile, Bangile, 161
Kanonkop Pinotage, release of, 137
Kellogg School of Management, ix, xii
Khula Enterprise Finance, 152, 156
Kinder Lyderberg Domini (KLD) Research & Analytics, 9, 12
Knight, Phil, 61
KPMG South Africa VC, 158
KWV. *See* Cooperative Wine Growers' Association
Kyoto Protocol, 205, 212, 246

Labor Congress of Thailand, 31
labor costs, 53; FDI and, 52; women and, 80

labor force: educated, 47–48; women
in, 79, 80, 82, 85
labor laws, 28, 66, 69; enforcing, 38,
63
Labor Protection Act (1998), 28
labor rights, 27, 29, 35, 37, 38
labor standards, xiii, 1; abuse of, 29,
60, 63, 69; addressing, 62, 71;
adherence to, 36, 49, 69; in
developing countries, 62–64;
economic growth and, 42;
economic/social effects of,
46–53; enforcement of, xiv,
30, 48, 62, 68, 70; evolution
of, 58–60, 64; FDI and, 65;
free trade and, 60; future of,
34–37; global integration and,
57; human rights and, 67;
impact of, 48–49;
implementation of, 27, 34,
35, 41–42, 52, 53, 60;
improving, 35, 37, 49, 61;
income inequality and, 53;
international, 35, 57, 58–60;
LDCs and, 70; minimal, 59,
64; MNCs and, 36–37, 38,
42, 53; NGOs and, 60, 62,
64; program strategy for,
67–72
labor-standards audits, x, xiv, 34, 67,
69, 127; efficacy of, 44, 46, 53;
faking for, 66; MNCs and, 51;
performing, 68; third-party, 63;
in Vietnam, 42–44; wage
growth and, 49
labor-standards programs, 69; effects
of, 61–62, 68
labor unions, 44, 68; consumer
pressure and, 57; factory owners
and, 29, 31; MNCs and, 71
Lancôme, 91
land grants, processing, 145, 146
land reform, in South Africa, 134–35
Lawler, David, 129
Law on the Protection of Rights and
Interests of Women (1992), 79
LDCs. See less developed countries

League of Nations, 59
Lee, Ching, 85
less developed countries (LDCs), 57,
62, 67; environmental programs
and, 217; investment in, 68;
labor standards and, 70; MNCs
and, 70
Levi Strauss, 57; charitable causes and,
2; Global Standards and, 43;
sweatshop scandal and, 43
Light House Union, 32
literacy, 125, 128, 130; financial, 111,
170
Liz Claiborne: Global Standards and,
43, 44; labor standards and, 31
local companies: labor rights and, 27;
types of, 33–34
London Business School, Old Mutual
and, 168
London Wine and Food Fair, 136
L'Oréal, 89, 91
Louis Vuitton, 35
loveLife, 179
Lowe's, supply chains and, 1

Magneti Marelli, ECM from, 239
Mahindra & Mahindra, 100, 110
Mamelodi College of Education, 129,
130; Ford and, 126, 127, 128
Mandela, Nelson, 151
Mandi, Anthony, 126
Manufacturing and Engineering
Related Sector's Education and
Training Authority (Merseta),
122, 123, 126
Mao Zedong, 256
Maraimalai Negar area, 103
marketing, ix, 8, 10, 67, 71, 110,
144, 146, 219, 220–21, 229;
costs of, 193; fuel-efficiency
standards and, 255; in China,
258, 259; overseas, xi;
responsible, 224;
social/political environments
and, 15; social, 179; strategic,
131
market share, 8, 69; increasing, 9, 62

Marriage Law (1980), 79
Marymount University Center for
    Ethical Concerns, 63–64
Mascot Systems, 104
Mattel, 86
Maybelline, 91
Mbeki, Thabo: HIV/AIDS and, 179
McDonald's, animal welfare and, 1
McKinsey & Co., 2
McKinsey Quarterly, 2
Merck: ARVs and, 193; price cuts by,
    193; river blindness drug and,
    11; WHO and, 196
Merseta. *See* Manufacturing and
    Engineering Related Sector's
    Education and Training
    Authority
MIC. *See* Mineworkers Investment
    Corporation
microlending, x, 156, 157
Mineworkers Investment Corporation
    (MIC), 166, 169
Ministry of Science and Technology,
    257
MNCs. *See* multinational
    corporations
Modise, Jacob, 167
morality, 3, 7, 8, 14, 115, 210;
    environmental/social standards
    and, 211
Motorola, Chinese women and, 86
MPVs. *See* multipurpose vehicles
MSD, IHD and, 181
MTBE (additive), 238
multinational corporations (MNCs),
    37, 41, 89, 98; BEE and, xv;
    child labor and, 27;
    China/FDI and, 77, 78;
    compliance teams and, 33;
    consumer awareness and, 229;
    CSR and, 99, 110, 111, 113,
    114, 115; emerging markets
    and, 65, 69, 97;
    environmental impact and,
    209; FLA and, 44; labor costs
    and, 61; labor rights and, 27;
    labor standards and, 32–33,
    34, 36–37, 38, 42, 51, 53;

labor unions and, 71; LDCs
    and, 70; NGOs and, 36, 60,
    63, 64, 65, 67, 70; profits
    and, 38; in Thailand, xiv, 29,
    35; in Vietnam, 43; women
    and, xv, 80–81, 82, 83,
    84–85, 86–87
multipurpose vehicles (MPVs), 252
Multiskill training programs,
    developing, 122–23

NAACP. *See* National Association for
    the Advancement of Colored
    People
Nadler, David, 129
Nallurahalli Literacy Initiative, 108
National Association for People Living
    with AIDS, 179
National Association for the
    Advancement of Colored People
    (NAACP), Economic
    Reciprocity initiative by, 148
National Commission on the
    Environment (Conama), 223,
    226
National Empowerment Fund (NEF),
    152, 156
National Qualifications Framework,
    168
National Union of Mineworkers,
    busaries for, 169
Natura, success for, 89
natural resources, 220; conserving,
    205, 213;
    extraction/consumption of, 223;
    sustainable use of, 226
Natural Resources Defense Council,
    Wal-Mart and, 2
Nedbank Corporation, 143
NEF. *See* National Empowerment
    Fund
Nelson, Alan, 135, 136
Nelson's Creek Winery, 135; black
    empowerment and, 136–37
Nestlé S.A., 220, 227
New Balance, Verité and, 43
New Beginnings Winery, xvi, 135–37,
    144

New Era Cap, labor standards and, 31
NGOs. *See* nongovernmental
    organizations
Nike, 35, 85, 86; audit process and,
    42, 47; boycott of, 61;
    education and, 46; Global
    Standards and, 43; human
    rights and, 68; labor standards
    and, 1, 31, 58; labor-standards
    audits and, 48, 49, 51; NGO
    revolution and, 61; sweatshop
    scandal and, 43; Vietnamese
    workers and, 45; violations by,
    61; women workers at, 47
Nissan, 122, 253; AMIC at, 124–30;
    community and, 129; CSI and,
    129; education/training and, xv,
    124, 125, 127, 128; literacy
    and, 128
Nitrogen oxide emissions, reducing,
    253, 254
"No botes la casa, recicla la caja"
    campaign, 225, 229
nongovernmental organizations
    (NGOs), 7, 68; consumer
    pressure and, 57; corporations
    and, x; CSR and, xiii, xv, 19,
    98, 111–12, 115; ecoefficiency
    and, 228; environment and,
    225, 255; health care and, 67,
    183; HIV/AIDS and, 180,
    181, 184, 196, 197; labor
    rights and, 27, 29–32; labor
    standards and, 31, 34, 42, 60,
    62, 64, 66; MNCs and, 36,
    60, 63, 64, 65, 67, 70, 113;
    policy fights and, 67;
    preempting, 71; recycling and,
    228; role of, 114;
    volunteerism/philanthropy
    and, 105; Wal-Mart and, 1–2;
    working conditions and, 38
Nordstrom: Global Standards and, 43;
    labor standards and, 31
North Face, 35
Nova, Avon and, 93
Novartis, IHD and, 181
Ntshangase, Jabulani, 139, 140

Ntsika Enterprise Promotion Agency,
    156

occupational safety and health (OSH)
    committees, 28
OEMs. *See* original equipment
    manufacturers
oil companies, accountability for, 17
oil crises, 234, 242
Old Mutual Business School, 168;
    black/Indian leadership at, 166;
    bursary programs at, 169;
    scholarships at, 172
"One Step Ahead" (Tetra Pak), 222
original equipment manufacturers
    (OEMs), 122–23
Orissa, aid for, 103
Otto, Michael, 211
Otto, Werner, 208
Otto Versand, environmental
    awareness by, xvii, 205, 207,
    208, 211, 213
outcomes, 129; ethics and, 19;
    performance and, 130; social,
    14, 19
outsourcing, xi, 43, 48, 104, 110

Parmalat, Tetra Pak and, 220
Patagonia: CSR and, 7; Global
    Standards and, 43; labor
    standards and, 31; social agenda
    of, 19
Payne, David, 64
performance, 100, 106, 129, 131, 237;
    environmental, 14, 17, 18, 19;
    financial, 4, 10, 13, 14, 19, 20,
    21, 210, 212; measuring, 127;
    outcomes and, 130; social, 4, 20
personal care sector, 90, 91
Petrobras, ethanol and, 242, 243,
    244, 247
Petrobras BR, 244
petroleum fuels, looking beyond, 210,
    233
pharmaceutical companies, 192, 195,
    196; HIV/AIDS market and,
    197–98, 198–99; investments
    by, xvii; margins for, 193

philanthropy, xii, 2, 105, 115
Phillips-Van Heusen, labor standards
    and, 31
Pinochet, Augusto: economic policies
    of, 222–23
Pizarreño S. A., Tetra Pak Chile and,
    225
Plachimada, India, 109
Plant Rosslyn, 124–25, 127
Platter, John, 139
Political Risk Services Group (World
    Bank), 51
pollution, x, 5, 220, 254; air, 251,
    252; cost of, 206, 251–52;
    decrease in, 206, 208, 218, 255;
    health care and, 251;
    productivity and, 251
Pollution Control Board (Ford),
    102–3
Polo Ralph Lauren, Global Standards
    and, 43
poverty, xii, 41, 98, 99
PPPs. See public/private partnerships
pricing: cuts in, 193, 195–96; global
    customized, 193–97;
    government-controlled, 194;
    preferential, 182
Private Equity Survey, 158
ProAlcool, 242, 243
Procter and Gamble,
    disability/retirement benefits by,
    2
product-differentiation strategy, 8, 9
production, 8; consumption and, 223
productivity, 66; improving, 10, 169;
    pollution and, 251
profits: CSR and, 21; environmental
    responsibility and, 218;
    maximizing, 3, 20, 99; MNCs
    and, 38; repatriation of, 2–3;
    social responsibility and, 20
progress, monitoring, 170–71, 219
protease inhibitor, 193
public/private partnerships (PPPs),
    159–60; hybrid, 152; SMEs and,
    163; weaknesses of, 160–62
public relations, xiv, 113, 148
Puma, labor standards and, 31

Randall, Duncan, 160
Rausing, Ruben: on packages, 221
"Recicla y gana una sonrisa" program,
    227, 229
recycling, 12, 101, 224, 225;
    automobile, 207; consumer,
    xvii, 229; corporate
    responsibility for, 222; external
    pressure for, 221; infrastructure
    for, 254; NGOs and, 228;
    political will for, 222; Tetra Pak
    and, 227–28, 229
Reebok, 62; Global Standards and,
    43; human rights and, 68; labor
    standards and, 31, 48;
    sweatshop scandal and, 43
regulation, risks and, 15–19
reimportation, 194–95, 197
Reisinger, Mike, 108
Renewable Fuels Association, 247n8
renewable resources, xii, 207, 218
reputational damage, 15, 17, 57
research and development, 193, 258;
    environmental, 207; reduced
    investment in, 196–97
rights: violation of, 16; widely
    accepted, 15
risks: avoiding, 210, 211; increased,
    15; minimizing, 15, 19; regu-
    lation and, 15–19; sharing, 13
river blindness, treatment for, 11,
    196
Roche, 181, 198
Roosevelt, Franklin D., 59
Roy, Raman: GE and, 104
Royal Dutch Shell: Brent Spar and,
    209; Greenpeace and, 16–17;
    human rights issues and, 17
Ruckelshaus, William D., 217
rules: circumventing, 66, 69–70;
    formal/informal, 16

SA8000 (labor standards code), 68
Safcol. See South Africa Forestry
    Company
safety, 37, 45, 62, 111, 123, 137, 141;
    standards, 33, 69, 101, 102;
    workplace, x, 106

SAI. *See* Social Accountability
International
sales models, retaining, 92–95
Samsonite, 32
Sanjeevi Health Centre, 103
Satyam Computer Services, 104
SAWB. *See* South African Wine and
Brandy Company
Sawit. *See* South African Wine
Industry Trust
Schering, IHD and, 181
scholarships, 170, 172
Sector Education and Training
Authority (SETA), 168
segregation, in South Africa, 151
Seguino, Stephanie, 83
Seia. *See* System to Evaluate
Environmental Impact
Selected Essays on Political Economy
(Bastiat), quote from, 41
self-employment, 50, 53
Senior Certificate examination, 170
Seventh Generation, CSR and, 7
Seveso Directive (1982), 206
sex education, 111
sex trade, 44
Shanghai, air pollution in, 251
Shanghai Automotive Industry
Corporation, 253
Shanghai Volkswagen (VW), 253
shareholder pressure, 12, 13
shareholders, 20, 60, 63; financial
performance and, 20; voting
rights of, 167
shareholder value, xiv, 3;
maximization of, 2, 7
Shell, 1; ethanol and, 244
Shell Germany, Brent Spar and, 17
Shell UK, Brent Spar and, 17
Shining Path, 226
sin stocks, 13, 20, 21n1
Six Sigma, 105
small and medium enterprises
(SMEs), xvi; apartheid and,
153, 154; black, 152,
153–55, 161, 162, 163;
economic development and,
152–53; funding of, 152,

155–62, 163; microlending
and, 157; monitoring of,
154; PPPs and, 163; UPF
and, 160; VC firms and,
157–58, 160
small-business sector, 151, 153
small-business loans, 156
SMEs. *See* small and medium
enterprises
Social Accountability International
(SAI), 30
social activism, 15, 21, 113
social development, 44, 151, 153, 218
socially responsible firms, 10, 17–18,
217
socially responsible investing (SRI),
11–12, 18, 20; CSR and, 12,
14; impact of, 12, 13, 14;
portfolios, 12–13
social responsibility, xi–xii, xiv, 3, 4,
9, 219, 227; in India, 98–99,
104; influence of, 113; profit
maximization and, 20;
reputation for, 69. *See also*
corporate social responsibility
social security, 36
social status, 94; automobiles and,
259; FDI and, 84–85, 85–86;
women and, 84–85
social welfare, 3, 140
socioeconomic classes, in Brazil,
90–91
solar-powered vehicles, 241
Songwane, Christopher, 125
Sonop vineyard, 140
South Africa Forestry Company
(Safcol), 138, 139
South African National Young Wine
Show, 136
South African Wine and Brandy
Company (SAWB), 140, 141,
144, 145, 147, 148
South African Wine Industry Trust
(Sawit), 140, 141, 144, 145,
147, 148; education and, 143;
funding by, 143
Spice Route Company, 139–40
SRI. *See* socially responsible investing

stakeholders, 17, 19, 37, 38, 62, 104, 138, 141; communicating with, 68–69; cost imposition by, 16; external, 7; information gap for, 71; workers' needs and, 70
Standards and Fundamental Principles and Rights at Work Sector (ILO), 58
Starbucks, sustainable sourcing and, 11
Starnberg Institute, 80
State Bank of India, GE and, 104
State Bureau of Machinery Industry, standards by, 254
Stockman, Norman: on SIW, 78
"Stop Trading Away Our Rights" campaign (2004), 31
strategic management, 8, 22n2
strategy development, 157, 169
sugar cane, 241, 244, 245
sustainability, 1, 2, 6, 112, 127–28, 208, 213, 220, 256; importance of, 226; promoting, 224
sustainable development, 2, 11, 12, 212, 227, 228, 229; economic growth and, 218; goals for, 219
Sustainable Productive Chain Project, 227
Sustentable, 224
sweatshops, 43, 48, 64
Swepston, Lee, 57–58
Synapsys, 93
System to Evaluate Environmental Impact (Seia), 223

Tae Kwang Vina Industrial Company (TKV), 42
Tata Consulting Services, 104
Technikons, 170
technology: adoption of, 258; availability of, 233; communications, 258; economical, 234, 245, 246–47; electric-car, 239; environmental, xvii, 212, 254–60; ethanol, 240, 246–47; flexible-fuel, 233, 239, 241, 242, 243, 245, 247,

247n1; investment in, 256; petroleum-based, 233; research-intensive, 257; solar-/wind-/hydrogen-energy, 210
Tectan, 225, 228
Tetra Pak, xvi; in Chile, 222–23, 224–26, 229; ecoefficiency and, 218, 220–22; environmental image of, 221, 222, 224, 225–26; marketing by, 220–21; overview of, 220–21; in Peru, 222, 227–28, 229; recycling and, 225, 227–28, 229; study by, 225–26
Texaco, ethanol and, 244
Thai Durable (Kreing) Factory, 32
Thai government: Asian financial crisis and, 28; labor rights and, 27, 28–29; political stability/economic development and, 35
Thai Labor Campaign: Thai Labor Organization and, 29; worker education and, 32
Thai Manufacturing Association, 35
Thai Trade Union Congress, 31
Thandi Initiative, 138–39
Thelema Vineyards, 139
Tiffany, strategy of, 4
Timberland: charity work and, 11; labor-standards audits and, 48; sweatshop scandal and, 43; Verité and, 43
Titus, Victor, 136
tobacco, 13, 211
Tommy Hilfiger, Verité and, 43
Toward a Sustainable World (Ruckelshaus), quote from, 217
Toyota, in China, 253, 257
Toyota Prius, 7
Trade Union Advisory Committee, 81
Trauma Care Consortium, 103
Treatment Action Campaign, 179
treatment programs, 122–24, 131, 167–69; cost-effectiveness of, 185; financial/health benefits of, 185

trifuel vehicles, 241
TRIPs. *See* Agreement on Trade-Related Intellectual Property Rights
Truter, Beyers, 137–38
Tshabalala-Mismang, Manto: ARVs and, 179
TudoAVON, 93

UCT. *See* University of Cape Town
"Um Beijo pela Vida" program, 94
Umsobomvu Progress Fund (UYF), 156; black entrepreneurs and, 161; mission of, 159–60; PPP model and, 160–62; SMEs and, 160
UN. *See* United Nations
UNAIDS/WHO. *See* United Nations AIDS/World Health Organization
Unilever, 89; Birds Eye brand of, 207–8; environmental awareness by, xvii, 205, 207–8, 211, 213; Tetra Pak and, 220
United Nations (UN): human rights and, 30; ILO and, 59; workers' rights and, 30
United Nations AIDS/World Health Organization (UNAIDS/WHO), 177, 181
"United Nations Norms on the Responsibilities of Transnational Corporations and Other Business Enterprises with Regard to Human Rights," 30
United Way, 101
University of Adelaide, 144
University of Cape Town (UCT), 144; Graduate School of Business, Old Mutual and, 168
University of Stellenbosch, 143, 146
Unocal, shareholder pressure and, 12
U.S. Association of Importers of Textiles and Apparel, 52
U.S. Department of Labor, study by, 80

U.S. Department of State, human rights practices and, 45
UYF. *See* Umsobomvu Youth Fund

venture capital (VC), 152, 158, 161, 162; black enterprises and, 159; financing by, 157; wine industry and, 146
venture capital (VC) firms, 159; SMEs and, xvi, 157–58, 160
Venugopal, Venu, 106, 107
Verité, 43
Versailles Treaty (1919), ILO and, 58
Vidya Integrated Development for Youth and Adults, 108; GE Fund and, 112; projects of, 107
Vietnamese Communist Party, 44
Vietnam Union of Friendship Organizations (VUFO)-NGO Resource Center, 64
Vineyard Academy, 138
VinPro, 141–42, 143, 145, 147
virtue, demand for, 7, 8–15
viticulture, 138, 146
volatile organic compounds (VOCs), 253
Volkswagen (VW): in China, 253, 257, 258; flexible-fuel vehicles and, 234, 235, 239, 240, 241
Volkswagen Golf, 258
volunteerism, 98, 101, 105, 108, 112, 113
VW. *See* Volkswagen

wages: FDI and, 82–83; gender gap in, 80, 82–83, 84, 85–86; growth in, 49; inflated, 47; minimum, 33, 52, 59, 61; unskilled labor, 16
Walk for Breast Cancer, 94
Wal-Mart: NGOs and, 1–2; shareholder pressure and, 12; strategy of, 4
warehousing strategies, 178
waste, reducing, 2, 205, 218, 222, 227

wastewater treatment facilities, 102, 103

water, sustainable use of, 208

WCOC. *See* Workplace Code of Conduct

wealth distribution, in Brazil, 90

Webb, Gyles, 139

welfare, xii, xiv, 99, 139

Wells Fargo, financial literacy program of, 111

White Paper on Land Policy, 134

WHO. *See* World Health Organization

Whole Foods: CSR and, 7; social agenda of, 19

WIETA. *See* Wine Industry Ethical Trade Association

Winds of Change, 140

wine industry, 133–34; BEE and, 145, 146, 147, 149; black participation in, 135–40, 141, 142; challenges for, 144–46; venture capitalists and, 146; working conditions in, 144

Wine Industry Ethical Trade Association (WIETA), BEE and, 141

Wine Industry Plan, 141

women: economic role of, 77, 78–79, 89; education and, 85; FDI and, 79–80, 80–83, 84–85, 85–86; financial/social status of, 77, 78–79, 80–83; independence/self-worth for, 87; in labor force, 78, 79, 80, 82, 85; MNCs and, 80–81, 83, 84–85, 86–87; social status of,

xiv, 84–85; upward mobility of, 85; worker unrest and, 80

Women's Development Bank Investment Holdings, 166

women's issues, 111, 114

worker rights, 30, 59, 71, 72; defending, 68, 69, 70; establishing, 31

workers, communicating needs of, 69–70, 71–72

working conditions, 12, 16, 62, 70; improving, 46; NGOs and, 38; purchasing decisions and, 64

working hours, limiting, 35, 45, 69

Workplace Code of Conduct (WCOC), 41, 43; provisions of, 44–46

World Bank: Political Risk Services Group of, 51; on pollution costs, 251–52; on SMEs, 153; on women/FDI, 81

World Health Organization (WHO), 195, 196

World Investment Report 2002 (UN), Vietnamese FDI and, 51

World Trade Organization (WTO), 60, 63, 190; ATC of, 35; labor standards and, 30

Wyeth, IHD and, 181

Xu Ewen, Sheng: on SIW, 78

Youth development programs, 170

Yum Brands, animal welfare and, 1

Zoellick, Robert, 52

Anuradha Dayal-Gulati is a clinical associate professor at the Kellogg School of Management, Northwestern University, and is affiliated with the Center for International Business and Markets. She is academic advisor for the Global Initiatives in Management Program and has worked extensively on Southeast Asia, China, and India. She coedited *Kellogg on China,* published by Northwestern University Press in 2004. She is currently editing *Kellogg on India,* the third book in this series. Her research interests focus on macroeconomic policies and their implications in emerging markets.

Mark Finn is clinical associate professor of accounting and international business at the Kellogg School of Management, Northwestern University. He is director of Kellogg's Global Initiatives in Management Program. His primary research interests are related to the quality and credibility of financial disclosures, especially in non-U.S. settings, and he has served as a consultant in the areas of portfolio management and securities litigation.

Daniel Diermeier is the IBM Distinguished Professor of Regulation and Competitive Practice, a professor of managerial economics and decisions sciences at the Kellogg School of Management, and a professor of political science at the Weinberg College of Arts and Sciences, all at Northwestern University. He is also founder and managing partner of Diermeier Consulting, which provides clients with analysis and strategy advice in crisis leadership, reputation management, stakeholder management, and regulatory and political strategy. His teaching and research, published in leading academic journals and media outlets, focus on integrated strategy, the interaction of business and politics, crisis leadership, reputation management, and strategic aspects of corporate social responsibility.